BUILDING ITGRC ECOSYSTEMS into the ENTERPRISE

Practical Approaches, Concepts, and Automation Techniques for Managing Information Technology Governance, Risk, and Compliance

Geno Pandolfi

*Dedicated to
my loving wife, Lee,
and our children,
Gene and Jessica,
and Baby Avery Lee*

Table of Contents

Preface i

Acknowledgements ix

1. Projects and Technology Delivery 1

    1.1 Introduction to IT Delivery Risks 1

    1.2 Delivery Life-Cycle Management Standard 3

    1.3 Roles in Project and Technology Delivery 8

    1.4 Project and Technology Delivery Process Controls 9

    1.5 Managing IT Capital Investments and Expenses 13

    1.6 Understanding Schedule Estimating Controls 16

    1.7 Resource Availability and Assignment Controls 18

    1.8 Quality Assurance IT Delivery Control Risks 21

    1.9 IT Delivery Ecosystem Concepts 26

    1.10 Identifying IT Project and Technology Indicators 30

2. IT Service Management and Change 36

    2.1 Introduction to IT Service and Change Risks 36

    2.2 Service Management and Change Standards.............. 38

    2.3 Services, Delivery, and Change Roles 39

    2.4 Service Management and Change Controls................. 41

    2.5 Service Request Processing Controls 44

    2.6 IT Assets Management Service Controls 47

    2.7 Usage of IT Configuration Management Controls........ 49

    2.8 IT Change Management Controls............................... 52

    2.9 IT Incident and Problem Management Controls 55

    2.10 Application Life Cycle's Role in Service Delivery 58

    2.11 IT Service and Change Ecosystem Concepts.............. 59

    2.12 Identifying ITSM and Change Key Indicators............. 62

3. Business Continuity Processes 70

    3.1 Introduction to Business Continuity Risks................... 70

    3.2 Business Continuity Governance and Policy 72

    3.3 Assessing Business Continuity Risk Impacts 74

    3.4 Understanding Gaps in Service Availability................ 79

    3.5 Business Continuity Process Recovery Planning.......... 81

    3.6 BCP Threat Vulnerability Assessments 83

    3.7 BCP Insurance Strategies... 85

    3.8 Identifying Recovery Dependencies in Processes 86

    3.9 BCP Testing and Demonstrating Recovery 88

    3.10 Managing Incident Emergency Notifications 91

    3.11 Evaluating BCP Concentration Risks........................ 95

    3.12 BC Management Ecosystem Concepts....................... 97

    3.13 Identifying BCP Program Key Indicators 102

4. Technology Resilience and DR 108

    4.1 Introduction to IT Resilience and DR Risks 108

    4.2 Technology Resilience and DR Governance 110

    4.3 Assessing Risk Impacts in Technology Resilience 112

    4.4 Understanding Process and Technology Gaps 118

    4.5 Technology Recovery Planning for IT........................ 120

    4.6 Understanding IT Data Center Risk Exposures........... 122

    4.7 IT Vulnerability and Operational Analysis 128

    4.8 Identification of IT Technology Dependencies........... 132

    4.9 Technology Recovery - Demonstrated Exposure 133

    4.10 Evaluating Technology Concentration Risks............. 136

    4.11 Technology Resilience Ecosystem Concepts............. 137

    4.12 Identifying TRDR Program Indicators 142

5. IT Information Security 149

    5.1 Introduction IT Information Security Risks................. 149

    5.2 IT Security Governance, Policy, and Standards.......... 151

    5.3 Assessing IS Risks in Technology Operations............. 155

5.4 Identity Access and Authentication Management 161

5.5 Application Security Assessment Process Controls 164

5.6 Security Controls for Data Backup and Recovery 168

5.7 IT Security Controls for Technology Changes 170

5.8 Monitoring Controls - Prevention and Detection 172

5.9 Managing Third-Party Supplier IT Security Risk 174

5.10 Emerging Information Security IT Risks 176

5.11 Information Security Ecosystem Concepts 179

5.12 Information Security Key Indicators 182

6. Third-Party IT Supplier Management 189

6.1 Introduction to IT Third-Party Risk Exposures............. 189

6.2 Requirement for Third-Party IT Supplier Controls....... 191

6.3 Approaches to IT Supplier Management................... 193

6.4 IT Third-Party Supplier Management Frameworks...... 195

6.5 Standard Third-Party Assessment Practices................ 198

6.7 Stratification of Third-Party IT Suppliers................... 206

6.8 Third-Party Compliance and Risks Controls................ 208

6.9 TSP Management Ecosystem and Data Concepts 210

6.10 Approaches to Managing IT Suppliers 214

6.11 Federal Regulator Third-Party Scrutiny.................... 218

6.12 IT Third-Party Supplier Key Program Indicators........ 220

7. ITGRC Executive Oversight.. 223

7.1 Introduction to ITGRC Executive Oversight 223

7.2 IT Risk Oversight Organizational Responsibilities 224

7.3 Management Framework for ITGRC Activities........... 225

7.4 Oversight Accountability for ITGRC Activities........... 227

7.5 ITGRC Risk Assessment Controls and Monitoring...... 228

7.6 Trusted Data Integration and Aggregation................. 232

7.7 ITGRC Management Ecosystem Concepts................. 235

7.8 ITGRC Management Reporting and Analytics 239

7.9 ITGRC Committee Meeting Structures...................... 240

8. ITGRC Enterprise Management 242

    8.1 Introduction ITGRC Enterprise Management 242

    8.2 Enterprise GRC Framework Concepts 243

    8.3 GRC Policies and Accountabilities 244

    8.4 Developing IT Risk Appetite Statements 246

    8.5 Standard ITGRC Operational Risk Taxonomies 248

    8.6 Enterprise GRC Program Indicator Structures 249

    8.7 Standards for ITGRC Risk Categories 252

    8.8 Enterprise GRC Ecosystem and Data Concepts 253

    8.9 Enterprise ITGRC Reporting and Analytics 257

9. Board ITGRC Governance 263

    9.1 Board Oversight Drivers for ITGRC Activities 263

    9.2 Board ITGRC Oversight Responsibilities 265

    9.3 ITGRC Board Roles and Accountabilities 266

    9.4 Board ITGRC Framework Controls 268

    9.5 Board ITGRC Risk Appetite Statement Controls 270

    9.6 ITGRC Program Board Activities 271

    9.7 Board ITGRC Program Monitoring and Reporting 272

Glossary of Terms 275

Index 299

About the Author 315

Preface

Risk is an opposing force to most human endeavors. Cavemen foraging for dinner risked being devoured by hungry predators. Explorers in search of the new continents risked shipwreck, starvation, and disease. Scientists invented rockets for space travel in the face of risk, although the risk involved was more keenly felt by the astronauts tucked in the space capsules than by the scientists who invented them. We humans are driven to control risk, whether to prepare for natural disaster, or in our daily life decisions. That's why an investor who buys shares of stock may prefer a share of a stable company over a share of a start-up, preferring a safe, modest rate of return over the slim chance of a windfall.

Not counting many of my early-life escapades, including those on motorcycles, I first became aware of technology risks as a young non-commissioned officer in the US Army in the early 1970s. At that early computerized point in time, the army's record system relied on tab-computer equipment, carbon paper, and mimeograph machines. These early tab-computers used data punch cards and were accompanied by the dire warning, "DO NOT FOLD, STAPLE, OR MUTILATE." Often black smears of roughly handled carbon paper were common in reproduction of documents. Some may recall the scene in the movie *Animal House* in which mischievous fraternity brothers pilfer a test mimeograph stencil?

The brown Army 201 folders that I processed were stuffed full of dates-of-service, orders, training records, promotions, disciplines, and payroll information, all vital and all at risk, not only of mutilation, but of being lost entirely. The cost of lost or damaged data was huge, both in wasted time and physical resources. Lost records required hundreds of hours to recreate from paper reports. Later, as a computer science student at Pace University in the 1970s, I then became fascinated by the processing of data, and use, storage, and security of data. A pivotal catalyst then to my study was a catastrophic fire at the National Records and Archive Center in St. Louis, Missouri, in July 1973.

This building housed a Department of Defense centralized archive center. It contained an estimated 51 million files (including army files) for many armed forces personnel. These personnel had served in the military from the beginning of the twentieth century through the early 1970s. This center had no recovery facility, fire detection, or fire-suppression systems. As a result, the fire, and resulting millions of gallons of water from the fire-fighting actions, permanently destroyed a large floor section of tab punch cards, computer tab equipment, and thousands of military reports that contained unreplaceable data in microfiche/film and indexes. It took several years to recover some of the files from microfiche/film with recreation from reports. However, some 16 to 18 million military files from veterans with services periods ranging from the early 1900s to the 1960s were destroyed and lost forever for these veterans.

Following my discharge from the US Army in the 1970s, my training began on basic computer operations with their associated operational risks. The training at the time was on IBM360s (S/360s), 16KB (16 thousand bytes of memory) machines. In these basic computers, that were introductory to the IBM360 line, memory was set by the computer operator for addressing RPG (Report Program Generator Language) programs. This language program was processed into the IBM360 computer operating system memory. The RPG program used several punch cards for sorting, placement, and/or finding specific 80-column input punch cards in the computer search deck. The program cards were fed with the RPG punched card program into a computer machine hopper, with a large stack of RPG program compiler punch cards. These program compiler cards were stored in a large card box of machine instructions via hundreds of punch cards to compile these simple programs into machine language. The IBM360 eventually evolved into much more powerful models with faster speeds and more memory, storage, and language flexibility.

The major risk exposure for these early IBM operational computers was the damage to the operational computer rooms and often computer circuit issues, and especially in higher-end model computers the potential for magnetic tape damage. However, for the basic S/360 the risk was the damage to the 80-column cards that served as data for compiling the RPG program into machine code. One of the biggest risks in this operation was from continued use and damage to the compiler punch card sequencing. The resulting key risk control was a manual concept to prevent card sequencing issues (misplaced cards) and damage to the compiler cards. The control for the compiler cards was to draw a pen line free-form down the center of the deck. This could then be used to examine, via line of sight, to check the line was not distorted, and that the sequence of the compile line was still intact. After repeated handling of the cards in daily operations and continuous feeds through the low-end hoppers, the decks would often fail, requiring replacement. Therefore, the additional IT operational risk control was to have multiple boxes of RPG compiler punch card boxes available, often 30 to 40 boxes stacked in the computer rooms as a standard back-up control.

From the 1970s thru 1990s, the computer technology advanced with expanded usage of additional programming languages into major coding languages, such as: Basic, Fortran, RPG, COBOL, and Machine Assembler code. IBM also introduced the next generation of their advanced S/370 series with more sophisticated capabilities including infrastructure cooling, random memory addressability, advanced tape libraries, disk storage, virtual operating systems/libraries, and expanded telecommunications controllers. Fifty years later, these core languages and many advanced IBM support environments still exist; however, programming languages have now evolved into multiple complex authoring tools, fourth and fifth-generation languages, web-based scripting languages, artificial learning systems, and specialized third-party proprietary logical development environments.

These have proliferated in almost all enterprise businesses and large corporations throughout the world. Online access was provided for both centralized and remote locations with dedicated communication lines and used standard centralized password security controls provided by IBM or third-party suppliers. As new enabling environments were introduced and businesses recognized the potential opportunities of remote user access and expanded process automation, the IT risk exposure grew proportionally. However, the risk management lacked a sophisticated approach and required manual identification and management of these new risk exposures.

Because of many new and expanding technologies, a large third-party supplier market eventually introduced more and more technology products. The introduction of these products and other new technologies began a trend that continues to this day. It has become a massive IT global supplier market, with specific technology subsectors, but has further complicated Enterprise IT management and risk exposure. The new product trends began to diminish much of centralized IBM command/control environments and the risk control enforced by use of standard IBM technologies. It introduced multiple technology environments into the IT organizations and processing environments. It opened the door to expanded risk exposures from the varying technologies and the non-standardized usage of technologies by many IT organizations.

The introduction of Apple computers, IBM personnel computers and software, and manufacturer clones generated an expansion of computer portability and non-centralized remote access control of many environments. This continued the expansion of third-party distributed telecommunications, distributed processing and client server technology, and the use of many more multi-purpose third-party products. These new products and technologies increased the proliferation of data risk access to the Enterprise.

Data risk was further expanded with the introduction of the all-purpose spreadsheets like VisiCalc, Lotus 1/2/3, and eventually, Microsoft Excel. These spreadsheets became the primary enablers for user development of financial and other data model activities. The spreadsheets' software also became the primary mechanism for risk based modeling and operational control tracking for most IT environments, together with other risk management activities, and various IT control processes.

Many IT and risk professionals often forget the simple origins of the IT industry and the single manufacturer technologies (e.g. IBM, etc.). These technologies often shared common manual IT management, risk control, and organization concepts. However, over the last fifty years, technology has progressed even further into 24 by 7 continuous operating environments, with mobile and global user access, and complex IT environments. Almost every generation has come to expect an "always-on" service level for automation and computer technology.

The technology proliferation of mobile and internet technology environments, real-time payments, email, and social networking sites, and introduction of mobile devices and smart-wearables in the "always-on" society have created an IT risk-based control quagmire. All of these technologies working at micro-second speeds, in often unheard-of volume, require more sophisticated risk management techniques. However, many Enterprise IT and risk management organizations still continue to control IT risk with spreadsheet documents. They move and report on a manual basis operational control and risk data, or via electronic-based attachments, and/or reports via email. These processes often use paper-based production of risk-based heatmaps, spreadsheet reports, and detail control reports. The concepts of the 1960s for manual control of documents, data, and the potential for transposition errors, presents many of the same delivery exposures in the twenty-first century, despite advanced technology sophistication, increased transmission speeds, user-based growth, product complexity, and multiple vendor technology environments. The new exposure creates risks that must be controlled and managed by all IT organizations.

Smart devices are now in the hands of billions of users, the devices often contain an average of fifty applications, execute multiple email/ social interactions, and access thousands of websites around the world. Because of this technology complexity, real-time processing speeds, massive data storage demands, large proliferation of devices, and federated cloud-sharing environments, in today's global operating environments, IT organizations require expansion of the controls with automated processing of this data.

With these enabling and complex technologies come IT challenges for managing the proliferation of web- and mobile-based security risks from tens of thousands of complex hardware devices and server environments. Demands are growing exponentially for delivery of newer and faster service technology; while IT and enterprise risk management organizations struggle to maintain control of these new and enabling technologies IT hardware manufacturers and software suppliers are rushing to introduce even newer web and mobile technologies. They are creating even more complexity within IT environments.

Some IT software and service suppliers are driving new automation of the various risk control and Ecosystem environments for IT Governance, Risk, and Compliance (ITGRC) management sectors. Additionally, the IT industry has introduced some best-practice-based standards and risk-based control environments to manage IT operational control and risk. However, to this day, the workhorse tool for many enterprise IT and risk management organizations continues to be the same spreadsheet structures introduced in the 1980s and 1990s.

In *Building ITGRC Ecosystems into the Enterprise*, the objective is to reinforce for IT and risk management personnel key IT operational controls and practices that are a basis for management of enterprise governance, risk, and compliance of IT services and operations. This book provides an understanding of the basic approaches and methodologies for managing IT governance, compliance, and risk exposure. It can assist in enabling IT operational control and risk management activities for development of processes, measurement of technology, system and control interfaces, policies, and standards. Finally, it provides a review of practical techniques for automating controls through sample technology concepts, and key performance (KPI) and risk management (KRI) indicators, comparative risk trends and leading measurements for ITGRC best-practice management.

While IT executive management still require risk-based decision processes and continued analysis to manage IT controls and risk exposure, it is critical to automate the environments. This is needed to reduce manual data handling and avoid manipulation in ITGRC environments and provide real-time risk assessment and management. It includes automation of hundreds of IT controls where possible and the validation of these controls, while providing real-time messaging from IT Ecosystems. It is a key attribute for efficient management in today's micro-second transactional and global usage of mobile technologies. Enabling ITGRC management with automated measurements and risk technology controls is vital to effective management of complex technology and the real-time exposure from today's IT risks to the Enterprise.

Acknowledgements

Thanks to my friends and fellow authors, Steven Lane Smith and Treena Crochet, who provided coaching, publishing insights, and creative thoughts in completing this book and the publishing process. Steven Lane Smith, is an accomplished author of four books and numerous screen-play scripts. Treena Crochet, has authored and published eight major interior design books, architectural college textbooks, and How to books.

Thank you to H. Lynn Ryan and Christine Sarnosky - my industry colleagues of twenty-five plus years, who generously agreed to review the book, and provide thoughts and suggestions. Lynn has held Executive Chief Information Officer roles and been a member of Corporate Executive Management in Banking and Financial Services Corporations, both public and privately held. Her expertise is in Enterprise-wide Information Technology Management, Governance, and Business IT Strategies

Christine has been engaged over the last twenty-years in managing and implementing multiple IT Operational risk, control systems, and processing environments. She has also managed and consulted on major IT System, ITSM, Infrastructure, and Cloud development/delivery environments in the financial services and travel industries.

Most of all, a big thank you to my wife Lee, for her continued patience and encouragement in completing this book. Thank you all!

CHAPTER 1

Projects and Technology Delivery

1.1 Introduction to IT Delivery Risks

Project and Technology Delivery Risk Exposure:

ALL ENTERPRISE IT organizations operate with a primary objective and purpose for the delivery of overall Technology services, innovative solutions, and processes to their Enterprise. Included in the major framework components for the Technology operational objective is the delivery of new functional applications, technology environments, IT services, and infrastructures. In this initial chapter, the focus will center on the governance and risks associated with the delivery of IT projects and initiatives, controls identification, implementation and maintenance of IT systems and technologies, and the associated oversight and management of those activities. The risk management process for this IT domain includes: (1) oversight for internal development of software applications or technology; (2) purchase and/or implementation of hardware, databases, software, or services from Third-Party suppliers; (3) Cyber and digital security; and (4) any required integration of services into the technology environments.

The delivery of IT initiatives for new or enhanced applications,

Third-Party software, IT infrastructures and hardware environments expose the Enterprise to numerous risks. The management of delivery risk by IT executives is a key operational risk component for the Enterprise. It can have a major influence in the lowering of IT and Enterprise risk exposure and environmental disruptions. The risks associated with project and technology delivery includes the potential losses that result from the IT implementation of systems, dependency upon key human process controls, and the associated exposure from control failures. These exposures can result from insufficient project control processes, lack of personnel, late project delivery, insufficient business process changes, poor systems and security engineering, and the lack of quality control testing for delivery of various technology environments.

Additionally, some of the more typical Enterprise exposures associated with potential project and technology delivery can result from:

- Project delivery cost overruns impacting Enterprise profits, Capital positions, and/or Shareholder value;
- Late delivery of projects to the market, and/or the inability of products and/or services to meet customer demand, and/or sustain Enterprise competitive positions and market advantages;
- Potential litigation and/or fraud due to poor management controls and oversight of delivery;
- Regulatory and compliance impacts from technology issues that are due to erroneous data reporting, lack of adherence to laws, poor project/technology delivery controls, and/or non-functional customer services;
- Operational cost increases due to incomplete or minimum business process reviews, procedural modifications, and/or policy updates;
- Insufficient assessment of Business Continuity and DR Technology requirements;
- Customer visibility and Enterprise reputational impacts from the failure to address and meet project commitments, and/or customer expectations for new product functionality, and/or poor performing product functions.

Organization Control and Accountability Delivery Risks:

In just about every industry, the IT disciplines for overall project delivery of new technologies and the project Life-Cycle management often rests with the Chief Information Officer (CIO) or Chief Technology Officer (CTO). Depending upon organizational structures, the CTO may report into the CIO. Both Technology officers may report into a more corporate senior Executive for IT or another Enterprise officer (e.g. CFO, etc.). Many large organizations utilize a Project Management Office (PMO) for controlling and administrating all IT projects for the Enterprise within the IT Organizations.

Regardless of the IT organizational structure, the delivery of new and/or upgraded IT services requires an Enterprise-standard project management approach and development methodology. Additionally, the overall management of strategic investments for delivery requires execution by the various IT teams, but also requires an overall oversight by a centralized risk management organization and a strategic investment organization. As many IT Delivery projects are capital-intensive, it is essential that proper financial and risk oversight be executed by the IT Organization. Therefore, use of a Capital investment oversight committee is a key Enterprise due diligence control element for any capital project. Many small and mid-size organizations may not utilize such control organizations but assign these responsibilities to an operational or financial executive.

1.2 Delivery Life-Cycle Management Standard

Use of Project and Technology Delivery Standards:

IT project Life-Cycle management and standards are one of the major controls available to IT organizations to help drive governance and risk management of IT delivery. Key to management of IT project and technology delivery is the overall due diligence and structures introduced to manage all IT initiatives, the overall project, and technology delivery Life Cycle.

The importance of IT to the Enterprise dictates the use of a framework for the development, implementation, and maintenance of Technology delivery initiatives. Use of IT delivery framework standards for project and technology delivery does not guarantee that organizations will manage their IT delivery activities. However, having a framework for managing project and technology delivery provides the ability for IT and Enterprise executives to exercise control and oversight over project and technology delivery activities and reduce risks. It allows for management controls to assist in increasing delivery success and decreasing delivery risk to the Enterprise.

A structured, communicated, and defined IT project and technology delivery framework, employee training, and repeatable processes can help ensure systems and technologies are delivered in an optimal manner, and systems will operate in a secure and efficient manner. Initiatives that utilize standard frameworks supported by organizational policies and procedures can help the Enterprise meet their strategic requirements. They can also assist in managing many of the risk exposures discussed in this chapter.

Project and Technology Delivery Life-Cycle Standards:

One of the key frameworks used throughout all industries and in many IT organizations is a Software Delivery Life Cycle (SDLC). An SDLC provides a systematic process to define the various delivery tasks associated with software and technology development projects. Many organizations employ an SDLC model or alternative methodology for managing projects. Projects can include: software and programming development; hardware and technology delivery; Cloud-implementation services; and Third-Party software acquisition projects. Figure 1.2 provides an overview of the key Project Delivery Framework Controls that will be discussed in this chapter.

Figure 1.2 Key IT Delivery Framework Controls

Typical project and technology delivery Life Cycles include the following major framework phases:

- Need based generation and business value for a new initiative or product requirements;
- Delivery initiation and requirements definition for funding consideration and prioritization;
- Scheduling, due diligence, and cost estimating for approval;
- Design and specification of applications, engineering design, equipment requirements, data design, service contracts, and technologies for delivery;
- Construction of applications and technologies;
- Quality Assurance and Application testing (Unit, System, Integration, Acceptance, Security. and Performance);

- Final Project delivery coordination, BCP/DR final plans, business process validations, and production implementation activities;
- Implementation and Post-implementation problem analysis and root cause investigative results;
- Support and software maintenance release phases (Post Implementation).

Each of these phases requires specific controls and performance indicators that enable oversight reporting and escalation of delivery anomalies. Most organizations will focus on two major elements for IT delivery: financial expenditures and cost overruns, and secondly, delivery time-frames and schedules. Both are key delivery risk-control attributes that require management oversight and due diligence.

Also, many IT organizations have implemented industry governance frameworks that allow consistent implementation, repeatable processes, and resource training to a common industry standard. One such standard is COBIT (Control Objectives for Information and Related Technologies). COBIT is a governance framework and supporting set of tools that allows IT management to set clear policy development and best practices for a SDLC management framework of IT controls throughout the Enterprise.

COBIT was created by the international professional association ISACA (Information Systems Audit and Control Association), to provide a set of common controls of IT industry frameworks. Another set of industry standards more focused on Technology Service Management and Service Delivery is ITIL (Information Technology Infrastructure Library). ITIL is used worldwide to set standards and guidelines that include Service Management, Service Technology Planning, Technology Delivery, and Support. The above two standards represent the most common and major IT frameworks used by IT Organizations.

Additionally, there are sub-frameworks and new technology delivery methodologies that are driving expansion of new delivery concepts in many IT organizations. Many of these methodologies involve the completion of SDLC project phases via iterative development methodologies. One such methodology that has evolved, is the Agile Development Methodology (ADM). It provides a set of principles and common practices where project needs and solutions are generated through collaborative teams, iterative work-streams, and with ongoing review/delivery of project tasks. Agile methodologies often require changes to standard IT procedures and processes. The introduction of ADM, as well as "DevOps" collaboration, has increased the complexity level of risk decision for CIO's and CTO's within the Enterprise. This is due to the growing market and business delivery pressures and the requirements for increased technology innovation.

These business pressures represent the need to balance management and funding of development, delivery risk, and the ongoing support of multiple legacy, mid-range, web, and Cloud infrastructure environments in product delivery. This has introduced new trends and management challenges for project and technology delivery and introduced additional governance management complications. These management concepts require IT executives to balance newer and faster delivery strategies for IT resources and risks, with some of the existing legacy IT "Waterfall" delivery concepts. These Waterfall concepts have been cemented in IT cultures for the last 40 years in both IT organizational delivery procedures and standards. Additionally, utilizing Outsourced development and delivery of projects can require additional procedures and challenges for IT management. All of these concepts require integration into today's management decisions, time-to-market, and accurate delivery practices in order to optimize the IT support and management model.

But regardless of the process used by the IT organization, many of these SDLC methodologies, concepts, and standards become key risk controls and audit elements for delivery oversight. They are key elements for understanding and control of these IT organizational activities. Additionally, management needs to understand, approve, and document anomalies in delivery initiatives. Isolating and reporting major variations to the defined IT controls is a best-practice risk management approach for IT delivery.

1.3 Roles in Project and Technology Delivery

While the IT Organizations are the primary organization within the Enterprise for execution of IT delivery through the SDLC, there are other accountable areas responsible for risk control and oversight for IT initiatives. These accountable teams are often outside of the IT organization and are focused often on audit, finance, and risk disciplines.

IT and Corporate Executive Roles:

Enterprise executive management are accountable for approving project and technology delivery initiatives and monitoring that these activities meet the strategic objectives of the Enterprise. These initiatives are often brought forward for approval and funding by IT and business executives who sponsor initiatives to the Enterprise executives. Senior IT management are also accountable to ensure the appropriate personnel and technology resources are available to complete the initiatives and provide for the ongoing monitoring of these delivery activities. Smaller and mid-size corporations may delegate this accountability to operational or financial executives. Often the corporate financial organization will provide overall standards and practices for management control of the delivery expenditures. They also have a major role in oversight of ongoing delivery expenses and investments.

Project and Technology Delivery Roles:

For large projects, a cross-business steering committee is often established for continuous assessment of objectives, business changes/

approvals, and management oversight of the project and technology initiative activities, review project issues or deviations, and ensure engagement of the required executives. These steering committees are the major accountable organizational structures for managing and reporting delivery project activity and for oversight of the various delivery risks associated with the initiatives. Often, they are made up of sponsoring business line management and key Subject-Matter-Experts (SME) (*e.g.* HR, Legal, Compliance, *etc.*) for the initiative, IT infrastructure and project delivery personnel, Information Security (IS) personnel, development managers, auditors, and IT risk managers.

One of the most important risk management roles for project and technology delivery is that of the IT Project Manager (PM) or Business PM for the delivery initiatives. These personnel are responsible for ensuring that the delivery meet the business objectives and goals for the initiative. They define, manage, and report the status and delivery schedule for tasks and phase activities for the initiative; manage allocations of delivery personnel and resources; monitor and report delivery function anomalies, escalate impacts and make project recommendations; review resource status and financials for the organizations. Often a cross-Technology project team is assigned with a system integration lead with participation of network, hardware, security, and database assigned resources. Lastly, the various audit departments provide an important risk role in that they are the final defense for overall management of effective system delivery controls. They perform testing of the controls and the control delivery environments during the technology/project development and initiatives delivery, and after the delivery initiative implementation.

1.4 Project and Technology Delivery Process Controls

IT Delivery Framework:

One of the key IT delivery framework processes is the management of IT delivery performance and risk management controls, via

Project Portfolio Management (PPM) system. The PPM concepts, along with the supporting software technology for managing the IT portfolio, are key IT delivery controls. In many organizations, this process level of control is known as the Demand Management Process (DMP). This process is used for controlling IT organizational, financial, and technology resources that are used in the delivery of technology. The DMP process helps to ensure oversight, annual planning, and project prioritization of all technology initiatives requested for IT organizational delivery, ensure compliance to policies, and meet regulatory requirements.

Project and Technology Delivery Processes:

The basic activity in the DMP is that of planning and control of the Enterprise project and technology delivery pool of resources and tasks. This is due to the large number of tasks to be completed within the chosen SDLC and the multiple personnel resources required to complete the various tasks. Effective resource planning is critical to meet the delivery objectives and expectations of the funded initiative. Key elements in the planning process is the ability to develop and use project plans that are aligned to the objectives and exposure associated with the delivery initiative.

However, it is a major challenge for large IT organizations to manage the entire IT delivery portfolio and technology resources for hundreds and even thousands of large and small technology initiatives, which include multiple complex and technology delivery tasks. It is crucial then to understand the risk posed by delivery of IT technology and services for the Enterprise. Typically, a delivery initiative begins the SDLC process with a business need or product idea that requires new technology implementation or updates to existing technology environments. This initiative then begins a task to assess the actual requirements for this business initiative and equally important, evaluates the business case for delivery of the initiative and the project scope

This initiation phase is when a project request is submitted for consideration by the key stakeholders and executives accountable for evaluating the delivery requests. They will justify the rationale for a project with the presentation of a business case, identify desired technology features and functionality, and scope of the overall initiative. The overall risk assessment process then begins with IT, affected business line areas, and Enterprise management determining that the business case justifies the scope by evaluating estimated costs and expenditures, Return on Investment (ROI), Return on Assets (ROA), Tangible/ intangible business benefits and areas impacted for the requested initiative.

Managing the Risk of Project Delivery Portfolios:

In order to manage large project portfolios and business needs, it is important that the Enterprise use a Project Portfolio Priority Management (PPM) process. The process should be automated with software that can prioritize and manage the overall resources of the IT organization and manage the multiple needs of many initiatives being delivered on a concurrent basis.

An example of a PPM Process environment, utilizing such technology is depicted in Figure 1.4 of this chapter section. With this suggested environment, various capabilities can be enabled by software that can provide support for the overall PPM environment and overall project management tasks. These products and services EW known in the IT market as, "IT Project and Portfolio Management Systems." They are available via Enterprise software site licenses and via SaaS (Software as a Service) within Cloud product offerings. There are numerous IT Third-Party supplier products in this sector. Key elements in the PPM process include the ability to initiate business needs through an IT Service Management (ITSM) or business needs processing systems that integrate with an IT Configuration, Change Control Management, and Deployment Systems to track business needs and the associated required delivery technology dependencies, and SDLC phases for the new requested technology services.

Figure 1.4 Project Portfolio Management Process

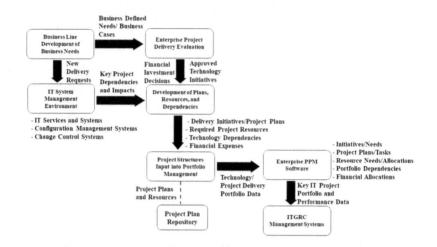

A major industry basis for planning and delivery of projects and technology used by many IT organizations are project planning software tools. The overall project plan developed for the initiative is a key element used for planning, resource assignment, task definition, task scheduling, and task/resource tracking. It is critical to the planning process and delivery portfolio. Many of the available PPM software products have the ability to integrate and import the project plans into their Portfolio Project Databases, or develop plans directly in the tools. They also often accept periodic updates of the plan into the PPM Database for tracking resource modifications and/or task updates and dependencies. Some of the key IT software vendors providing products in this IT PPM market space are Enterprise Software suppliers, such as: BMC, CA, HPE, IBM, and Microsoft. The Enterprise Software suppliers provide Cloud-Based solutions to their customers. SaaS suppliers, such as: AgileCraft, Innotas, Changepoint, WorkFront, Clarizen, and One2Team provide focused Cloud-Based solutions. Many of these products include key PPM functions that include: Project analytics, project plan integration, business need initiation and tracking, project estimating, delivery workflow controls processes, project communication repository, financial and budget tracking, personnel time management and tracking, what-if planning and analysis, operational delivery deployment, and technology release controls.

IT organizations should understand that selecting the IT software and service provider needs to be based upon the requirements of the Enterprise, and the ability to integrate these products into the Enterprise IT Delivery Management Ecosystem environments. Over the last five years, the industry has seen several consolidations and acquisitions in support of both vertical market integration and expansion of software vendor strategies with the introduction of new and emerging Cloud services and other technologies.

1.5 Managing IT Capital Investments and Expenses

Enterprises are required by regulatory (*e.g.* IRS, etc.) and industry audit standards to manage software and technology expenditures, and to account for these capital investments via specific rules and structures. It is required to reflect both the expense and depreciation of IT investment assets and include impacts to the Enterprise's financial books. Specifically, decisions as to when to capitalize certain investments in hardware, development labor, and software, and when to expense such investments. These are key decision processes that can impact approval of a Technology initiative ROI or ROA, during the described initiation phase.

Capital Expenditure Process and Controls:

In most Enterprises, the process to approve and capitalize specific technology investments is known as, and governed by, the Capital Expenditure (Capex) Process within the Enterprise. The process requires investments for project/technology delivery to be evaluated by a financial and/or technology steering /or corporate Capex committee. Smaller to mid-size organization may utilize a CFO in this accountability. This review is recommended prior to moving forward with any specific initiative and/or major IT project. It is a key risk control for managing technology requests and/or major capital investments by the Enterprise. Most Enterprises align their strategic planning for technology to the overall strategy for the operational businesses and financial objectives of the Enterprise. Some major financial controls used to evaluate the technology investments for most Enterprises are: ROI, ROA, Net Present Value (NPV), for IT investments, and/or the overall technology investment payback period.

Prioritization of Project and Technology Investments:

For most large Enterprises, both financial and personnel resources for projects and technology initiative investments are finite resources. This is an important consideration for understanding the technology investment portfolio to classify or categorize the investment initiative based upon the financial controls and to prioritize the justified business cases. This is also an important risk control for managing the finite project resources available to IT departments, and to understand the risk of the entire development delivery resource pool. As such, it is recommended that a technology delivery portfolio of business cases be structured into a risk prioritization pool that provides for understanding key business priorities and risk to the Enterprise, such as: financial revenue/profit, regulatory and compliance issues, technology obsolescence, product innovation, operational optimization, business beneficial, nice-to-have initiatives. Having a Portfolio Prioritization Model can help manage the overall delivery pool risk to ensure resources are allocated to the most important and beneficial delivery initiatives.

Control of Technology Investments Financial Risks:

Once the investment is approved for the initiative and the planning completed for tasks and resource assignment, these decision directions and financial allocations become key project and delivery controls. The expenditures need to be tracked in detail and reported to key stakeholders and the various steering committees as a key control. A periodic reporting control is often employed for monthly and annual expenditures (for multi-year projects) to the various stakeholders for capital and expense acquisitions. These delivery risk variables often become a paramount focus for all PM's and delivery managers, technology executives, and corporate steering committees, in terms of managing the financial risk and exposures for the delivery initiatives. Additionally, Legal, Vendor Risk Management, and Procurement areas may establish further tracking requirements for project risk management.

The majority of the available PPM software products and service concepts have the ability to track expenditures of the various technology delivery initiatives. Many of the products also have the capability to link the various resources' time-on-task reporting concepts for correct allocation of labor resources associated with the delivery initiatives. Delivery of technology initiatives often require specialized technology resources to support delivery of these initiatives. As such, the Enterprise will use internal employee developers, support technology personnel, and often supplement internal resources with external consultants, programming, and system integration professionals. These expenditures need to be tracked against the delivery investment portfolio as a key component of both the technology capital investments and operational expenditures for the initiatives. In large IT projects, it is suggested that these resources be tracked with some type of service tracking or reporting product. This can be beneficial for tracking time and expenditures for external resource delivery of services, enable effective planning for personnel recruiting, and for providing feedback to the PPM environment and over delivery expense controls.

A key delivery control is ensuring synchronization between the procurement/financial environments and the PPM environment to reconcile the capital and expense system costs. This requires a synchronization of these variables to the Enterprise's financial books (general ledger) and PPM or project/technology tracking mechanisms.

A key component of this synchronization and a requirement in some organizations is the ability to effect chargebacks or allocations to the appropriate Enterprise organizational cost centers for appropriate tracking of expenses. This requires that project expenditure anomalies are controlled and managed, and correct oversight exists to avoid impacts to the P&L of the Enterprise, and the delivery meets the objectives of the proposed initiative. Ensuring that delivery initiatives are prioritized to the key Enterprise objectives and strategies and management of the detail capital expenditures and operation expense impacts are crucial to understanding and managing the risk associated with delivery initiatives. Ultimately it enables financial departments to plan effectively for annual and upcoming funding requirements.

1.6 Understanding Schedule Estimating Controls

There are two major components to management of the initiative delivery time risks associated with scheduling that are core to managing the initiative. First, the estimating of the delivery time-frame and cost estimates; and second, the tracking of time to the predicted schedule and any scheduling anomalies.

Delivery Schedule Estimation Process:

The delivery estimation process, while a key part of the overall PPM process, is an important framework component. It requires a realistic approach to be able to quantify and predict the on-time delivery of projects and technology. This is needed for the development and delivery of Enterprise software projects where major efforts need to be expressed in objective terms of resource hours and costs to deliver the initiative. The project time-frame estimates to deliver specific aspects of software delivery, including: requirement definition/collection, technology design, coding, testing, implementation, and documentation are key to project plan development, iterative plans, capital and operating expenses, and pricing technology procurement.

Many projects fail because of unrealistic time estimates, conflicts with daily production impacts, and meetings. Project plans should allow for contingencies in resource downtime and loss in the estimates.

Therefore, the PPM estimating process can make or break the actual delivery of a project and is one of the most difficult component phases in the overall SDLC for delivery of projects and technologies. It requires definition of specific objectives to be achieved by the delivery initiative, and a key understanding of the high-level business requirements and technologies. While project and technology delivery are not a pure science; it is a skill set based upon experience, as a key determination for successful delivery of any technology initiative. It requires a scientific approach and controls for estimating the delivery of projects and technology. Project management must balance both art and science, and sometimes it is even considered a "Black Art". Because of this, numerous PM training and approach methodologies are available for IT PM's, throughout the IT Industry. Six Sigma Certification is one example of such certification available to PM's, for training on the delivery of quality projects to the Enterprise.

Delivery Estimate Framework Structures:

Some of the basic estimating framework control elements to understand for management of time and cost estimates for any delivery initiative includes: Definition of Project scope and objectives; Sizing of the initiative; Itemized work efforts, dependencies and tasks; Estimates for software delivery; Level of personnel experience for the project; Specific scheduling constraints for resources, and time-frame limitations; Resource and labor allocations; Project hours and budget detail; Defined delivery assumptions and planning contingencies.

Schedule Process Estimating Technology:

Because of these process needs, there are some focused software technologies and tools available in the marketplace to assist

Enterprises in utilizing a more scientific approach to project and technology delivery scheduling and cost estimating. Some examples of these software suppliers include: Cost Expert Group, Galorath Seer Software. Also, several PPM software suppliers integrate scheduling and estimating subset functions in their tool suites.

These solutions provide project modeling functions, estimating algorithms, plan tracking and reporting, plan simulation capabilities, schedule import/export, and/or integration capabilities to other PPM tools. Many of these solution Third-Parties provide project knowledge and historical project initiative knowledge bases to help increase the likelihood for success in planning and estimating schedules. These are often based upon standard project structure templates and experience- based database environments.

Agile development methodologies planning is different in that the estimating methods deal with delivery of smaller segments in their scope but it still feasible and advisable to establish comprehensive scheduling and estimated time frames for each delivery segment.

The importance of the delivery estimating is a key control for managing the overall risk of delivery for IT department. It should not be underestimated as a key control by IT management. An informal guess, or "Swag Estimate," for delivery is not the desired practice in implementation of a standard and repeatable risk management process for the Enterprise. The ability to remove as much uncertainty out of the delivery schedule and estimates are important objectives, for both initiation of the project for approval, and also for the successful implementation of the delivery initiative to the Enterprise. It is a major control for managing the risk of IT delivery.

1.7 Resource Availability and Assignment Controls

One of the work-force technology initiatives implemented over the last fifteen to twenty years has been the migration by many IT organizations and Enterprises to a more remote technology work-force. It has been a major trend from the use of traditional in-house technology employee bases. The costs are high for maintaining, as well as, providing the availability of large IT workforce resources for multidimensional technology delivery. This has increased the need to both outsource various Life-Cycle delivery services and the increased use of external consultants and/or technology contractors. Today, companies face the challenge of tracking and managing outside resources that may not be resident onsite, or located at the Enterprise IT offices, as well as employees "hoteling" and/or working from home, and/or at remote corporate sites. Additionally, many IT organizations utilize "resource pools" and competing project demands require careful contingency planning.

However, for appropriate resource management, IT organizations need to understand the availability of those internal work forces and outside contractors and consultant. Also, they need to establish resource verification procedures. This is especially true for a "Follow the Sun" off-shore approach or large outsourced projects for ensuring appropriate project planning and control. It also important to understand what time is being reported and expensed on task assignments, what projects they are working on, and tasks delivery for the various project and technology delivery objectives, workloads, and schedules.

Resource Availability Control:

Managing large projects requires tracking to the original target schedules and ensuring the availability of the required resources. It is a key risk management control for successful delivery of the initiatives. In order to understand this delivery risk, it is important for the Enterprise to maintain a pool database of available internal IT employee resources and any assigned technology contractors or consultants.

Some of the discussed products have the ability to track all IT staff, external personnel, and the associated project and technology delivery task initiatives scheduled for engagement. They can allocate time and activity to projects based upon the schedules. Several tools can track non-delivery administrative activity, such as: training, time off, vacation, jury duty, holidays, etc. and also categorize these activities and time on project. Having the ability to understand resource available free time is then critical to resource assignments and control of all delivery initiatives.

Resource Assignment and Time Accountability Control:

In addition to the understanding delivery resource availability, another key delivery control is having the ability to allocate resource assignments to multiple activities. It is also important to maintain the ability to track and account for all workforce resource activities on the various delivery initiatives. This requires having the capability to track time-on-project or tasks for the entire project portfolio and is a key management initiative for PMs and delivery managers. It is a key to understanding the overall capital and expense allocations associated with workforce resource activities. Since this is a key control for PPM, software products should also provide the capability for tracking time on the delivery initiatives and against project plans defined for the initiatives. Also, a large number of both Cloud service and boutique software suppliers can provide automation of the entire external talent acquisition process. This represents the service process of resource availability through requirements to resource engagements to time reporting/billing for supporting the IT external services industry and clients.

Whatever approach is taken by the IT organization or Enterprise, it is a key control to have the ability to understand both internal and external resource availability for assignment to the delivery initiative schedule. Additionally, it is important to have the product ability to track the time on task for the initiative, and ability to integrate the time activity for controlling time and costs associated with any other PPM products.

1.8 Quality Assurance IT Delivery Control Risks

Ensuring the quality delivery of software, automated business functions, and IT technology is another key control component in the SDLC initiative. Quality Assurance (QA) testing for the delivered technologies is a key measure of success for delivery of any initiative. It ensures the initiative objectives are delivered to the expectations and business requirements that were defined for the delivery initiative. Software QA testing is necessary, as most delivery initiatives are resource-dependent on human activity. In any human endeavor, mistakes can be made, and technology delivery has the potential for multiple delivery issues. But mistakes in technology and software delivery can be expensive to the Enterprise. In some cases, they are dangerous to the public, depending upon the type and scope of the delivery initiatives. It can open the Enterprise to a large number of risks as defined in this chapter.

The majority of the major Enterprise and IT organizations are under tremendous pressure to reduce both capital and operating expenses in the delivery of their services and products. However, they need in many instances to improve the quality and speed of their technology deliveries. As such, the level of delivery quality and reporting of testing anomalies is a key risk control to understand and manage delivery. This includes understanding testing trends and ongoing testing activities as they relate to the quality of project and technology delivery.

Quality Assurance Delivery Testing Controls:

QA testing control is then a key component of the SDLC. The IT delivery framework validates the delivery of software and technology components are capable of meeting the requirements of the business and operating in the production environments of the Enterprise. There are varying levels of testing that are performed during the delivery Life-Cycle of software and technology products. These are performed by various stakeholders involved in the delivery of the technologies.

These levels of Testing controls include:

- Unit Testing/Code Reviews - Individual construction program testing completed by the programmer and engagement of other delivery team members. It requires detailed knowledge of the internal program architecture, design, and code that is being delivered to the environment.
- Integration Testing - Provides testing of integrated modules of the complete applications or federated environments to validate the combined functionality after construction and object packaging, and individual programming module integration. This is useful in multi-tier levels of software delivery e.g. web-based interfaces, server-side application, and database or host processing tiers, such as client server type systems. Testing is often performed by a collective development group or delivery teams.
- System Testing - Full testing of delivered system environments are often performed by a third-party or Enterprise QA team. The delivered system or environments are tested to the business use cases and requirements developed by the business units and sponsors.
- End-to-End Testing - An advanced level of systems testing. It requires testing the complete delivery environment and system interfaces and/or all federations, using the network topology, communication with hardware and security devices, other dependent or federated applications and integrated systems and databases. It is often performed with a host of teams coordinated by the Enterprise QA testing team.
- Web, Digital, Mobile Device Version Testing - Continual testing to ensure the new product or code release functions correctly within the various manufacture and/or vendor product, software releases, and versions.
- Acceptance testing - Is a major checkpoint for program testing and is performed to verify the delivered technology or system

meets the expectations and the specific delivery requirements of the business and ensures validation of the technology. The business line users make the determination to accept the system from the results of this type of testing. This may require extensive engagement by the business line. Major disruptive test anomalies are to be documented for executive go-forward decisions and risk analysis.

- Performance/Stress Testing - This testing is used to measure the full potential performance level and exponential growth impacts to application and system environments. It is used to manage a range of processing loads for determination of environmental potential failure and/or performance degradation (e.g. response time to users, transaction through-put, etc.)
- Cyber Penetration/Security Testing - Penetration testing for web applications and external internet sites validates the resilience and effectiveness of security technology or system controls designed into the delivered environments for defending against software and environment intrusion. It also isolates IT and Enterprise security violations and potential system/application vulnerabilities.
- Regression Testing - Once the software technology is implemented, this testing is conducted to ensure the environment continues to meet functionality and performance objectives. It is used post-system-maintenance or for introductions of new releases of the Technology. Typically, an organization will maintain regression test databases for validation of baseline functions.

Automation of Quality Assurance Testing Risk Controls:

For large Enterprises, due to the importance and complexity of QA testing controls and high volume of concurrent projects, many IT organizations employ the use of QA Management and Testing Software. Given the levels of testing controls used in the overall delivery testing

Life-Cycle phase and large number of potential testing permutations, it is essential that automated testing technologies be supported for completion of delivery testing in an on-time manner.

Even smaller Enterprises require some level of testing automation, regardless of their size. This is due to extensive application testing conditions required to ensure a quality level of delivery for their Technology products. Spreadsheets are often used by some organizations to track various testing scripts and testing defects. However, for large IT environments, the level and volume of quality assurance demanded by the Enterprise's customers and stakeholders can precludes usage of spreadsheets for large organizations for control of these testing environments.

Quality Assurance Management and Testing Tools:

To support, time-to-market, large testing bases, and the multitude of heterogeneous technology environments, many PPM software suppliers have integrated Quality Assurance and Testing Automation software components into their PPM products and/or aligned with focused and boutique testing tool vendors. The various solution suppliers in this market space are focused on several major software functional characteristics for QA testing:

- Primary QA Management Tools - Used to manage and plan various testing activities, and aligning testing resources to delivery releases and testing scripts;
- QA Defect Tracking - Mapping to the delivery requirements and alignment of testing failures, to include detail defect tracking, categorization, and reporting, to include automated and advanced dashboards and analytics;
- Functional Testing - Automation that provides testing script development and generation of requirements and business test cases to identify defects in delivered technology;

- Automated Stress and Load Testing - Technology that provides simulated user transaction and database volume testing with large populations of test data, to include auto-generation of large test data scripts;
- Application and Security Environmental Testing - Can detect security vulnerabilities and control issues in application and technology environments.

Some of the key software and service vendors focused in this QA testing market include: IBM, Cross Check Networks, HPE, Microsoft, Oracle, CA, and MicroFocus, White Hat Security, Synopsis, and Vericode. Many provide integrated QA tool sets and kits that have a vertical integration with multiple components of the testing environment in their products. Several of these supplier's support Cloud-Based services. Some have also incorporated Agile testing methodologies, into their product offerings.

Third-Party Quality Assurance Testing Services:

In addition to the various QA testing software suppliers in this solution space, the industry has seen the emergence of several QA testing service suppliers over the last ten years. They can perform outsourcing of various levels of testing activities for the Enterprise. These vendors will perform several of the key testing functions, specialized platform testing (e.g. graphical user or mobile application testing, etc.), desk-top software testing, web-application testing, application security control and penetration testing services.

The following service suppliers provide QA service offerings to support Enterprises looking to outsource and provide focused testing activities: IBM, Infosys, Capgemini Group, Cognizant, Deloitte, CSC, TATA, Qualitest, and several large accounting practices. However, the level of exposure to delivery risk may introduce increased risk and create a more complex delivery project environment for IT initiatives. This can be true if utilizing off-shore suppliers, and should be evaluated prior to the use of any Third-Party supplier services (see Chapter 6.10 reference Controlling Risk of Third-Party suppliers)

Regardless of the level of testing performed by the Enterprise or types of tools and services employed to support delivery testing, the most effective risk control for ensuring quality is the ability to perform continuous testing and report the results of testing activities to IT and corporate risk executives. This includes the levels of testing performed, test cycle results, level of defects encountered in this testing, and mitigation efforts for discovered anomalies and defects prior to project and technology delivery.

1.9 IT Delivery Ecosystem Concepts

IT Project and Technology Automation Drivers:

The DMP, PPM, and QA management/test tool software markets are mature industry sectors. Many Enterprise that maintain large IT departments have implemented some, if not all, of the varying software tools in order to manage large project portfolios. These have been leveraged to increase the effectiveness and optimize the delivery of technology to their customers and stakeholders. In fact, time-to-market for project and technology delivery has become an overwhelming driver for introducing new testing products, software, and services technology to the market. This combined with maintaining and increasing quality is a primary objective for almost all CIO's and CTO's in most Enterprises.

Additionally, the rapid state of technology change and innovations and the shortage of IT resources has driven the overall SDLC automation for many organizations. However, a key to this delivery is to ensure the appropriate performance and risk controls are embedded into the SDLC environments. Section 1.10 references some of the key performance indicators recommended for reporting and oversight at an Enterprise level for the project and technology delivery Life Cycle. To obtain that level of reporting and oversight the project and technology delivery requires an Ecosystem of several of the Technologies discussed in this chapter, and that is reflected in the summary Ecosystem discussed in this section.

IT Project and Technology Data Control Concepts:

There are key data sources and categories of data and information recommended to be included in an IT Project and Technology Delivery Ecosystem. These range from other major IT management environments to the required Financial Control Systems that includes:

- IT Service Management System - Represents data associated with the various requests for services to support the initiation of the delivery initiative. This includes the originating businesses and sponsors, business case key linkages, financial justifications, and workflow control associated with the various service task assignments for required hardware, network, equipment, infrastructure, and deployment support. It includes required delivery time frames, development resource dependencies, and technology delivery implementation status.
- IT Configuration Management Systems - Provides complete inventories of application associated data and required technology and application dependencies, and configuration data associated with hardware, networks, security, and software. It ensures compliance and linkage to IT Change Control tracking.
- IT Change and Release Management System - Provides key tracking and authorization controls and work flow for implementation of project and technology delivery into the various production environments. This includes: code packaging control for releasing those changes for the project applications, new technology objects and structures, scheduling changes to production environments.

- Financial Control Systems - Represents the consolidated level of required financial data controls for managing activity associated with all project delivery. These include: Capex management for tracking all capital expenditures approved for the delivery; updates to asset depreciation schedules in General Ledger (GL) accounting for all charges to specific GL accounts, both capital and operating expenses; charge back to required Cost Centers; Accounts Payable for processing all project and technology services and assets; and software expenditures to Third Parties.

IT Project and Technology Delivery Ecosystem:

There are key Third-Party software products available for use in controlling the overall project and technology delivery Life-Cycle. Because of the size of many large IT organizations, high volume of delivery initiatives, and associated demands on the financial capital and technology resources of the Enterprise, the automation of the Delivery SDLC with Trusted Data sources are key to strong IT performance and risk controls.

An automated PPM software suite that includes initiative demand prioritization and risk assessment, project scheduling, tracking, and resource assignment is essential to best-practice delivery activities. These products can be enhanced and/or integrated with resource time-tracking and allocations software components, external resource-tracking software and service components, business requirement development and management components (some include integration to QA testing tools), and delivery Life-Cycle workflow software. Another recommendation is to ensure linkage or interface of the PPM environments to key IT management systems and financial control systems. This can ensure on-time reporting of IT and financial data for ensuring efficient management of the environment and financial records of the Enterprise.

Use of IT QA Management Software and Testing Tools is a key processing control for the on-time delivery of projects and technology. It is also used for driving activity for functional quality testing of all project and technology deliveries. The large volume of functional test scripts, logic coding variables, and design permutations required to validate the delivery environments to business requirements is a driving factor for automation of the Quality Assurance phase. This includes: management of all Testing phases; Testing Script Generation Tools and Load Factor Testing; Performance Testing; Application and Technology Vulnerability and Security Testing, to include Penetration Testing, Defect Management, and Tracking controls.

Each of these components enables the increased optimization of the Quality Assurance process and overall control of the risk associated with poor-quality project and technology delivery. Figure 1.9 provides a summary concept for an IT Project and Technology Delivery Ecosystem, integrating the various Trusted Data Sources discussed in this chapter.

Figure 1.9 IT Project and Technology Delivery Ecosystem

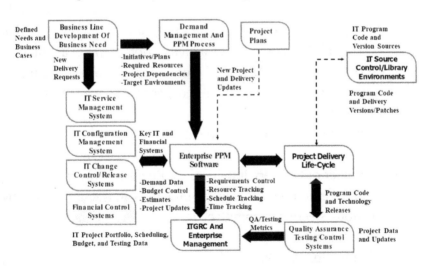

1.10 Identifying IT Project and Technology Indicators

The ability to ensure efficient, timely, and quality delivery of projects and technology for the Enterprise is the major driver for automation of the IT delivery environments. Additionally, it is essential that the Enterprise's financial exposure for any delivery initiative risk is one of the most critical exposures required to be managed, to ensure minimum risk to the financial results of the Enterprise.

As discussed, key Enterprise capital and/or financial committees, IT delivery steering committees, and the overall Enterprise and IT executives are at the core for oversight of delivery performance and risk reporting. Enterprises providing efficient and strong oversight over IT delivery initiatives are capable of demonstrating strong capital, financial, and operational performance to their stakeholders, shareholders, and customers.

Project and Technology Portfolio Performance Indicators:

One of the major program performance items is to be capable of providing key Performance Delivery Indicators and Reporting that relates to overall delivery initiative activity prior to approval and post approval of the initiatives. Some of these indicators are suggested as basic structure of key compliance and performance metrics in the program control framework and includes the following key Delivery Demand Initiative Performance Indicators:

- Number of Delivery Initiatives for Review - Provides tracking as to the number of Delivery initiatives in-que for review by various steering committees to include Financial/Cap-Ex, IT risk and strategic committees. Ranked by business case justification (e.g. revenue, obsolescence, regulatory, compliance, infrastructure, discretionary, process improvement, etc.) and key financial ratios (ROI, ROA, Payback Period, etc.).

- Delivery Initiatives Approved - Outlines the delivery initiatives approved by the capital and/or IT strategic committees for funding and implementation; includes approved financial commitments (capital and operating expense); accountable business sponsors; IT target environments; and delivery time frame.
- Delivery Initiative Financial Accounts - Identifies specific delivery accounts for charge-back and tracking of each of the financial accounts and associated delivery target initiatives.
- Number of Delivery Initiatives Disapproved/Postponed - A key performance indicator to understand the level of delivery initiatives that were not approved to move forward, due to insufficient Delivery information, insufficient Enterprise benefits (both tangible and non-tangible), and/or additional due diligence required.
- Types of Delivery Initiatives - Identifies Discretionary and Non-Discretionary Application, Infrastructure, and Operational delivery initiatives (Number, Costs, Hours)

To facilitate annual IT budget preparations in large Enterprises with a high volume of initiatives, an aggregate list of delivery projects can be used with categories of justification and potential delivery size. And as necessary, isolate financial benefits associated with the initiative. This type of performance and risk exposure reporting can assist IT and financial executives in better understanding of resource and funding requirements for the annual budgetary processes, deferred and carry-over project funding, and performance/infrastructure business improvements.

Delivery Portfolio Performance Activity Indicators:

- Delivery Initiatives In-Process - Defines each of the project and technology delivery initiatives in-process, to include: Project definition, current Life-Cycle phase, status indicators, approved initiative funding, funds expanded to date (capital and operating), phase schedule date, overall target deliver date, and justification business category.

- Delivery Initiatives (Over Budget) - Isolates all delivery initiatives that are exhibiting financial variances, and defines the categories of variance and reasons, variation percentages and amounts, and estimate summaries.
- Delivery Initiatives Late - Isolates all delivery initiatives that are past schedule either on the Target delivery date or exhibiting variances to delivery phase Life-Cycle delivery dates, reason for variances, and proposed time-frame mitigations.
- Delivery Initiatives with Issues - Identifies all delivery initiatives that are experiencing delivery issues that could lead to either future budget variances and/or late phase or initiative delivery.
- Initiatives Completed and Delivery Scheduled - Defines delivery initiatives in a completed stage and by scheduled delivery, final financial accounting of projects, budget vs. actual expenses, and any identified contingencies.

Also, as a matter of good IT governance, all delivery initiative activity performance and reporting should allow for identification and sorting of delivery initiatives for the top twenty-five highest-priority initiatives. These can be isolated in any of the various Key Delivery Performance Reports to generate priority executive attention and management focus.

Delivery Quality Assurance Testing Performance Indicators:

- Delivery Initiatives by Active Test Category - Identifies all Delivery initiatives for each of the key test cycle phases (e.g. functional, user acceptance, etc.).
- Delivery Initiatives Late Testing - Isolates all delivery Initiatives that are past their scheduled test cycle phase delivery date,

encountered during the test cycle phases by severity, and mitigation time frame to complete the QA testing phase.

- Major Delivery Initiatives Defects - Identifies all delivery initiatives by category of defects encountered during the test cycle phases by severity.
- Summary Delivery Testing Cycles Completed - Defines all of the targeted delivery testing cycles completed with indication as to the numbers and severity of defects encountered during the various targeted QA test cycles.

Delivery Initiative Key Risk Indicators:

The identification of delivery project and technology key risk indicators are essential to allow the project teams and more important IT and Enterprise risk management the ability to ensure an efficient risk management of delivery initiatives. This provides for management oversight through each of the various stages of the delivery Life Cycle. It is of paramount importance to avoid major delivery delays that can impact the Enterprise's strategic objectives and financial condition.

Some typical delivery risk concepts have proven to be difficult to quantify through the various delivery SDLC stages, but are recommended, based upon the author's past experience, to require understanding and evaluation in all Enterprise project and technology delivery.

A sampling of these risk concepts that can require additional focus for recognition of any delivery initiative assessment include:

- Initiative introduction of new technologies and/or lack of organizational resources experienced in the new technologies;
- Delivery of large and multi-year projects are by their nature complex and require strong project management methodologies, tools, and oversight, and are often responsible for multiple project strategy miss directions;
- Poor requirement definitions, and/or undefined requirements

that are not included in designs and/or defined for QA testing;
- Lack of engagement by sponsoring business lines and/or executives, and poor testing participation by the business, and/or misunderstanding of target deliverables;
- Predefined delivery dates with insufficient availability of delivery resources and/or unrealistic delivery time-frames to meet the predefined time-frame;
- Lack of competitive product knowledge and customer expectations;
- Flawed technology designs and/ specifications for applications and/or technology;
- Insufficient testing cycles and/or scripts, and/or bypassing of key testing cycles to meet specific delivery dates.

Some of these risk concepts can be difficult to quantify but can be categorized as subjective risk qualifications. They can be identified for specialized monitoring and qualification for executive reviews. These can be isolated, as "Qualified Risk Initiatives", for specific delivery monitoring and reporting to executives.

Additionally, the following key risk indicators are suggested for delivery metrics that are both quantifiable and best-practice industry indicators of potential IT delivery risk:

- Budgeted Delivery Exposure Risk Indicators - Reviews the level of budgeted capital and operating expense to the overall percentage completion of the delivery initiative and delivery phase, and the Actual vs Budgeted (Current and YTD), variance for the phase, with revised estimates for initiative delivery within specific risk tolerances.
- Delivery Schedule Exposure Risk Indicators - Isolates all late delivery initiatives, phases and projects, and the additional time-frame required to complete the Initiative, and resource allocations, with estimated impacts of the late delivery.
- Quality Assurance Exposure Risk Indicators - Defines the

level of risk by defect severity of all projects with the highest severity indicators that precludes delivery of the initiative. This includes Severity indicators that could cause impacts to customers, regulatory, legal, brand/reputation, financial exposure; and indicate estimates for mitigation, business line and Enterprise impact categories.

- Performance/Load Delivery Testing - Identifies the results of all application and technology performance and load testing, and performance level for each application and technology in the delivery initiative, identification of performance category and estimates for mitigation and delivery impacts.

- Vulnerability and Security Penetration Testing - Provides the results of application and technology vulnerability and penetration testing by category of security risk and vulnerability, mitigation strategies, and estimates for mitigation of the detected vulnerabilities, and delivery impacts.

- Summarized Risks and Recommendations - Summarizes initiatives by Risk category with indicators to proceed or cancel based upon impacts.

IT Technology and Project Delivery performance and risk indicators are essential barometers for understanding the core exposure of IT delivery initiatives. They require identification of the highest exposures for initiatives, and aggregation of the overall performance and risk in the IT delivery portfolios. Utilizing automated IT Technology and Project Delivery Ecosystem components can be a major value add for effective IT management of the delivery portfolio.

CHAPTER 2

IT Service Management and Change

2.1 Introduction to IT Service and Change Risks

MANAGING THE IT environmental and system modifications associated within the Technology Service and Delivery Change (SDC) Life Cycle is one of the major risk management controls available to the Enterprise. Delivery of IT Services and Changes are often discussed as a major component of the IT Service Management (ITSM) Life Cycle. With the delivery of changes into IT operational environments, regardless of the type of IT modifications or service introductions, the use of standard change control processes is essential to IT governance. The management of the risk and the understanding of the level of changes to the production environments allows IT organizations and the Enterprise to manage the impacts of ITSM related activities.

IT Change Control, by its nature, requires a process to define, document, and validate the changes being made to assess the resulting demands on the infrastructure production environments. This provides insight for potential business disruptions, reduces the potential for unauthorized production modifications, and can assist in reduction of human and technology issues. Many of the major IT services outages and problems encountered today in IT organizations can be attributed to modifications and changes made to IT infrastructure, operating environments, production applications, networks, and system operating environments. Additionally, IT operational changes can impact the entire ITSM Life-Cycle when appropriate IT control measures are not in place for understanding the nature of IT changes, impacts to Business Continuity/IT DR, and the overall risk to the Enterprise.

ITSM Organizational Control and Accountability:

The primary accountability for change management aligns to the individuals or support teams that are responsible for implementation of the production or environmental service changes and any support teams that are associated with the change. Typically, these individuals or teams are accountable to the executive management of the support organization within IT, either a CIO, CTO, or some other IT departmental or divisional executives. Even outsourced infrastructure functions require oversight by IT executives. It often depends on the nature of the change, whether it is a new or upgraded technology being migrated to production, new security patches being implemented across environmental frameworks, upgrades to existing or new hardware solutions, network service upgrades, and/or implementation of and/or patches to operating systems and database environments.

In the majority of IT organizations, the discipline and methodology for management and oversight for controlling the IT ITSM Life Cycle falls into the domain of the Production Management department. Within this organization there is typically a Change Control Officer and a Change Control/Production Support team that uses a dedicated IT systems environment. These personnel are accountable for ensuring that there exists a daily change process and policy for managing all production and environmental changes to the IT environments They also manage the overall change Life Cycle for production, and any IT DR environmental changes.

ITSM Life-Cycle Accountability:

As a matter of good IT governance, the ITSM Life Cycle requires that a complete set of policies, standards, and processes be in place to provide and facilitate IT services and changes. These standards and processes help ensure that a change or request for service is positioned with the correct priorities and tracked from its initial origins within the Enterprise. This includes: the various IT departments required to support the change, the ongoing status of the change, and the dependencies of the change. Once a change is implemented, the process includes the follow-up and resolution of potential problems or disruptions as a result of the change. This can include the root-cause analysis of the reasons for the change disruption and/or any failures. Almost all of the ITSM Life-Cycle management described above will reside within the overall CTO or CIO organization, but in some IT organizations it is shared between the CTO and CIO, if both rolls exist. This is dependent upon the IT organizational structure.

Regardless of the organizational structure of the IT organization, having an integrated set of standards and processes for control of ITSM functions and resulting changes, provides the IT organization with the ability to leverage a complete business view of the IT Service functions. The ITSM Life Cycle enables IT organizations to better support the Enterprise and prioritize IT service changes and resolve issues associated with those changes.

2.2 Service Management and Change Standards

IT Service Management Standards:

As discussed in Chapter One, the major management and service delivery standard used throughout IT industry is ITIL. There are other variations, such as the Microsoft Operations Framework or IBM Tivoli Unified Process. In addition, some organization may also use the COBIT standard. However, COBIT can be more focused on overall global IT governance, but it does incorporate ITIL concepts. As such, the ITIL standards are often more used to provide the basic structure of standard ITSM Life-Cycle controls for many large Enterprises. Often, ITIL and COBIT are used together as a best-practice control approach in IT organizations. There is also a large ITIL infrastructure and development industry base population who are certified in various methodologies within the ITIL standards.

ITIL Standards for IT Service and Change:

The ITIL standards are an IT industry methodology that focuses on five key IT service governance concepts: Strategy and Objectives; Service Design and Plans for meeting objectives; Service Development and Transitioning for introduction of services into the target environments; Service Operations for managing the various targeted services; and Continual Service Improvement for optimization of IT service levels and delivery of continuous process improvements.

2.3 Services, Delivery, and Change Roles

IT Service Management, Delivery, and Change Roles:

An IT organization is the primary organization within the Enterprise that is accountable for execution of IT Service Request Processing and Changes to the various IT operating environments. This accountability includes providing appropriate hierarchical management and executive approval, and the knowledge as to the severity, risk, and the potential impacts of the change. There are other organizational and accountable areas responsible for both risk control and oversight over IT changes. In fact, changes to the various IT environments are some of the highest volumes of issues that are often reviewed by IT executives, risk managers, and/or an Enterprise Risk Management Committee (RMC), all of which have direct accountability for understanding the level of risk for any changes promoted to the various production environments, and the potential for resulting business impacts.

Additionally, changes and the resulting remediation process are often at the root of many internal and corporate audit focuses along with the review of all controls associated with the IT ITSM Management environments. In most Enterprises, the immediate accountability for oversight of production and other environmental changes is a Production Change Control Board (PCB) or committee. Best practices in ITSM require the use of some type of review structure that is comprised of multiple IT specialist review officers and/or support teams. These boards are often made up of a Primary Change Control officer, various infrastructure personnel that include Network, Security, Architecture, Database, Hardware, Operating System, Data Center Facility, Capacity, Testing, BCP/DR/ Technology Resilience, IT Risk, and other various support environments.

The primary objective of the PCB is to assist the delivery teams (application and/or infrastructure) in assuring that all of the key IT implementation steps, policies, and the processes of the IT organization have been completed by the responsible delivery execution teams, and all impacted environments and teams are aware of the change. The meetings of change control teams as a committee or board ensure there are appropriate levels of collaboration and awareness about these changes to the production environments. They assist the IT organization and Enterprise in the assessment and mitigation of risks associated with the changes. They meet in a formal periodic process to ensure collaborative discussions, validate management authorization, and a documented audit trail for future evaluation.

2.4 Service Management and Change Controls

Controlling Risk in IT Service Management and Changes:

The key control processes for management of the overall IT ITSM environments include major Service Management Delivery Processing Framework component processes. These processes are summarized in Figure 2.4 and are the key summary controls for managing the process and ITSM Framework.

Figure 2.4 Key IT Service Management Delivery Controls

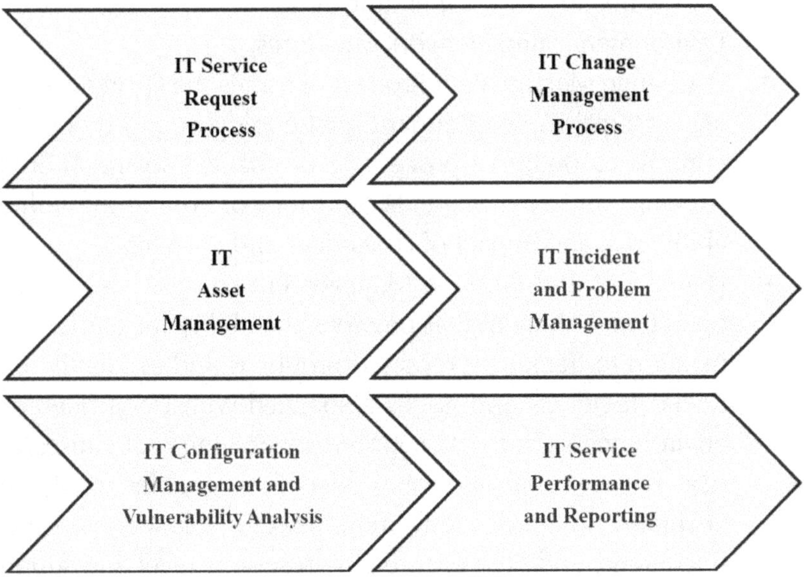

IT Service Request Process	IT Change Management Process
IT Asset Management	IT Incident and Problem Management
IT Configuration Management and Vulnerability Analysis	IT Service Performance and Reporting

These key IT Service Management Control Processes include:

- Service Request Process - The Service Request Process controls the origination of requests for IT services and changes to the IT production environments, and assignment of activities to the appropriate ITSM teams.

- IT Asset Management Process - Provides categorization and inventory of all IT assets via a structured process from ordering of those assets (Hardware, Software, Network, Equipment, Security, Applications, and PDA's, Phones, etc.) through implementation. It includes current environmental diagrams and schematics where appropriate for the environment. The eventual disposal or sunset of the environment is another key control within the ITSM Life-Cycle for IT environments.

- IT Configuration Management Process - Allows the IT organization and Enterprise to control the key technologies and/or subsystem physical attributes and logical relationships, to include architecture; integrated components; dependencies of Hardware, Software, Operating Systems; Third-party Services/ Environments; and Network Structures.

- IT Change Management Process - Ensures the IT organization and Enterprises use standard methodologies and procedural controls to optimize processing of changes to the IT infrastructure and environments, and for controlling the vulnerability risk and impact of IT services and changes.

- IT Incident and Problem Management Process - Is a critical operational element that provides the ability for the IT organization to track user reported problems and to identify particular incidents and issues associated with ITSM operating environments. This data supports identifying root causes, assists in restoration of normal operations, enables timely and accurate communications, minimizes the impact on business operations, and help ensure a high service level and support for business users and customers.

- IT Service Delivery Performance and Risk Report Process - Provides IT services delivery measurements for identification and quantification of levels of service to the Enterprise. These indicators represent IT services, issues, and process improvements, to enhance IT ITSM Life-Cycle governance and risk management.

ITSM Management uses these key processing controls to provide a business view of IT technology architecture, system delivery, and environmental changes. It also allows for prioritization of the delivery of IT services, management of the risk and prioritization for the response to issues, and escalation of problems as needed to the appropriate delivery organizations. Use of the key processes with key integrated automation tools and technologies allows for enhanced risk and governance controls. It also enables IT organizations to manage IT service requests and changes through the entire ITSM Life Cycle.

ITSM Third-Party Software Suppliers:

The IT ITSM Life Cycle is supported by hundreds of ITSM Management technology suppliers. It is a growing industry market sector with some software suppliers providing mature niche tool sets. Key technology software suppliers providing tools in this area include, but are not limited to: BMC, Computer Associates, Cherwell Software, HPE, LanDesk, IBM, Innotas, Microsoft, MicroFocus, Rally, Servicenow, and Vision One. Many of these suppliers include a partial or complete set of technologies for many of the key ITSM Life-Cycle processes, controls, and provide integration to other Third-Party products. Still others offer an integrated suite as part of the overall ITSM Life Cycle discussed in Chapter One.

Additionally, many of the Third-Party suppliers have moved their solution into the Cloud to provide not just Enterprise on-premise solutions, but SaaS solutions for their customers. Some of the suppliers are one-hundred percent Cloud-Based services and there are continually emerging provider Cloud solutions. This can complicate Enterprises looking to complete full integration of the process with the overall project and technology ITSM Life Cycle. It can result from the increase in the risk of external supplier product integrations and federations with internal environments. Enterprises looking to use Third-Party products to control their ITSM Life Cycle should evaluate each of the products, as some are focused in ITSM Service Request

Management, IT Procurement, Asset Management, Change Control, Help/Service Desk, Incident Management, Knowledge Management, Detection Analysis, and/or Metrics Reporting. As indicated, it is one of the largest IT technology provider markets in the IT Industry, and as such, a careful analysis and plan is recommended to use these controls environments and to ensure appropriate integration and automation capabilities with other IT environments and Ecosystems.

2.5 Service Request Processing Controls

The Service Request Processing Framework allows for the primary management of IT service delivery, consistent and repeatable processes, and consolidation of the service approach for the IT organization. It ensures that services are delivered when and how the various agreed-to services are delivered to the Enterprise. Typically, the Service Request process is an internal customer-focused methodology for delivery of IT services. The process provides a structure for collaboration and interaction of IT technology and delivery personnel and internal customers.

Usage of IT Service Management Catalogs:

IT services delivered to internal users and customers will often take the form of supplying a list of standard available services (e.g. Develop new application environments, order new telecommunication networks, build environments, etc.) and/or asset acquisitions (e.g. purchase new hardware servers, new laptop computers or software license, etc.). It also includes explaining how the users or customers can obtain the required service or asset, the costs of those services or purchases, the level of services to be performed, and standard delivery times. This information is often organized into a Service or IT Delivery Catalog, which is often enabled to the internal users or customer via a Service Catalog Management System (SMS). Often the Service Catalog will be enabled for self-service by the IT organization via a standard "online shopping cart". It enables the internal users and customers to order the services or items directly from their desktops or mobile devices. Some IT service requests are more advanced types of technology service requests. These are complex and major efforts, and as such, may only be initiated as a request for a new project application or full technology environments. This is due to the requirement to engage multiple technology service and/or application teams. These complex requests are then large projects and can initiate as full project and technology delivery SDLC type processes, as discussed in Chapter One. The initiatives and supporting efforts will potentially break out into multiple service and change requests linked back to a central major project. This is true where application development, new hardware and software infrastructures, security considerations, and network environments are required for delivery of the full functionality and service for the user or customer.

IT Service Management Level Agreements:

One of the key elements in the ITSM Life-Cycle process is the use of SLA's. An SLA is an agreement between a technology service area and the Enterprise customers that details the key elements of the service and includes the standard delivery response times, availability parameters, the key steps with assigned parties to be engaged for the services, expected time estimates required to complete the requests, and key performance reporting requirements associated with the delivery of the service. Some IT organizations use a "Scorecard" approach to minimize the resource requirements needed to ensure SLA administration because of the labor-intensive nature to maintain SLA's.

IT Service Management - Delivery Change Life Cycle:

Figure 2.5 provides a concept of a Business ITSM Request Processing Cycle from request initiation through the approval of the key request for service process elements. In this sample process, the business identifies and requests the service through the use of an IT Service Request Automated Management System (SRM), using an IT standard Service Request Catalog. The SRM process performs an analysis of the various risks of the Service Requests and based upon predefined Service Parameters for the requested service, assigns the required delivery time frame, priority, risk exposure, cost, key technology delivery assignments, and target dates.

Figure 2.5 IT Service Delivery Request - Change Cycle

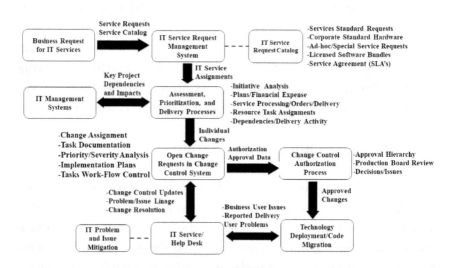

The service request then flows through the required Service Management Life Cycle that drives the delivery IT tasks and activities, and then flows into the Delivery Change process. This change environment documents, authorizes, and controls the assignment of tasks for the changes to the production environments. The process also includes use of a Service or Problem Help Desk for internal users and/ or customers to report any issue with Service Changes. It also provides for identification of any resulting service incidents or problems, escalations of issues to appropriate support teams and executives, and provides problem management tracking and reporting associated with the Service Changes. Controlling the level of severity associated with the problem and/or issues and the aligned priority response can be a major control for reducing the outage time and team response time, and for mitigation of the resulting impacts.

2.6 IT Assets Management Service Controls

Managing IT assets is a key framework control process of the ITSM Life Cycle, because it provides the IT organization with the structures to document and manage the life cycle of each IT asset. It enables the IT organization to track assets from the originating request through the ordering of the IT assets, all upgrades, production migrations, and movement of the assets, and the final retirement of the IT assets. Asset management also provides the IT organization with a complete inventory history of the IT assets, including those areas that have owned the assets, with the service histories, the costs of the asset, and current status/location of the assets.

IT Asset Control Framework:

Key processing within the IT Asset component framework of the ITSM Life Cycle includes use of the following controls:

- Hardware and Software Inventory Controls Process - This is a comprehensive inventory of all computer hardware including: Laptops, Desktops, Servers, Thin Client Displays, Network Appliances and Devices, PDA's, Mobile and Smart phones, Tablets, Printers, Scanners, Phones, and other IT operating equipment. Also, part of the inventory are IT software and applications, both purchased and developed internally; and this includes: desktop software, server-based software, open source software, Operating System and Database software, SaaS environments, and Mid-range/Mainframe software utilities.
- Procurement and Purchasing Control Environments - Consolidated procurement environments for IT Hardware,

Devices, and Software that links directly to standard SMS cataloged equipment and software with their linkage to the IT Inventories for receiving procured assets for the Enterprise, and linkage to Financial/Accounts Payable systems.

- License Compliance Management Control - Provides tracking of purchased software and the associated licenses for that software, open source agreements for ensuring the tracking and allocation of licenses, ongoing maintenance fees, and software support contract cost controls. It is a critical element to avoid the risks of large fines and supports contract negotiations, even when purchased in a decentralized business environment.
- Contract Management Controls - Inventories service and maintenance contracts for Third-Party Asset Service Repair and Contract support for acquired hardware, equipment, and software. This includes maintenance contract services for renewal, terminations, and extensions.
- Asset Identification/Discovery Control - This control can automatically detect software, hardware, and network equipment/devices and allows for reduction of manual reconciliations and ensures accurate recognition of hardware, software, network appliances/equipment and other general equipment, such as printers, and other equipment installed within the Enterprise network, and facilitates auto-integration with Configuration Management controls.*

*(Many Enterprises outsource printer, copier, and telecommunication equipment through leased managed services, but the inventory and control of these assets are key to service, network and security management).

IT Asset Management is enhanced by the integrated automation within the overall IT ITSM Life Cycle. Utilizing automated inventory software with asset identification and detection allows the Enterprise to manage their assets and control the financial and technology ob-solescence risks associated with managing large IT asset portfolios. Linkage of the automated software/asset data collection and detection with the procurement environments simplifies the data collection process and avoids the potential risk of not conducting IT asset tracking.

IT Asset Life Cycle Third-Party Suppliers:

There is a mature and expanding Third-Party Solution Provider market that provides software focused in the key Asset Management Life Cycle. It includes: Asset Tracking, Inventory Audit Management, Compliance Management, Contract Management, Asset Cost Tracking and Depreciation Management, License and Maintenance Management, and Procurement Management. Many of the Third-Party suppliers are focused on providing an all-in-one solution to the market place. Some of these suppliers are emerging and new suppliers enabled by the emergence of Cloud services, and the use of SaaS environments.

Understanding the Life Cycle of an Asset (Order-Receive-Inventory-Track and Disposal) allows organizations to manage their IT financial asset allocations, ensure linkage to financial depreciation schedules, validate compliance with open source and standard Third-Party licenses, logistical management, and track use of all IT assets and the integrated relationships in the ITSM Life Cycle. Additionally, a key focus for many IT organization audits focuses on the capability and effectiveness of IT Asset Controls, and the impacts on Business Continuity, Disaster Recovery, and Information Security processes.

2.7 Usage of IT Configuration Management Controls

Management of the physical configurations in the various IT environments is an integral component of the IT ITSM Life Cycle. Configuration Management is a framework component process for maintaining control over the physical deployment and operational structures associated with all IT Assets implemented in the multiple production and recovery environments of the Enterprise.

The management of the physical configurations of application software, hardware, operating systems, databases, security structures, and operating environments is essential to track the physical nature and status of the implemented assets. Configuration, virtualization, and Cloud-based issues have been associated with some of the largest number of root causes for environmental failures and disruptions, and as such, is a key focus for managing the risk in the ITSM Life Cycle and is the subject of many Enterprise IT audits.

ITIL Framework Configuration Items:

Within the ITIL Framework used by many IT organizations, Configuration Management defines the physical setting and baseline structures of the assets. It defines the architecture of the system, components, and structures deployed for the assets (applications, software, hardware, equipment, and network). In most ITIL based Configuration Management environments, these definitions are known as Configuration Items (CI's). Once defined, the CI establishes the baseline structure for the deployed asset and as changes are introduced thru the ITSM Life Cycle. Changes within the IT operational environments are inevitable and require accurate recording of the versions and status of each of the modified CI's.

Software Life-Cycle Configurations:

Key controls for Software Management requires a process to define and trace changes to in-house applications, operating software, licensed software, open source software, security software, and hardware/network utilities. The final delivery of the software or release to production sets the baseline version configurations for the software and controls all future releases of the software to production, as well as, changes to the key components of the software. Specific settings require unique identification for all software, naming and identification conventions, configuration variables (e.g. type software, language, operating environment, etc.), linkage to specific hardware, network, and operating components (e.g. TCP/IP addresses, storage sizes, memory allocations, etc.), CI status, and approval/audit levels. Maintenance of a complete operating software configuration environment is essential to both COBIT and ITIL frameworks, and a key requirement for understanding the risks posed by software for Cyber, Business Continuity, Technology Resilience, and Data exposures.

Configuration Management System and Database Controls:

As part of the ITSM Life Cycle, a Configuration Management System (CMS) or environment is often composed of both software and databases that are used for collection, storage, management, and analysis of all IT physical configuration data and other CI's in IT environments. A CMS environment will often use, a Configuration Management Database (CMDB), as its control point structure for storing all CI's. It is a centralized relationship database of CI's for the entire IT operating environments. However, in many IT operating environments the CMDB maybe a collection of federated databases and system environments, such as: Information Security CI's, Network CI's, Application CI's, Database CI's, Security Appliance CI's, and Hardware CI's. The concept being that the overall control of the CMDB environment is best suited to the native technological base needs of the target operating environments. In fact, some CMDB tool suppliers in the overall ITSM software market use a federated model of CI type databases. This is due to the unique nature of each of the CI's and for effective management usage of automatic discovery tools for detection of CI data within the native environments, and for usage in data collection tool environments.

Key Benefits of IT Configuration Management Environments:

A key performance benefit of utilizing CMS and database controls is that it provides for increased system reliability via effective controls of IT assets; provides for consistent standards enforcement for centralized monitoring of asset status/functionality; promotes more efficient management of complex system, application, and infrastructure environments.

From an IT risk perspective, use of CMS environments allow for discovery of configuration issues prior to an incident. It also allows for rapid detection of invalid configurations that can then impact availability and performance. It provides for understanding CI dependency impacts from licensing and/or obsolescence conditions for software Life Cycle planning and financial impacts. It can also assist in improving Systems Availability, Capacity, and Security Operations, with identification of IT asset and Cloud environment vulnerabilities.

2.8 IT Change Management Controls

IT Change Management provides the overall primary risk control point and understanding related to the management of the exposure from implementations and modifications of technologies into IT operational environments. This includes implementation and update of production, recovery, end-user business, and operational technology environments.

The ITSM Management process ensures that service changes are documented in a formal structure as to the change objectives, impacts to technology and business, risk assessment and severity/complexity of change, key change participants work activity priorities, hardware/ network/ security patches, management evaluations and approval coordination activity.

An effective change mechanism process provides a best-practice approach for ensuring that IT changes are assessed and that there are no unauthorized changes. It can reduce unplanned outages, increases the success rate of changes, minimize the potential for emergency or reactive technology changes, and can assist in reduction of project delays and risks.

Key Structures in the ITSM Change Process:

Some of the key components of the ITSM process requires that specific knowledge regarding the IT changes be obtained for both coordinating knowledge transfer to all accountable stakeholders and management, but also for controlling the IT changes. These key components and controls includes:

- Change Originator - Identifies who is accountable for requesting the IT change and the sponsor of the change;
- Change Objective - Defines the primary purpose and goals for the changes;
- Change Reason - Identifies the primary reasons or problem the change is being implemented to resolve or implement;
- Change Risk - Qualifies the severity and assessment of risks associated with the change (See Change Severity and Risk Analysis);
- Change Benefits - Identifies the overall business and/or technology benefits associated with the change;
- Change Accountability - Defines the individual assigned resources to the various tasks required to deliver the changes, including sub-operational implementation teams and areas;
- Change Technology - Identifies the required technologies and environments required to implement and deploy the changes, identifying the key CI's and Resilience/DR Technology Tier (see Chapter Four);
- Change Dependencies - Relates all dependent changes required to interact or are a serial dependency, or related to the changes;

- Change Hierarchy - Provides the required hierarchy of managerial approvals required for awareness and acknowledgement of the change;
- Change Time Frame - Identifies the target implementation time frame (dates/time implement and validate) for the changes and/or dependent or inter related changes.

Identification of these key IT change elements allows the ITSM Change Management process to convey to all participants the critical criteria for the proposed changes including the PCB. The PCB will make the final determination in most Enterprises as to the release of the changes to production, with the coordinated approval and notification to the required managerial hierarchies.

IT Change Severity and Risk Analysis:

Since IT Change Management is one of the key risk controls for IT management of technology exposure for the Enterprise, there are several considerations for understanding the risk associated with IT Changes. One is that it is critical to understand the severity and technology exposure from the changes. This often requires a Technology Change Severity assessment be conducted as part of the IT management change process It includes understanding the delivery changes; the probability for a system or technology failure from the change; types of conditions or events that could arise to impact operations (e.g. employee health/safety, operational and environmental disruptions, contractual delays, and/or financial impacts, etc.).

Additionally, it is important to understand the overall nature of the proposed change. This includes assessment of the technology and plan complexity as it relates to the related CI changes; contingency or back-out plans; potential issues or failures; historical analysis of similar previous technology changes and the associated successes; and or problems resulting from the change.

Typically, most Enterprises use some simple risk-scoring mechanism that identifies the Severity of the Change (*e.g.* High, Medium, or Low, *etc.*); and the extent of Potential Impact (*e.g.* Essential to Business, Critical Business, Not Business Critical, *etc.*). Some Enterprise even use the Technology Resilience/DR Tier's (see Chapter Three) to assist in understanding the impact to the Enterprise. Also, the risk assessment may introduce the Complexity of the change (*e.g.* Complex, Moderate, Simple, or Business as Usual, etc.). In any event, assessing the risks associated with the IT changes is an important component of the overall ITSM framework. It is often a key automated component in most Enterprises and exists in many of the available IT Third-Party software tools.

ITSM Change Process Automation:

As ITSM Service Changes are one of the major and mature components of ITSM product offerings from Third-Party Service suppliers, there are several with mature Change Management components in the software products. Some of these suppliers includes: BMC, Cherwell Software, Computer Associates, HPE, IBM, and Micro-Focus.

2.9 IT Incident and Problem Management Controls

The focus of this ITSM framework component is about delivery of services to assist internal user and customer businesses across the entire Enterprise. This process is a primary customer or user-facing process to manage reported and/or detected technology incidents and reported issues. It is also about assisting the end-users or customers of the Enterprise with the implemented technologies. Typically, many Enterprise use a series of processes, technologies, and environments to control end-user prioritization and tracking of issues, workflow for resolution of IT incidents and reported problems.

IT Servicing and Help Desk Usage:

Some of these processes include the employment of an IT Help or Service Desk or an IT Call Center to respond to inbound customer queries and/or reported issues from the internal Enterprise users. Regardless of the concepts used to support the customers, this process is the primary point of contact and customer service portal for the IT organization to manage issues associated with changes.

In many organizations, it is also used as a point of control for assisting users and customers in support of various IT technologies and products. Typically, these are software-based tools that allow the IT service or support environments to enter reported customer or user issues, system errors, and/or key support items reported by their customers. The issues can then be assigned to a particular support area for mitigation and resolution but often can be handled by the service desk, depending upon the complexity.

Often services desks are organized into multiple support tiers, where the lowest tier handles standard user issues with technology (e.g. password resets, etc.) to higher tiers where more significant knowledge is required to resolve the issues. However, to increase efficiencies in many IT Organizations, internal users and customers have been empowered to use Self-Service Portals and Help Technologies, and/or Automated VRU's (Voice Response Systems) to leverage technology to resolve frequent customer issues or questions quickly. These can reduce the impacts on IT budget expenditures, while increasing efficiency in the overall customer responses.

Issue Tracking, Ticketing, and Analytics Systems:

Many IT Organizations also use an issue tracking and/or ticketing environment to track all reported problems (issues or incidents), task assignments of allocated resources to problems, and actual status/resolution of the problem, once closed by the accountable mitigation team. The Tracking and Ticketing systems provide the ability for assessing the severity of the issues or incident, and other key information about the issues (e.g. impacted customers, time and date, repetitive analysis, impact on SLA's, associated CI if appropriate, and change references, etc.). The Issue Tracking technology can track the workflow of an assigned ticket to resolution, perform statistical analysis and reporting about the severity levels of tickets, and types of incidents. Also, the tools can provide monitoring of the progress on ticket resolution, amount of time engaged on the problem, and level of response and quality of service.

One other component is key for these Tracking and Ticketing environments and that is the use of automated interfaces or integration with key IT Environmental Monitoring and IT Operations Analytics Technologies. These management systems can automatically detect issues or problems with the various IT environments, and as such, have the capability to generate automated problem tickets based upon the issue detected, setting a severity, and automatic assignment to the accountable IT environmental team to mitigate the monitored or detected anomalies. Use of management environments integrated or federated to the Issues Tracking/Ticketing environments, are IT best practice concepts for decreasing the potential risk of operational outages. It is a key control for understanding operational impacts for all ITSM services.

Problem Management and Knowledge Repository:

A Problem Management repository and support team are often used to assist in identification of problems, issues, and to track the actual resolution of the problem. It is also used in many Enterprises to provide information and knowledge as input to the Service process via identification of previous incidents or problems and grouping that knowledge with other IT information. These structures can provide quick resolution to similar occurring problems to resolve customer calls or queries. It also supports root cause analysis for evaluating future and consistent recurring problems or questions to reduce

problem-response time for internal users and customers, and for identification of key risks within the ITSM process.

Use of Incident Management, Help Desks Technology and IT
Ticketing, and Problem Management with the use of Problem/
Knowledge-based repositories, either via internal developed systems
or Third-Party products are core components of the ITIL framework.
The appropriate support and management of user- and customer-
reported issues, monitoring of the varied technology environments,
and restoration of IT services in a rapid and effective manner, are key
ITSM core performance activities for IT organizations, and control of
ITSM risk.

2.10 Application Life Cycle's Role in Service Delivery

During the last ten years the IT Software Delivery Life Cycle
(SDLC) associated with the delivery of new software and application
technology has evolved into a concept of Application Development
Life Cycle (ADLM). This is a direct result of the evolution and maturity
of the IT SDLC and IT ITSM methodologies in the industry. It is due to
the fact that many of the key aspects of the delivery paradigm for new
software and continuous ITSM releases are similar and require use of
identical IT resources. The processes have proved that the Life Cycle
of hardware, software, and applications experience many of the same
support and technology needs.

Some of the key processes and components that are similar to the
ADLM includes:

- Identification of business cases, project or change portfolio;
- Aggregate planning of technology and delivery projects;
- Project estimating, and tracking of time and financials;
- Requirements definition, and workflow management;
- Application, software, and technology change management;
- Testing defect tracking and QA testing management;
- Licensing and open source software controls;

- Configuration and Software Version control management;
- Issue Problem Management delivery technologies.

Due to these drivers, many Third-Party suppliers are focused on merging their product delivery into a suite of ADLM technologies. This includes many of the Third-Party technology suppliers reviewed in both in Chapter One and Chapter Two of this book. From an IT ITSM Management perspective, the ability to leverage tools and technologies into a holistic IT Management environment is a win-win for IT and internal customers, but more important, it also assists in reducing the overall risk to the Enterprise.

2.11 IT Service and Change Ecosystem Concepts

IT Service Management Technology Control Drivers:

The ITSM Management software market is an emerging technology supplier market with a large number of new and existing Cloud-Based SaaS suppliers. This includes a core cadre of mature and Enterprise-level sector suppliers. Many of the Enterprise on-premise software suppliers and some of the Cloud-based suppliers are striving to develop a full solution suite for consolidating many of their SDLC, ITSM, and ADLM component products. This allows them to provide an all-in-one focus for their customers. Depending upon the level of automation implemented and the level of integration, IT organizations and Enterprises may wish to consider full suite implementations that meet their objectives, or selective use of key Third-Party product components where there maybe gaps in their overall ITSM control environments.

As IT organizations are working to accelerate the speed of delivery, increase the quality of the delivery, and enhance and align IT resources for optimum productivity, the use of ITSM Management technology is essential for both performance and risk control. The level of changes in many large Enterprises is on the order of 40,000 to 50,000 primary changes annually. The ability to deliver a standard process control of the ITIL based processes, as a result of the high volume and complexity of the IT environments, necessitates usage of automated and integrated and/or federated technology to support the ITSM management environments and processes.

ITSM Ecosystem and Data Control Concepts:

The sample ITSM Life-Cycle Ecosystem depicted in Figure 2.11 builds upon the concepts introduced for a Service Request to Change Management, as part of the IT Service Delivery Request to Change Concept (Figure 2.5). The suggested Ecosystem provides a concept that integrates and/or federates the key IT management components of the overall ITSM Life Cycle. It a Trusted Data concept for linkage to key IT and other Enterprise IT Ecosystems.

Figure 2.11 ITSM Life-Cycle Ecosystem

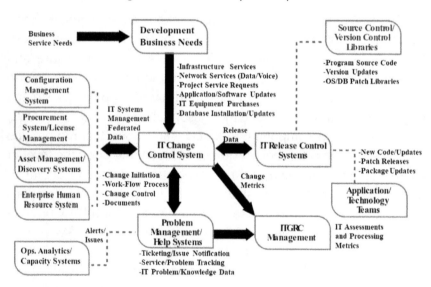

There are key data sources and categories of data and information recommended to be included in the IT project and technology delivery Ecosystem. These range from other major IT management environments to the required Human Resources and Financial Control Systems. Chapter One defined the use of the same Trusted Data Sources and IT management systems for project and technology delivery management. However, what is key for the ITSM Management Life Cycle, is that many changes can be repeatable and routine—or, as defined in the industry, Business as Usual (BAU) standard services (e.g. install desktop applications, set up network access, etc.). However, these may not flow through the full project delivery Life Cycle but may start initiation as a business-process Service Request input from the business. It can have the same level of resource prioritization and flow through a more expedited routine process cycle for implementation without many of the larger project delivery governance and financial project level requirements.

What is important is that the application, project, BAU requests, and ITSM Life Cycles build upon the various Trusted Data Sources and concept interfaces, and federated system structures to enable full delivery of controls for IT services to the internal customers.

Beginning with a Service Request from the IT Service Catalog through work assignment to the appropriate Technology delivery area, with control of IT Asset Management, Procurement (as needed), and Licensing controls, IT organizations are able to leverage the same key ITSM controls. This is enabled by piggybacking upon the exact same controls associated with the ITSM processes to ensure a consolidated view of risk for the IT organization and Enterprise.

Therefore, projects, applications, BAU requests, and technology delivery should be required to open change control activity and approval based upon the controls established for the ITSM framework. Code deployment for new project applications or routine application upgrades are required to use the same Release Control Process for scheduling and packaging the changes for release and propagation to the IT operational environments. They should also use the same Source and Version Control IT Libraries, standard production migration, and common packaging/support areas for implementation of the changes.

IT organizations are then able to leverage the Problem Management, Help Services, and Service Ticketing components of ITSM Life Cycle for all the discussed types of delivery into the IT operational environments. The IT organization and Enterprise are then able to maintain a holistic view of all ITSM Life Cycle performance and risk to ensure consolidated control views of all delivery activities.

2.12 Identifying ITSM and Change Key Indicators

In this chapter section, the Key Performance and Risk indicators are defined for some of the IT best practice and basic concepts for overall control and management of ITSM Management performance. The ability to ensure efficient processes and managed environments is a major driver for automation of the ITSM Management environments. Additionally, it is essential to ensure the management of Key Performance Indicators (KPI) to understand the level of resource activity allocated to support the ITSM processes, performance to predicted time-frames, and to ensure the quality delivery of service by IT executive management.

KPI's for managing IT ITSM Management include the following key categories: IT Service Management Request Process, IT Asset Management Process, IT ITSM Process, IT Environmental Incident Process, and IT Incident and Problem Tracking Process.

IT Service Management Request Process KPI's:

Service Management Request Process KPI's allows IT management to understand the level and status of services being provided to the Enterprise. These KPI's include:

- Service Requests - Number of Service Requests received daily, weekly, and monthly, with breakdowns by requesting business areas and types of service requests;

- Major Service Requests - Isolates the number and types of major or complex Service Requests received for IT servicing, and associated Releases;
- Repetitive Service Requests - Defines the numbers and types of repetitive requests for similar services;
- Service Requests Assigned - Provides the number of Service Requests assigned by area and estimated SLA for delivery of the Service Requests;
- Unassigned Service Requests - Defines the number of Service Requests that are past-due for assignment;
- Delinquent Service Requests - Isolates and ages by delivery dates due, all Service Requests and assigned IT support areas, days past-due and reasons for delay;
- Completed Service Requests - Provides the number of Service Requests completed with isolation by types of services, duration, assigned area, completed SLA time, and resources (resource time and costs);
- Missed Service Levels - Identifies SLA's that were missed and the documented reason for the missed SLA, along with the IT support area and type of service requests.

IT Asset Management Process KPI's:

The IT Asset Management Process KPI's provides management with an understanding as to the overall IT Asset portfolio, asset aging level, asset categorizations, and deployment status. These can include:

- Assets Ordered - Identification of IT Assets ordered by type and unit costs, and associated reference to Service Requests and CI reference;
- Assets Received - Records the receipt and number of IT Assets, procurement reference, and deployment locations, and assigned Enterprise area receiving the IT Assets;

- Deployed Assets - Identifies and records the number of IT Assets installed by type and location of installment for inventory accounting, and by IT support area, asset movement, and associated Service Request linkage;
- Sunset Assets - Identifies and records by location the number of IT Assets removed from operation, and salvaged and/or disposed of due to obsolescence;
- Depreciated Assets - Isolates and ages IT Assets based upon the Enterprise's financial depreciation schedules, assigned owners, location, cost-center and types of IT Assets;
- Assets End of Life - Defines the type and numbers of IT Assets removed from current operation, remaining IT Asset life, and retained for redeployment from Asset inventory;
- Outsourced Assets - Tracks assets with outsourced services/leased from vendors (*e.g.* printers, copiers, *etc.*)
- Assets Missing Configuration - Isolates any IT Assets that are missing configuration-management linkage for the CI.

IT Configuration Management Process KPI's:

Configuration KPI's provides IT management with an overall level of configuration detail and summary status for all physical and logical configuration and assists in driving compliance to architecture standards, ITGRC, and vulnerability management.

- CIs - Identifies the number of and named Configuration items by type (*e.g.* Application, Servers, Desktop, Storage Devices, Laptops, Routers, etc.), sub-components, dependencies, virtualized and logical indicators, replication targets, and overall status, last change date, and target configuration change dates;
- IT Asset Reconciliation - Defines the number of and identified CI's by type that are missing reference reconciliation to IT Assets inventories, and identified missing CI linkage (e.g. applications to physical/logical servers, Cloud environments, etc.);

- Incomplete Configurations - Identifies the number of CI's by type that are missing key data variables or are incomplete, not defined, or missing dependency references, etc.;
- Configurations Changed - Defines the number of CI's by type referenced and updated due to an implemented change reference.

IT Change Management Process KPI's:

Change Management Process KPI's allow management to understand the overall level of change and velocity of changes being introduced to IT operating environments, and level of risks to the IT organizations and overall Enterprise: These include:

- Number Service Changes - Defines the number of changes opened for implementation, change requestor/area requesting, and type of change, including emergency changes, with due date;
- Severity Changes - Isolates the number of changes by Severity and assigned area;
- Approved Changes - Defines all service changes approved by management and time/date of approval, if they exist, and appropriate approval levels;
- Unapproved Changes - Defines all service changes awaiting approval, with identification of changes past the expected approval timeframe;
- Production Board Changes - Isolates the number, type, and time frame of changes submitted for Production Change Board approval;
- Approved/Unapproved Board Changes - Isolates the number of changes approved by the Production/Change Board for implementation, and defines changes not approved by the board with reasons for rejection;

- Completed Service Changes - Defines the numbers and types of changes completed and time-frame completed, and definition of resources expanded to support the changes;
- Changes with Problems - Number of changes with reported issues and description of issues, assigned issue IT support team, and definition of problem impact;
- Changes Incomplete - Number and types of changes that are incomplete with aging by time-frame, and assigned IT support team;
- Changes with Missed SLA's - Identifies the changes that missed the service delivery SLA and reasons for missing SLA, where SLA's are utilized to track both internal and external services. Outsourced SLA's depends upon the available vendor details and associated data costs.

IT Incident and Problem Management KPI's:

Incident and Problem KPI's allow management to understand the complexity of incidents and problems, criticality of incidents, and response to these incidents, and the level of impacts to the Enterprise These include:

- Received Incidents - Defines the number of reported incidents and problems by type of issue and assigned IT support team;
- Incidents Resolved - Isolates the number of incidents resolved by area (e.g. service desk, IT support team, resolution time etc.);
- Incidents Resolved within SLA - Isolates the number of incidents resolved within SLA, type of issue, and IT support mitigation team;
- Incidents Unresolved - Isolates the number of incidents not resolved and aging of incident by due date, type of incident, and IT support team;
- Incidents Missed SLA - Isolates the number of incidents

resolved but with missed SLA's, indicating reason for missed SLA, and IT support team;

- Incidents Escalated - Isolates the number of incidents escalated to senior management, and targets area issues associated with escalation, reasons for escalation, and IT support team;
- Major Outage Incidents - Tracks major outages and associated post-mortem status and mitigation actions/dates;
- Automated Environmental Alerts - Identifies the number of automated monitoring alerts from IT management systems tools, associated ticket reference numbers, and assigned IT support team;
- Resilience Automated Alerts - Identifies IT Resilience and Storage Alerts from IT Operational Analytics tools, and associated ticket reference number and assigned IT support
- Security Automated Alerts - Identifies IT Security issues and detected vulnerabilities in network perimeters and traffic, software, and hardware environments from IS sensing software and security analytics packages;
- Capacity Automated Alerts - Identifies IT Capacity Issues from IT Operational Analytics Tools, and associated ticket number and IT assigned support team.

Key Service Delivery Change Life-Cycle Risk Indicators:

The identification of the ITSM key risk indicators is important to understand for the overall risk to the IT organization and in support of future IT organizational strategies. Project and Technology Life Cycle Delivery risk is much more focused on the financial and project impacts for management of full Project Life Cycle risk. ITSM risk is focused on the risk of technology delivery and operational activities. Controlling the risk to the full delivery point is essential for the IT organizational areas, as issues associated with the ITSM Life Cycle are often escalated visibility for the IT organization, Enterprise executives, and customers (external/internal) on a broader and larger scale.

There are two key risk control activities that are central to understanding all risk activities, but that are essential in the ITSM portfolio of risk for the IT environment. The first is understanding where the risk exists in the overall ITSM Life Cycle, and second, how the IT organization is provisioned to avoid the risk associated with ITSM activity.

The following Key Risk Indicators are recommended best practices for understanding and/or avoiding risk in the ITSM Life Cycle:

- ITSM Severity - Providing a comprehensive report of all future changes by Severity and Exposure is a key to understand the portfolio of IT risk on a daily, weekly, and monthly basis, and the ratios by Severity to all ITSM changes. A primary KRI for executives as it relates to the entire ITSM cycle, allows executives to understand their operational delivery risk profiles.

- Emergency ITSM Reasons - Isolates the number and detail of Emergency Changes required for rapid delivery, reasons for change, target environment for these changes, and authorized management levels, and ratio of Emergency Changes as a percentage of all ITSM change activities. A key requirement for executive understanding of the level of change due to major issues and/or required environmental patches to correct production issues, and as a potential indication of poor or incomplete delivery controls.

- Recurring ITSM Issues - Identifies all Problems and Incidents that meet a ratio of recurrence either in terms of past-due delivery, similar root causes, and/or continued anomalies. Allows executives to understand where there are predictive issues associated with their environments, and recognition of potential delivery and/or environmental issues.

- Service Delivery Downtime - Identifies the various Service Delivery Technology environments based upon the duration of outage for the category of services, and/or CI's, including Applications, Technology Environments (e.g. Network, Services, Security/Network Appliances, Operating Systems/ Utilities, Database Environments, etc.). Indicates to executives where they are not meeting key service levels and identifies exposures for the Enterprise, and potential technology environmental issues.

- Asset Management Levels - Isolates by Category of Assets the status of the IT Asset and includes Asset Depreciation Time-Frames, Budgeted IT Asset variances, target Obsolescence Levels (*e.g.* time frame, *etc.*). Provides management with key understandings of the IT Asset portfolio to assist in understanding the risks to the IT portfolio for both strategy and planning, and potential environmental risks.

- Capacity Management Levels - Identifies the level of Capacity targeted for the IT operational environments vs Performance and Issues, including: Networks, Servers Capacity, Storage Capacity (Disk, Tape, Replication), Operational Redundancies, CPU Processing Levels, Data Center Infrastructures (power, raised floor, cooling, UPS and Generator capacity) and Support environments, and Security environments), and validation against Future and Current business volume projections, isolating Capacity issues and/or projecting potential variances. Allows executives to understand operating environments risks posed by inadequate capacity that can impact service delivery, operational performance, strategy and financial performance, and for future strategy/budget planning for the Enterprise.

IT organizations utilizing a standard and consistent ITSM Life-Cycle methodology and risk assessment process will help ensure the Enterprise has a consistent and repeatable process to assist in reduction of the risks associated with IT technology delivery. A mature ITSM Life-Cycle process with appropriate performance and risk monitoring, allows the Enterprise to forecast and manage the risks of IT Service Delivery to the organization. As such, a mature ITSM Life-Cycle methodology can assist in transitioning the IT organization behaviors from a reactive or fire-fighter responses to a predictable operational focus, reduce overall Enterprise operational risks, and optimize IT financial expenditures.

CHAPTER 3

Business Continuity Processes

3.1 Introduction to Business Continuity Risks

BUSINESS CONTINUITY PLANNING (BCP) is a process that is used to help ensure the continuous operations of business and/or recovery of business services or processes. It includes continuous services to business customers for product delivery by Enterprises during adverse events. These types of events can include natural disasters, local/regional utility outages, manual errors, cyber and technology issues, and other man-made events *(e.g.* active-shooter, terrorism, *etc.).* Most recently, the focus has expanded to increase understanding for continuity planning for crisis response and risk management for these events. This is due to introduction of global and enabling web-based business technologies; 24/7 mobile operations; and the increasing dependency upon Third-Party servicing of operations and technologies (*e.g.* call-center support, Cloud-Services, etc.); the expansion of global terrorism concerns; and increasing dramatic climatic conditions and events (*e.g.* hurricanes, flooding, etc.). It has also increased the business drivers to determine how the risks of these impacts are identified, evaluated, and reported, together with the speed of the risk determination, and the oversight of BCP activities and guidance by management in most Enterprises.

A priority for IT organizations is to ensure that the business and operational processes supporting the Enterprise have been risk-assessed accurately, and also, that appropriate planning and mitigation are developed for the various internal business organizations. This chapter will focus on the practical approaches to development, maintenance, risk assessment, operational delivery of effective BCP control programs, supporting Business Continuity Management (BCM) technologies, and reporting of key BCP performance and risk indicators. An Enterprise-wide business process approach that develops governance frameworks for not just technology recovery, but for business processes recovery, business process testing, crisis management, and various business communication, and notification strategies are critical to building a viable BCP Program to control these risks to the Enterprise.

Business Continuity Risk Organizational Accountability:

Depending upon the culture of the organization, the BCP governance and accountability can be organized within different departments across the Enterprise. These include Procurement/Real-Estate, Finance, or IT organizations, or even the Enterprise risk departments. Again, this organizational structure is dependent upon the business culture and industry. In the financial industry, within the last few years there has been a consolidation effort to house both BCP and Technology Disaster Recovery (DR) planning and exercise execution within the IT departments but maintaining risk-management oversight within the Enterprise's risk organization. This is due to the implied and expanding dependencies and convergence of technologies between the IT and business activities.

However, in 2014, with the introduction of the Dodd Frank Law regulations and other regulatory direction under disaster, the financial industry has been implementing organizational strategies, which consolidate and create a Second Line of Defense (SLOD) oversight organization for BCP and technology resiliency programs within an Enterprise risk structure (See Chapter Eight). This includes key second lines for oversight of IT key operational technologies and Information Security (IS). The heightened standards require the need for independent organizations that manage these governance programs and the risks associated with these strategies.

The new regulations and direction go as far as stating that a first-line executive IT officer or CIO should not control both execution and oversight of certain risk control activities for these governance areas. This concept could apply to any industry that is looking to ensure overall independent governance control of technology and operational risk activities for key IT business domains, such as BCP, DR, Technology, and Information Security.

Regardless of the organizational accountability for the governance of the Business Continuity program and accountability for reporting the risks associated with Business Continuity, a pre-requisite to good corporate risk management is to maintain governance and operating standards for these IT domains, and over decentralized business operations.

In any event, the operating business and/or service divisions must be accountable for the recovery strategies of their operations with alignment to their businesses. They likewise have accountability for executing the recovery of their operational areas and the ongoing continuation of services to their customers. Additionally, an oversight accountability is required that includes the management of the Business Continuity governance frameworks or programs, executive focus at the corporate level, and processes as governed by an Enterprise risk program.

3.2 Business Continuity Governance and Policy

The requirements for governance over the BCP program should be organized into a strong BCP Enterprise policy and governance framework. To ensure the BCP policy has the required exposure and appropriate level of control over this risk, the BCP policy should be approved at a minimum by an Executive Stakeholder Committee.

A Board of Directors approval is recommended, but at a minimum in lieu of Board approval, Board oversight over BCP policy is necessary to ensure compliance by all stakeholders and operating divisions. In the banking industry, it is a requirement that the BCP policy be approved annually by the corporate banking or holding company Board of Directors. Regardless of the policy accountability and/ or governance approval layer it is important for all BCP programs to have the visibility and support from top-down Enterprise executives in order to drive communication of policies to all employee levels.

The BCP policy should establish a governing frame work of accountabilities by a centralized group, operational units, and executives for this risk area. The policy frame work should establish:

- An Enterprise methodology and defined roles for BCP participation for organizations and participants (a RACI structure is recommended);
- Requirements for a Business Impact Analysis (BIA) and business risk assessment and priority recovery process;
- Specific BCP planning and BCP exercise requirements;
- Appropriate risk assessment and management concepts, criteria, and executive oversight requirements;
- Identification of BCP program performance and risk reporting and monitoring requirements;
- Required employee training curriculums for program participants including BCP planners, approvers, plan testers, business process management, recovery resource teams, and risk officers;
- Program hierarchical approval levels, and specific escalation oversight and accountability;
- Essential reporting levels and identification of program anomalies and exception requirements.

Additionally, the BCP policy and framework should establish specific periods of time for evaluations, exception review, planning, and exercise time periods, with required levels of participation for the various components of the program.

3.3 Assessing Business Continuity Risk Impacts

Each business division with operational and service accountability should be required to perform a BIA risk assessment before introduction of any new services or operational processes. This should also be accomplished with risk impacts when the business updates these operations or service processes. The BIA process should be governed by the overall Business Continuity Policy for the program. It can be a foundation for Business Continuity Risk assessments of the corporation. Figure 3.1 provides a sample conceptual flow for a standard BIA and Risk Assessment process.

Figure 3.1 BIA Risk Assessment Process Concept

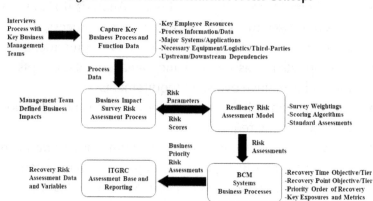

Business Impact Analysis and Risk Assessments:

The BIA and risk assessment process should capture essential planning data components as to the resources required to maintain operations in the face of a potential worst-case solution impacting the operational processes and/or service. These components should include:

- Required core personnel resources;
- Necessary forms and documents;
- All data and information requirements;
- Business processing capacity capabilities;
- Essential office and logistical requirements;
- Required equipment and supplies;
- Dependent technology, assets and resources;
- Key upstream and downstream dependencies.
- Third-Party processor dependencies.

BCP BIA Risk Assessment Component:

The risk assessment component of the BIA should be designed into the BCP framework to capture the impact and risk for a particular business functions and process that are objective and standardized across the Enterprise. The BIA risk assessment process must be capable of determining the Recovery Time Objective (RTO) for the particular process and thus the importance and recovery sequence for this process within the overall Enterprise requirements.

Most corporations will often assign a Business Recovery Tier Category for their processes in order to determine the maximum allowable recovery time and prioritization for conducting recovery of the business processes. These can be grouped into specific Tier categories. As an example, the Recovery Tiers are numbered throughout most industries from Low to High. In this example, Tier Zero represents the most critical business functions and most critical recovery priority for the corporation and Tier Five represents the business processes and functions of some of the least important processes to the corporation.

The process will also determine, a Recovery Point Objective (RPO), for data or information required by the process, and a Recovery

Priority Sequence (RPS) required to ensure appropriate alignment of resource needs to ensure meeting the targeted RTO. Figure 3.2 provides a sample conceptual set of standard BIAs Risk Assessment tiers and other risk parameters.

Figure 3.2 BCP BIA Risk Assessment Tiers

Risk Assessment Recovery Tier	Recovery Tier	Recovery Time	Recovery Point	Priority Sequence
Critical	Zero (0)	< 2 Hrs	Zero Mins.	1 ,2
Urgent	One (1)	02-04 Hrs	1 Mins. Or Less Less	3,4,5
Very Important	Two (2)	04-24 Hrs.	5 Mins. Or Less	6,7,8
Important	Three (3)	24-48 Hrs.	1 Hrs. or Less	9,10,11
General	Four (4)	48-72 Hrs.	24 Hrs. or Less	12,13,14
Non-Essential	Five (5)	>72 Hrs	24 Hrs.	15,16

The BIA risk assessment process should also identify any potential impacts to the RTO to include: any special process dependencies and requirements, provide appropriate metrics reflecting the degree of impact to the RTO, and derive the RTO from consistent impact metrics across all business lines. It is also recommended that the BIA process use and identify relative weights/measurements for each of the Tiers and logic to assign consistent recovery objectives. These should be based upon aggregation of the various metrics and risk scores associated with the BIA.

Business Impact Survey Component:

The BIA risk assessment process, in most Enterprises, spans the range from simple to complex structures. This is dependent upon the sophistication of the BCP program and Enterprise risk management programs. The actual BIA risk assessment in a simple form is a series of 15 to 25 key business survey questions in a document form reference for the target business process or function. It allows the Enterprise to determine the priority of the processes to the Enterprise and the maximum allowable downtime for critical business processes, recovery point objectives, backlogged transactions potential volume, and the potential losses/costs associated with a process due to a potential business outage and/or downtime.

The BIA survey questions are often completed by the actual business line operational or service management team with oversight from the BCP organization. However, it also can be derived through a BIA interview process conducted by the BCP oversight organization. Depending upon the exact data point, specific weightings will be implied as it relates to the various priorities of importance to the Enterprise. In the most complex process, the BIA format for many Enterprises uses automated data-capture techniques and rules-based algorithms to ensure objectivity and consistency in the risk determination process. Additionally, major dependencies should be identified and understood to ensure continuous operations. These will be discussed in more detail later in this chapter.

Key risk condition categories that are addressed in most standard BIA processes are based upon impacts to any of the following:

- Revenue - Impacts to direct revenue and/or Profits from loss of the operational services or business, due to business disruptions, critical resources, or personnel;
- Customer Service - Impacts to external customer service processing or activity, internal SLA's, or final product delivery from service interruptions;
- Legal - Resulting impacts to existing contractual agreements with customer, partners and/or potential litigation and other exposure to legal ramifications from operational impacts or disruptions;
- Regulatory - Impacts from failure to meet appropriate regulatory requirements and/or potential fines associated with regulatory compliance disruptive events;

- Reputation - Impacts from service or business disruptions that would have a major impact to the reputation or brand of the Enterprise, customer loyalty, and also stakeholder equity and/or stock valuations;
- Infrastructure - Key supporting infrastructure environments that could result in direct revenue or profit losses to the corporation, or major service failures;
- Employee Safety - Any disruption or incident that could be harmful or impactful to employee health, safety, or well-being.

Business Impact Risk Assessment Determinations:

Each survey, regardless of the results, needs to assign an RTO and weighting to the business process and functions. The BIA should be able to determine the mission-critical processes for the most important functions to the Enterprise. The RTO outcome must also not be in dispute by the business line and should be the result of at least a qualitative understanding by the business. However, the assessment should use quantitative business measurements and supporting metrics. No subjective determination should be allowed in the process without specific review by an authoritative control SME groups, and with executive management knowledge and acceptance of the results.

The BIA when implemented in a standard manner and with the correct oversight, should become a standard reference information base and trusted asset in the determination of all business risk priorities across the Enterprises. It should identify business processes and function as a repository of data for mapping all process inventories and business functional flows across the Enterprise. Also, the BIA should include identification of the various upstream and downstream dependencies (e.g. Processes, Technology, Third Parties, and Employee Resources, etc.). Later in this chapter (3.10) we will identify this key integration points for IT risk aggregation with these key data sources.

Secondary Challenge to Service Risk Assessments:

After the business functions and processes have been risk assessed and RTO, RPS, and Recovery priorities established for the Enterprise along with key risk exposures, each business line should review and evaluate the assessments. It is suggested as a good practice for the organizational area accountable for the BCP Subject-Matter-Experts (SME) review BIA results with the business lines to ensure correct assessments. They should also challenge the business lines on any dispute of the results.

The challenge process will help maintain detailed reasoning and challenge discussion points in a documented, and if possible, automated repository to ensure consistent due diligence regarding the risk assessment process and to support future corporate audit activities. This ensures a consistent evaluation review process as well as a level of quality control and a creditable review framework. It provides the ability for corporate accountability of the risk assessment baseline for other risk areas that can depend upon this cross-operational process within these BCP processes. The challenge process also allows the BCP SLOD organizations the ability to update processes on a continuous basis, provide an iterative risk assessment process, update and revise framework guidance, and provide any additional training required to ensure continuous improvements in the BCP program frameworks.

3.4 Understanding Gaps in Service Availability

A key determination in understanding the risks associated with IT and operational services delivery is an evaluation of any gaps between the availability of technology and applications used by the various business processes and the RTO requirements for those processes. This is often discussed as a discrepancy in RTO's for the various target technologies or applications (See Chapter Four) but is understood to be the Dependency Gap between the required technologies needed for the business process to conduct normal operations. It is important to understand these gaps, as the non-availability of the technologies could have a major impact to the delivery of the required operational services to customers or other stakeholders that are downstream or upstream from the business process.

Comparing the RTO between business processes and technology/applications, and Third-Party suppliers are standard processes in all BCP program frameworks. It requires that a similar process for RTO assessment be conducted for technologies and applications of Third Parties. Utilizing an automated gap analysis process for understanding these gaps is a best practice and one of several common concepts used by some Enterprises. When this gap analysis is automated, it allows a rapid determination of processing gaps between the dependent technologies and/or Third-Party suppliers and business processes for efficient risk management. This is often the case in large IT organizations.

Gaps between the technologies, Third Parties, and the dependent business processes requires specific identification, but it also requires development of mitigating process controls and special strategies. This is to ensure appropriate resolution to gaps in availability of the processes and the inherent risks to business processes.

Mitigation of the gaps can take the form of re-architecture and/or reengineering of the Technology environments. This can ensure availability to the required business processes. Mitigations could include: mirrored and active processing environments; development of automated alternatives to support the processing components that are dependent upon the technologies, third parties or other downstream processes, and can include special automated backup reporting and alternative processing environments. Also, the development of manual work-around procedural tasks and activities may be required until the technology, third-party, or dependent processes becomes available for the target process (e.g. alternative offsite backup staff, document and tested work flow procedures, etc.).

These mitigation alternatives need to be assessed based upon the risk of financial impacts vs. investments and the resulting residual risk associated with mitigation and overall impacts to the Enterprise. In many cases, the associated risk of the various dependencies will be elevated to executive management. Management may then consider the investment cost for mitigation vs. the probability of an event, and then evaluate acceptance of the risk. A sample Technology Dependency Gap Analysis is provided in Figure 4.4 of Chapter Four.

3.5 Business Continuity Process Recovery Planning

Once the BIA is conducted, the accountable business lines need to develop documented plans to recovery their businesses. These plans are known, as BCP recovery plans (BCP's). They need to document the recovery strategies and functions to be performed, and procedures required to execute the plan priorities for critical and non-critical services, processes, and functions in the event of a business disruption. BCP's should address the various risks and threats to the business process. Additionally, they also describe the specific responsibilities and procedures to be used in the recovery of the targeted business process, and the resources required to allow continuation of services and business functions with the appropriate recovery resources.

The BCP should be flexible enough to address various types of inherent risks and threats to the business response to specific scenarios and planned recovery objectives. Plans should identify specific steps to take after an event or process impacts to minimize service disruption, mitigate damage, and identify recovery alternatives and actions. Enterprise should focus on continuation of business operations, recovery of the business as required, and the resumption of normal operations with the appropriate planning strategies.

Specifically, these plans need to identify the risk and define procedures for recovery when any of the following events could impact operations or services of the Enterprise:

- Key local and regional utilities are unavailable (power, tele-communications, water/road public infrastructures, including transportation, etc.);
- Logistical facilities, operational centers or offices, and/or geographic operational areas unavailable to support the business;
- Equipment malfunctions and service repair delays (hardware, telecommunications, security devices, operational equipment);
- Data and/or essential documentation or records are corrupted or unavailable, or lost;
- Critical work force or large employee absence (e.g. pandemic events, etc.) impacts to operations or service;
- Computer applications and availability, operational disruption of business processes, and cyber events;
- Third-Party provider technology, support, or services are unavailable to continue operations and/or support business processes.

BCP constructs, structures and key components recommended in the construction of BCP's should include the following:

- Plan overview that describes the purpose of plan and key resource owners and management;
- Descriptive information about the business and/or process targeted for recovery planning and key processing strategies;
- Plan revisions (plans often are updated frequently) - Organizations should maintain versions and change tracking for all plan updates for regulatory and audit review;
- Recovery team members and other required contacts and their contact data (phone, email, SMS), and personnel job functions/titles;
- Assembly locations for employees (evacuation points) in case of major location impacts, active shooter protocols, evacuation routes, and response to incidents, such as fires, bomb threats, etc.);

- Command Centers instructions and locations for key management of the continued process service and recovery;
- Damage assessment and emergency declaration process resource definitions and procedures;
- Go/No Go decision processes for recovery and escalation procedures;
- Alternate Work Area Recovery WAR (alternative displacement sites from the primary process location;
- Business function process RTOs defined during a BIA process;
- Recovery procedures and strategies (e.g. work from home, split operations, transfer work to other site, transfer to hot site, relocate to vendor site, implement manual procedures, etc.);
- Dependent processes and technology definitions;
- Vendor contact lists with checklists of recovery steps;
- Communication requirements and frequencies (internal and external communications);
- Resources required for completing the recovery of the process or function;
- Restoration procedures and return to primary locations for these processes.

3.6 BCP Threat Vulnerability Assessments

One of the major BCP concepts is the requirement to understand the threats to the business from specific events and also the assumptions developed to support planning for response to those threats. A key element in understanding the risks from these various events is for the BCP framework to include a Threat Vulnerability Assessment (TVA). This provides for assessing the probability and potential for impact to critical and non-critical business functions and facilities. Vulnerabilities in a BCP framework translate to assessing the threats from potential hazards to the business operations, employees, and infrastructures. Once identified, they require development of mitigation plans and strategies to address these threats. Enterprises should consider automation of the TVA processes to ensure rapid under-standing, and to provide efficiencies in processing large volumes of threat and hazard data to the Enterprise.

An example of an automated BCP TVA automation processing concept for assessing the risks to specific business processes and op-erating facilities is depicted in Figure 3.6.

Figure 3.6 BCP Threat Assessment Automation Concept

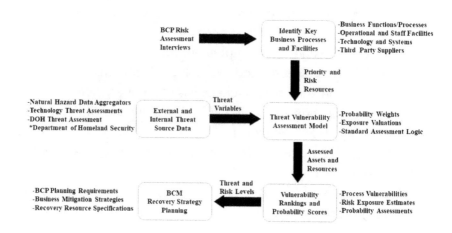

In this process, the risks to all organizational facilities from spe-cific natural threats, hazards, and man-made threats are assessed and prioritized based upon an automated process of measuring the prob-ability of these threats. Once the threats are identified and prioritized, the business can define the appropriate strategy to respond to those enterprise risks.

One example is a threat for power outages that are common im-pacts to the Enterprise and a major form of disruption to many orga-nizations, as these may impact business operations and technology data centers. Therefore, these threats need to be evaluated for these operations and technologies. Additionally, there are specific types of natural hazards such as floods, hurricanes, tsunamis, and earthquakes that can cause major operational facility and work-force disruptions, along with operational impacts and data center availability.

A TVA can be used to identify high-probability impacts to locations, and then to the Enterprise. Then organizations can develop specific strategies to plan for recovery from high-probability inherent risks for these types of events, rather than just perform overall all-hazard type planning. Such types of threats can have unique requirements to mitigate impacts and plan for continuity of operations.

3.7 BCP Insurance Strategies

Often the Enterprise will offset the potential risk of specific types of threats with the purchase of types of liability insurance. This is used as a control to assist in the recouping of losses that may not be mitigated or prevented by the Enterprise. They are risks that are not controlled or foreseen in the planning and recovery strategy definition process, or where mitigation is often a high cost for low-probability events.

The determination as to the requirement for insurance and other loss-recovery strategies needs to be based on the probability and exposure of the potential loss as determined during BIA risk and TVA process. Management should understand the exposure from various events and review all insurance options to ensure the level of coverage is appropriate for the risk appetite of the Enterprise. Enterprises also need to understand the potential financial losses from specific threats and determine the level of reimbursement and investment required to mitigate losses from the event.

However, management should also consider any other contributing continuity factors as to the loss of services from disruptions or incidents. This includes impacts to their customer base, reputation, and/or shareholder valuations. Where insurance may offset losses from an event, it is only one of many strategies available to executives, to offset business interruptions. But, executives may want to balance the understanding that insurance will not recover or maintain the business services of the Enterprises for their customers, it assists in offsetting potential financial impacts to the Enterprise.

3.8 Identifying Recovery Dependencies in Processes

Another major element in BCP risk management from disruptions of service or business operations is the identification of key technology, Third-Party, and/or operational processing dependencies. Most BCP programs require that during the risk assessment processes, Mission Critical (MC) process dependencies be identified, as either upstream or downstream dependencies in many organizations. MC processes and resources are defined as those that require immediate availability in terms of service or can include requiring services be available within 24 hours due to impacts. However, these should be outlined in the BCP policy and framework, as to their definition based upon the needs of the Enterprise. Many organizations designate this based upon the defined RTO definitions, but these can also be defined by other risk characteristics of the Enterprise (*i.e.:* high visibility customer process needs, or special regulatory requirements, *etc.*).

Upstream dependencies are determined when mission-critical business processes and functions are prerequisites for completion of a targeted business process function or to provide critical services for customers, or product delivery of product. Downstream dependencies are determined when the business process or function is a prerequisite for completion of a full operational mission-critical service function (*e.g.* customer order to delivery, *etc.*).

In addition to processes, Third-Party provider services, and technologies can also be found to be MC to the specific targeted process. Later in this book, we will explore in detail the risk process for understanding and managing Third-Party IT service vendor management (Chapter Six). As in MC processes, Enterprise Third-Party risk management policies and frameworks need to define definitions for MC vendors and their characteristics. These policies should be synchronized with the BCP programs. Key technologies, IT services, and applications also are often prerequisites and/or a dependency for MC functional needs of the processes and customer service functions for these various technology domains.

During the BIA process, this dependency analysis should be a key outcome and provide for an initial process that captures information required for further planning. This can then avoid additional steps and retro analysis during the BCP and overall risk management process. There are many BCP Management (BCM) tools available in the technology marketplace to support automation of the BCP framework and dependent capture process. These tools can allow one-time capture of automated risk assessments, BIA, and required dependency elements for a particular process. Figure 3.8 depicts a concept that is available in many of the off-the-shelf BCM software products that are available in the IT marketplace for one-time capture of BCP dependency information and data.

Figure 3.8 Sample BCP Dependency Capture Model

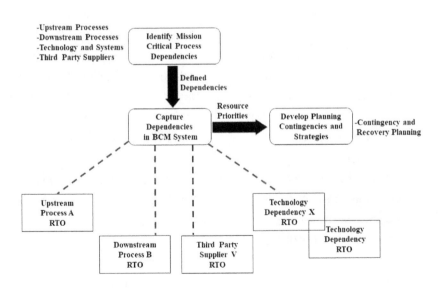

Once defined in the BCM system and processing model, the dependency processes, technologies, and Third-Party supplier data and information become a Source Record of critical data for the BCP risk assessment process. These can also be used for centralized linkage and validation of MC processes to technology, suppliers, and dependent processes across the Enterprise. Utilizing one single and trusted source of MC processes can substantially improve risk management in the Enterprise.

3.9 BCP Testing and Demonstrating Recovery

Understanding the exposure from BCP programs and planning for continuity of business operations requires a risk management practice that ensures that the recovery and continuity plans are validated strategies prior to any real impacts or events. This is accomplished through a rigorous testing program, periodic updating of the program, and updates that result from BCP testing, and key reporting of the testing results to executive management.

Testing strategies should include business decisions and directions that must be defined within the BCP policy and framework. This includes the level, type, and frequency of testing required to ensure the business objectives can be achieved during a business interruption or disaster across the Enterprise. These decisions should be based upon the level of risk that have been defined during the BIA risk assessment process, and threat levels/probabilities of risk occurrence for the Enterprise.

BCP testing also requires definition of testing objectives, detailed testing scripts, and schedules based upon those defined levels of risks and framework of the Enterprise. Most BCP programs are recommended to conduct testing of their BCP's at least annually. However, many operational functions and business processes may require a more frequent testing pattern that is based upon the criticality of the processes or business functions. Also, the level of inherent risk associated with those processes and functions may drive the frequency of testing requirements, such as, very high risks defined in the BIA assessment process.

There can be multiple testing methodologies employed in the development of testing strategies for ensuring the validity of BCP's and exposure across the Enterprise. These include the following levels of testing structures and concepts:

- BC Plan Desk Checks - Represents a standard type of testing in any BCP program. It includes meeting as a group or team with the BC planners and/or accountable stakeholders that step through and walk-through the components of the plan and provide feedback for plan updates.
- Tabletop Exercise - An advanced type of testing where a team and the second line BCP SME's meet to test specific components of a plan. Normally is based upon a predefined threat or disruptive scenario and includes role-playing and simulated response by team members; team knowledge and activities, and recovery team interaction; simulation of recovery responses and critical steps; documentation of issues and addressing of detected plan gaps.
- Functional Testing - Requires actual engagement and transfer of personnel in the business line to other sites, including other geographic facilities or alternate locations execution, as required by the plan; execution of specific plan strategies to recover the business function and processes; executing specific controls and activity; simulated or actual communication to personnel; participation of teams in dependency processes, Third-parties, and technology resources, includes application testing; engagement of Crisis personnel and communication as needed to manage the testing scenario; and tracking/reporting of all issues encountered for plan remediation and reporting of plan exposures.
- Full-Scale Testing - Enterprises or business units are often mobilized to change locations and conduct all portions of the

BCP's and specific strategies by implementing processing of information, data, and transaction, and use of back-up sites and Third Parties; physical transfers of work that are required by the plan or work-from-home strategies; and execution of interdependent processes, Third Parties, and technology resources. It should include application testing validation of Crisis Management responses and required management notifications; executing actual communication mechanisms for contacting response teams, management, and stakeholders; decision-making by business and executive management engaged in the testing. This type of testing is often reserved for Mission Critical type BCP's or Third-Party interactions.

All testing results can then be reviewed and evaluated based upon the testing scope and objectives. The testing results should be analyzed, measured, and reported to senior management and the Board of Directors based upon the requirements of the Enterprise BCP policy and framework. These can include key metrics of the testing results as to the specific objectives for the tests; evaluation of the information, actions, response team resources; Third Parties required communications and technology executed during the testing. Also, it can include identifying any gaps encountered in the BCP's or recovery strategies. BCP frameworks should provide for upgrades to the plans and tracking of these changes and expected dates for completion of retesting. Therefore, testing of BCP's is a major requirement for demonstrating and understanding the exposures to the Enterprise and the risk mitigation steps to deal with inherent risk to the Enterprise from business disruptions.

When executed and reported in a correct manner, BCP testing allows the Enterprise to better explain the business risk from potential business disruptions to all stakeholders, government regulators, and customers. More and more end customers and regulators are becoming concerned about the business resilience of their servicing enterprises.

As a result, many are requesting participation and engagement in Enterprise BCP tests to validate any risks to their organizations and the continuation of support and services from their supplier entities.

3.10 Managing Incident Emergency Notifications

The BCP policy and framework should ensure that all stakeholders, employees, and customers can be contacted and/or notified during a major business incident or disruption of services. It is imperative during a major incident or natural hazard event that all employees, with a focus on mission-critical employees and key stakeholders, should be notified about such events. They need to be contacted about the status of the Enterprise, provided instructions for response and managing their personal safety, and also advised on the next steps to take during the declared incident. Failure to communicate during such events is a major risk to any Enterprises in ensuring a proper response protocol and an organized approach to managing responses to any particular disruption. Emergency communication is key for effective management of any incidents.

Typically, most Enterprises will engage the services of an Emergency Mass Communication or Notification System (ENS) Third-Party suppliers to enable these types of services and assist in mitigating notification risks. These are similar to public safety or emergency management public notifications systems (e.g. Reverse 911, etc.) metropolitan systems where all citizens are contacted via burst communication on their home phones during major events (such as: Tsunami Threats, Active-Shooter, Shelter in Place Orders, etc.) or that have subscribed to the Wireless Emergency Alert (WEA) government services for notification services to cell-phones.

Some of the key Third-Party ENS suppliers providing services include: Adhoc, Air Bus DS, EverBridge, MIR-3, Mission Mode, Send Word Now, VoloRecovery, and XMatters.

All of these suppliers provide some type of software and/or communication push services for effective mass emergency notification via multiple channels that includes: SMS text, phone, email. Enterprises need to engage for these services and/or products with the suppliers. Many large enterprises will integrate these services with the appropriate BCM system environments by subscribing their contact information for required notifications, and also link their BCP's directly to these service suppliers/products. Regardless of the size of the Enterprise, the employee or stakeholder data must be entered and maintained current in these service suppliers' systems by the contracting Enterprise. Also, standard communication scripts are suggested to be developed for quick usage in certain types of incidents.

Just as in the testing of BCP's and recovery strategies, it is important to ensure that employees, key stakeholders, and key customers can be contacted during major incidents and business disruptions. It is suggested that these integrated services be tested on a frequent basis to ensure appropriate contact data is current, the services are functional, and personnel know how to respond to such notifications. As with any program testing, clear results of the test objectives, and follow-up mitigation are required, along with specific testing metrics to executive management. These metrics may include number of personnel contacted, issues with notifications, incorrect contact data or information.

Use of ENS type solutions require some level of federation or integration with the Third-Party suppliers to provide the key contact information for these environments. Figure 3.10 depicts a conceptual model for automating the information flow and managing the integration of ENS with BCM system environments.

Figure 3.10 Emergency Notification - BCM Concept Model

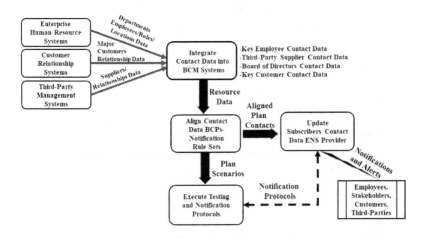

In this model, the target BCM system receives key emergency contact and notification data from a federated or integrated system for ensuring single Trusted Data and information from a validated source system. Depicted in this concept model are Three key target environments for hosted data that are identified for integration with the ENS process. These target sources systems include:

- Enterprise Human Resource System - Contains a single maintenance source for employee and stakeholder business unit data, employee work location, emergency and contact phone numbers, emails, and SMS text data. This includes the Board of Directors and senior executive management of the Enterprise;
- Customer Relationship Management System - Contains the data and information about major and high visibility customers, and the contact data to include: addresses, contact names, phone numbers, and emails, and type of customer (e.g. VIP, High Revenue, etc.);
- Third-Party Supplier Management System - Provides key Third-Party supplier and vendor contact data to include:

addresses, contact names (primary/secondary), phone numbers, emails, and type of vendor (*e.g.* mission critical, key process supplier, etc.).

Once the data is forwarded from the target source systems, it is integrated with and aligned to the appropriate business process and functions of BCP's in the BCM system, and notification protocols aligned with the contacts and plans. The contact data is then subscribed to the ENS environments and contacts data updated in the Third-Party ENS environment. It is important that periodic maintenance updates be processed with the Trusted Data Source environments, and connections established to ensure consistent data updates to maintain current data for employees, stakeholders, and key customers. Enterprise that lack an Enterprise system environment should maintain at a minimum complete master records or files of this data, with consistent updates.

The ENS environment, once updated with the required contact data, is enabled for execution of active emergency contact notifications to employees, stakeholders, and customers. The process can then be executed based upon the strategy or protocol employed (*e.g.* direct execution with the Third-Party ENS provider via their protocols; notification scenario executions, etc.), or directly from the BCM systems environments, via plan execution of these notification strategies.

Results of all exercises and/or actual notification events should be documented to ensure the demonstrated ability to contact employees, stakeholders, and customers to management and/all stakeholders. By providing this base of information, Enterprises can ensure their due diligence in meeting the expectations and demonstrated mitigation of risk to notify and contacting personnel is validated for major disruptions and incidents.

3.11 Evaluating BCP Concentration Risks

Increasingly, operational Concentration Risk has become a major concern for many IT and Enterprise risk organizations in the areas of BCP, Resilience, Third-Party, Cyber, and Technology risks. In this chapter section, we will review key evaluations as it relates to BCP Operational Concentration Risk. There are several types of concentration risk that are focused on the sources of the risk to the Enterprise or business. One type of concentration risks is known as Location Concentration Risk. This can arise from the concentration of geographic exposures to business functions from various types of business threats (e.g. hurricanes, floods, pandemics, geopolitical etc.). Additionally, the concentration of these threats at particular facilities or locations where there are larger number of MC can cause a concentration risk. If a particular business has a high concentration of MC business processes at a particular location exposed to these high-probability threats, it could overweight the exposure of the business to a higher probability for required recovery investments and/or a potentially larger number of business failures.

An example of Location Concentration Risk would be a series of customer regional call centers, distributed throughout the United States to support a particular service (e.g. Service A). However, services located and concentrated at the same facility, as Call Center A, are other business call centers with multiple other products serviced by other call center teams. The consolidation of these various call centers in the same location can create a significant concentration risk to the Enterprise and the Enterprise's ability to recover these businesses from a major event at these locations due to multiple process impacts. These can often overwhelm the Enterprise's ability to continue business operations in an uninterrupted manner even with use of redundant call centers.

Additionally, Dependency Gaps between technology and operational services delivery can also be a cause for larger concentrations of risk and exposure for the Enterprise. This Technology Dependency Gap risk can present a concentration of multiple major technology failures that support particular processes, thus increasing the financial exposure or service outage delays. It can also place the Enterprise into a higher risk profile and recovery investment model for these technologies requiring increased redundant strategies requirements for data and operations, depending upon the various business needs.

Each of these Concentration Risk types have the potential to impact a larger number of mission-critical business processes, including multiple downstream MC processes on a wider scale. They can also press the capacity capabilities of the recovery teams and/or recovery strategies and the ability to service the businesses and/or customers. It is critical then that businesses understand these threats, gaps, and the potential probabilities at all locations and the level of concentrated risk at these locations.

The Enterprise must then have sufficient capacity to meet RTOs and RPOs needed by the Enterprise to handle a larger number of potential transactions, data, information, or processing impacts due to impacts of high-probability threats. There may also be higher concentration risk at those processing and business locations that require more capacity to manage these risks. A key series of elements that should be captured as part of the BIA process is the processing capacity of both the production and recovery locations.

Therefore, when performing BIA risk assessments, it is essential that the planners and risk stakeholders understand the processing capacities and volumes at all locations, and with Cloud-based provider locations. They should have the ability for recovery sites or sister processing sites to be able to accommodate increased processing throughputs and also larger concentrations of processing impacts during a service disruption. These may require alternate sourcing of processing capability and/or external Third-Party supplemental resource contingency processing capability.

3.12 BC Management Ecosystem Concepts

BCM Operational Automation Drivers:

Throughout this chapter, key BCP framework processes and controls have been reviewed and explained in automation for these key program processes. These automated processes include: Business Impact Analysis and Risk Assessment Process; BCP Plan Dependency Capture Model, Threat Vulnerability Assessment, and Emergency Notification Management Model.

Many elements of the BCP framework can be automated in the processes. This is almost a necessity for large Enterprises where there are tens of thousands of processes, technologies, business assets, and employee resource populations. In fact, one of the key elements to maintaining a strong and effective BCP framework is the recommended integration and/or federation of key operational process and system components of the framework. In this chapter section, we will review a full BCP Operational System Ecosystem Model and key data concepts within these automation models.

Available BC Management Software and Services:

The BCM software market has seen some consolidations in the last five years, but for the most part is made up of some twenty-five or more Third-Party suppliers of software. They provide various products for BCP Development, ENS, plan testing, risk assessment, issues tracking, and management of various types of business continuity and crisis type events and recovery.

The majority of these products can provide functional automation and manage or enable many of the key BCP framework components. For other organizations or Enterprises in transition, many of the Third-Party suppliers provide SaaS services but most provide for execution at the client's data center. Several of the suppliers provide a

Cloud-Based hosted environment for their clients and BCP migration services. Also, several of the Third-Party suppliers either provide or embed ENS components as part of the product suite, and/or provide standard application interfaces directly with several of the key ENS Third-Party suppliers reviewed in this chapter.

A partial list of some of the key software Third-Party suppliers that market either software or Cloud-services includes: BC in the Cloud, Continuity Logic, eBRP Solutions, Dell/EMC (RSA/Archer), Fusion Risk, Metric Stream, Modulo, Recovery Planner, Strategic BCP, and SunGard AS. Most of these suppliers have the capability to assist in automation and management of the BCP framework for the Enterprise to some extent, and potential integration with the Enterprise risk management environments within the Enterprise.

It is recommended that no matter which product is selected or used for the BCM environment, if any, the product should be configurable for the Enterprise or client customers. By configurable, it references the need and ability to tailor the various key data components of the BCP framework to the Enterprise's internal business terminology, program status levels and items, business identifiers, and other key business and process functions. Several of the BCM products referenced have the capabilities to support large configurable data components for their client. Additionally, it is recommended that the risk assessment components of the BIA be flexible and adaptable to the Enterprise's risk management assessment methodology and environment. As in all off-the shelf products, it is recommended that customization be avoided due to the version control issues encountered in future releases of the BCM product by the supplier, and to minimize Enterprise release testing issues.

BCP Trusted Data Sources and Concepts:

It is suggested that for large Enterprises with a large population of data elements and repositories, that the BCM software be automated with federation or integration of key information from key trusted data sources of the Enterprise. As such, selected Third-Party supplier products should be integrated with minimum development activity with other Enterprise IT environments within the BCM ecosystem.

Some of the key data sources and key categories of data elements recommended to be included in the Business Continuity Management Ecosystem includes:

- Human Resource Data (Enterprise HR System) - Supporting BCP's development and recovery team assessment, and integration with the ENS framework components for employee organization, location, job/role, employee, and stakeholder contact data.

- Threat Vulnerability Data (Recommend Value - Add Hazard Service Aggregator) - Provides data regarding specific natural threats probability and severity along with specific technology assessment data and man-made threats (e.g. DHS alerts, etc.). Source of the data can be internal or sourced from an external data provider (e.g. National Weather Service, USGS, Department of Homeland Security, etc.), or Value-Added Data Service Aggregators (e.g. CoreLogic CDS, etc.).

- Risk Profile Data (Enterprise Risk Management Systems) - Provides data in reference to operational risk categories, risk assessment weightings and governance levels to aggregate Key Performance and Risk Indicator metrics and data for the Enterprise.

- IT Operational Management Data - (Enterprise Configuration Management System, Incident Management, Change/Release Management, Service Management) provides essential data required for BCP and dependency linkage for BCP and integration with the DR Technology Plans and Technology Components, to include application lists and identifiers for dependency mapping of technology and RTO's and for plan reference, risk assessment, testing resources, and reporting.

- Third-Party Supplier Data (Third-Party Supplier Management and Inventory Systems) - Provides information for identification of key Third-Party suppliers including locations, products/services, performance status and risk attributes, and key nomenclatures for referencing during planning, testing, risk assessment, dependency mapping, and cross-reference of BCP and testing results for Third-Party supplier management.

- Knowledge or Training Data (Training System) - Recommended for assignment of training that maybe required by the BCP Policy and framework of the Enterprise. Provides the required courses, employee data, and roles in the program and/or potential recovery operations for assigned role training.

- Customer Relationship Data (Customer Relationship Management System) - Used for identification of major customer relationship information (Customer Names, Address, Other Contact Data, Relationship Identifiers, etc.) for BCP and ENS operations.

- Organizational Structures (General Ledger or Organizational Systems) - Provides hierarchical structures of the organizations, cost centers, and other organizational levels to enable stakeholder ownership of businesses processes, and planning, risk approval levels.

BC Management Ecosystem:

Figure 3.12 provides a conceptual overview of a BCM Ecosystem for managing the entire BCP environment. In this environment, a core BCM product from one of the vendors can be used to automate and conduct key framework component processing such as: Business Impact Assessment Process and Data Collection, Business Impact Risk Assessments, BCP Components and Recovery Strategies, Business Continuity Plan Testing Scripts and Results, Threat Vulnerability Assessment, Emergency Notification and/or Service Integration, Incident Management, and Issue Tracking.

Figure 3.12 BC Management Ecosystem

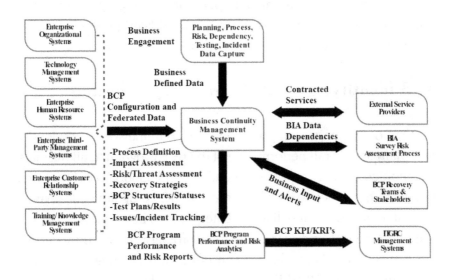

The BCM software product can then be integrated or configured to federate with many of the key Enterprise data sources discussed in the previous chapter section and provide for well managed Business Continuity Operational Management Ecosystem. As discussed for smaller Enterprises with less data resource populations, a SaaS model may work well for automating the process for them. Note that the majority of the listed BCM product suppliers of SaaS services for BCM management will provide upload capabilities for much of the base integrated Enterprise data sources. The ability should exist to configure BCM data to Enterprise information and/or the ability to enter direct data to configure a BCM Ecosystem for the environments.

Regardless of the BCM Ecosystem used for managing the BCP framework, the Ecosystem supporting the framework environment should have the ability to aggregate all of the BCP program compliance and risk data variables. This is required for delivery of periodic operational and risk reporting to all business stakeholders and business executives and for Board oversight. It is recommended that whether a BCM Ecosystem is implemented in an integrated or federated Ecosystem, SaaS Supplier environment, or even a paper-based framework system, that all operational BCP program controls, and performance and risk metrics, be consolidated for the Enterprise into an ITGRC or Enterprise environments.

3.13 Identifying BCP Program Key Indicators

One of the major components of a BCP framework is the ability to explain the overall performance of the BCP program to all business stakeholders, senior corporate executives, and the Board of Directors. This section will define the most common BCP program performance and risk indicators that will allow Enterprises to better understand the compliance level and activity in their program. It can provide key risk exposure levels for decision and direction by Enterprise executive management. All BCP program frameworks must be capable of articulating trusted and Key Performance Indicator (KPI) and Key Risk Indicator (KRI) data to management.

General Business Continuity Program Performance:

A major program performance item is to be capable of providing KPI's as to basic or simple construct counts for the program and to allow general profiling of the program and understanding of the program compliance level. An important characteristic of these indicators is to understand the performance level in the program of individual business units, overall divisional or sub-corporate, and even Enterprise subsidiary levels for BCP performance.

These indicators are suggested as basic structures of key compliance constructs for a BCP program and includes:

- Business Continuity Processes in the Program - Number of target Processes in the BCP program, including work in-progress processes to program;

- Business Continuity Processes in Program with Key Dependencies by RTO - Number of BCP target business processes with key Dependences in the program by RTO (list processes);
- Business Continuity Plans in Program - Number of BCP's accepted into the program, and work in-process plans to program;
- Business Continuity Processes Risk Assessed or In-Process of Risk Assessment - Number of business processes in the BIA process both Risk Assessed in program and BIA's work in-process;
- Business Continuity Processes by Recovery Time Objective - Target business processes in program by RTO groupings;
- Business Continuity Plans by Recovery Time Objective within Business Divisions, Provides number of BCP's within business line divisions within RTO;
- Business Continuity Plans and Processes Compliant/Non-Compliant with Program Framework, include Late Compliance (Aging delays) - Number of BCP's and target business processes compliant and non-compliant to the BCP framework with identification of late Items and days aged;
- Business Continuity Plans and Process with Issues and/or Late Issue Resolution (aging delays) - Number of BCP's and targeted business processes with issues, and those with issues that are unresolved by their mitigation Due Date, and issue days aged;
- Business Continuity Plans and Process Detail Issue Tracking - BCP's and targeted business processes listed with detail tracking of issues by issue category;
- Business Continuity Plans and Process Issues Escalated for Management Action - BCP's and targeted business processes with issues that have been escalated for management activity and resolution.

The importance of these indicators is twofold. First, they provide an overall level of understanding for operational and senior executive management, as to the size and complexity of the program; and second, they provide a level of compliance and an indication as to BCP program stability, quality, trending, and overall direction.

Program stability and trending are important, as the BCP program frameworks can be resource-intensive operations depending upon the level of program complexity and committed personnel resources. These are necessary metrics for understanding resources that are used for planning and for budgeting purposes that are essential to manage program frameworks in large Enterprise programs. Key Performance Indicators also provide an overall direction of risk where performance can be a predictive warning sign of potential risk and exposure for operational risk management exposure and business line or division concentration risk

Demonstrated BCP Program Testing Performance:

Another major Key Performance Indicator set is for tracking the overall validation testing of the program. As discussed in chapter section 3.9, demonstrating the efficiency and performance of the program is a major requirement in any BCP framework and requires various levels of testing and/or exercise performance to ensure a viable BCP program. The major KPI's for understanding both the overall performance of the program and compliance level for business requires a complete series of Testing KPI's. Again, it is important to understand levels of performance by individual business units, division, and subsidiary Enterprise Levels.

Key Performance Indicators for Testing includes the following suggested variables:

- Business Continuity Plans and Processes Tested (Passed/ Failed/Incomplete) - Number of BCP's and targeted business processes Tested with Indications as to Testing Passed, Failed and/or Incomplete;

- Business Continuity Processes Testing Compliant with Framework; include Late Compliance (aging delays) - Number of BCP's and targeted business processes tested within Compliance of Framework, and number of Non-Compliant to Framework (Identify List of Plans/Processes) with aging of Non-Compliant Plans/Processes;
- Business Continuity Plan and Business Processing Testing Categories - Defined number of tests of BCP's and business processing conducted by category of testing (e.g. desk checks, functional, etc.);
- Dependent Processes, Third-Party Suppliers, and Technology Tested - Number of Identified Dependencies Tested within the targeted business processes;
- Business Continuity Plans and Processes with Testing Issues - Number of BCP's and targeted business processes tested but reporting Testing Issues required to be mitigated per the BCP framework and within framework time-frames;
- Business Continuity Plans and Processes with Testing Issues Escalated for Management Action - BCP's and targeted business with Testing Issues that have been escalated for further managerial action and/or mitigation;
- Business Continuity Plans and Process with Testing Issues and/or Late Resolution (aging of delays) - Number of BCP's and targeted business processes with Test Issues with Late Resolution with aging of Late Plans/Processes.

Depending upon defined thresholds in the BCP program framework, these indicators could be indicative of potential risk to the overall business unit or Enterprise, signal a negative trend of performance and compliance by specific organizational areas, and/or signal increased risk exposure to the Enterprise. This is based upon the types of compliance and testing issues encountered in the test process.

Key Business Continuity Risk Indicators:

As an aggregation point for the BCP risk profile of the Enterprise, the Key Business Continuity Risk Indicators allow executives to explain and drive the risk management profile for the program. The KRI's provides the program capability to measure the level of risk sensitivity for particular business activities, provide predictive warning and risk trends for potential business disruptions, and analysis of overall Enterprise operational risk data components.

Therefore, BCP KPI's measure how well the BCP program and businesses are doing; the KRI's provide a view of potential or inherent risk to the businesses and resulting residual risks. Key Risk Indicators suggested as major risk measures for most Business Continuity Programs include:

- Business Continuity Plans/Processes with Recovery Strategy Issues (Within Threat Levels) - Number of BCP's and targeted business processes with Recovery Strategy Issues defined by Target Threat Area and Threat Severity;
- Business Continuity Plan/Process RTO Dependency Gaps (Process, Technology, Third-Party, etc.) - Defined number of BCP's and targeted business with RTO Gaps between Targeted Dependencies with Identification of the Targeted Dependency and Gap RTO's;
- Business Continuity Plan/Process Testing Failures by RTO - Identification of the number of BCP's and targeted business processes with Testing Failures results and within RTO category and with identification of Plans/Processes;
- Business Continuity Plan/Process Testing RTO Misses - Identification of the number of BCP's and targeted business processes that missed recovery within the designated and risk assessed RTO, with identification of plans/processes;
- Business Continuity Processes with RTO Testing Discrepancies - Number of Targeted Business Processes with RTO Testing Discrepancies;

- Business Process Detail Tracking of Testing RTO Failures and RTO Testing Delayed Remediation - Tracking of targeted business process RTO Failures/Misses during Testing and with aging of days and remediation target dates;
- Level of Risk Acceptance by Business Lines (Defined Inherent Risk with no Mitigation) - Number required remediations and identification of business processes where business lines threats require remediation and for which business line executives have accepted the Inherent Risk;
- Business Continuity Process Severity Threat Levels - Identifies business targeted processes within various Threat categories and Severity Levels;
- Business Continuity Process Risk Concentration Levels - Identification of targeted business processes with Risk Concentration Levels by Category of Risk, Severity of Risk, and Concentration Levels (at Location, within Business Division, with Mission Critical Process Groupings).

Utilizing standard KRI's for the BCP program allows holistic management by Enterprise executives of interdependent, complex risk relationships of the Enterprise. It can demonstrate that the BCP program exposure is under control. This can make it possible for business managers and executives to structure implementation of operational and strategic growth plans with confidence. Engaging and orientating senior Enterprise executives and the Board of Directors to these key BCP program elements ensures these are part of the IT and Enterprise Risk management process.

It is suggested that all BCP program KPI's and KRI's be integrated into the ITGRC Ecosystem, and that Enterprise risk control environments include aggregation of these program and risk metrics as key components of the BCP program components. Managing BCP risks are one of the core fundamental aspects for any Enterprise and needs to be a core foundation consideration for development of any business and technology strategy. Automation of BCP Ecosystems with the appropriate Trusted Data is key in large Enterprise risk management activity.

CHAPTER 4

Technology Resilience and DR

4.1 Introduction to IT Resilience and DR Risks

FOR MOST ENTERPRISES, Technology Resilience and Disaster Recovery Risk has historically been managed as a discipline in terms of planning for continuation of IT operations and services due to major Data Center disasters. This concept continues in the industry today and is valid in terms of planning for Data Center construction and preparation for major disasters and the loss of Data Center operations. However, in the last fifteen years the concepts of Disaster Recovery (DR) have expanded to include availability of IT services and that of Application architecture and the overall concept of IT Resilience across the Enterprise. As such, the concept of Resilience and DR planning, as a process, is to recover from major processing interruptions. It is embedded within IT Resilience strategy, along with ensuring the continuous uptime and availability of IT networks, applications, storage, hardware servers, mainframes, Third Parties, Cloud-Based services, and key supporting environmental infrastructures at operational locations. Additionally, technology resiliency has evolved in some Enterprises to become a basic principle for strategic investment planning.

One of the major and potential IT Resilience risk areas is understanding the exposure levels of Technology Obsolescence Risk, for applications, databases, infrastructures (security, hardware, network, and/or Data Center facility plant), and Third-Party infrastructure environments. These levels of Obsolescence Risk can complicate and expand the risk for Enterprise technology exposure. This is due to the fact that technology obsolescence may contribute to a higher potential for failure and can create a Single Point of Technology Failure in various environments. It can also include potential licensing and product upgrade vulnerabilities across multiple technology environments. These exposures are all prevalent in network, security, hardware, software, and Data Center environmental portfolios, where aging and expired support components have reached maximum life for the technologies.

Additionally, understanding the potential risk from Dependency Gaps in RTO's and data availability for the technology supporting key business processes, along with Third-Party supplier dependencies, becomes an additional Technology Resilience Risk factor. A major risk exposure for Resilience Technology for any Enterprise is the ability to provide full availability of technology operations and support in specific real-time application and technology infrastructure environments. It is imperative for effective recovery of environments, because of the potential for functional design flaws and/or human errors in recovery architecture, software design, and technology strategies.

The existence of the ubiquitous 24/7 technology exposure and continuous operating mobility environments are now defined expectations from customers and stakeholders. Therefore, almost all Enterprises are focused on managing the availability risk of their services, functions, and automated technology processes. By far, the increased exposure to consumer' wireless access, internet-enabled applications, and "always-on" technologies have been a major market driver for the expanded requirement for management of Resilience exposures to the Enterprise. Additionally, the expansion of end-user services by Enterprises into Cloud-Based services has expanded the requirements to manage Resilience exposure within the Enterprise. This includes oversight of Cloud Third-Party supporting environments contracted by the Enterprise.

Organizational Accountability for IT Resilience Risk:

IT risk management in the financial industry is migrating to isolate this risk discipline and oversight into an independent Second Line of Defense (SLOD) organizational risk oversight centered within the Enterprise risk management group. However, from an execution perspective, almost all Enterprises center the execution of Technology Resilience and/or recovery planning focus in the IT organization. Unlike BCP management, which is often housed in various organizations, such Finance, or Procurement, Technology, Risk management, or Corporate Real Estate organizations.

In almost all other industries, IT combines the management and oversight of Resilience risk management, planning and recovery operations in the IT departments of the Enterprises. These organizations set the standards, operating principles, and guidance for DR and Technology Resilience efforts in IT environments. The IT operational business and/or service divisions then are accountable for the recovery strategies and planning for their operations. They likewise have the accountability for executing the recovery of their operational areas and the ongoing continuation of services for the Enterprise. It is recommended that an Enterprise accountability be included to ensure the oversight of the Technology Resilience governance framework program, executive focus at the corporate level, and as governed by the Enterprise Resilience program.

4.2 Technology Resilience and DR Governance

Just as in the overall governance of the Enterprise BCP program, the Enterprise IT Technology Resilience/DR (TRDR) governance should be organized into strong IT Resilience Enterprise governance and policy frameworks. However, due to organizational differences that may exist in many Enterprises, the BCP program policy and governance may be contained in separate and distinct governance documents, frameworks, and guidelines. The financial industry often consolidates these documents and frameworks into one Enterprise policy document and overall governance program. This concept, regardless of the organizational execution structure, is recommended for all Enterprises. This will ensure that both the BCP and TRDR policy and governance frameworks are in tight alignment to promote good Enterprise IT risk management.

Whether centralized in IT, or decentralized, the governance and execution frameworks require extensive collaboration between BCP and TRDR SME groups. They should operate from a strong TRDR policy component of a consolidated Business Continuity Policy or linked processes in separate BCP and TRDR policies. In the financial industry, federal regulators define specific TRDR requirements as major structures of a well-structured business continuity program and framework.

A TRDR policy component should establish a governing framework of accountabilities for technology operational units, executives, and for technology risk oversight accountability. Additionally, the policy should outline specific requirements for evaluating new technologies and definition of standards and protocols for introducing Resilience strategies across the Enterprise.

The TRDR program policy and framework should establish:

- Enterprise approaches and roles for TRDR in all organizations (a RACI structure is recommended for this component of the framework, similar to BCP);
- Requirements for a Technology and Application Risk Assessment (TARA) and Dependency Gap Analysis Process;
- Strong Alignment to BCP BIA risk assessments;
- Specific Technology and DR protocols, planning, and testing processes and requirements;

- Appropriate risk assessment and risk management concepts, criteria, and oversight requirements for technology applications, hardware and network infrastructures, and Data Center environments;
- Identification of TRDR planning and program performance;
- Definition of TRDR risk monitoring and mitigation requirements;
- Required training curricula for program participants (planners, approvers, testers, technology management, technology support and recovery resource teams, and risk officers);
- Program hierarchical review and approval levels, and specific escalation oversight and accountability;
- Requirements for managing Resilience technology environments, and capacity/performance evaluations;
- Essential reporting levels and identification of program anomalies and exceptions.

Additionally, the TRDR policy and framework should establish specific periods of time for evaluations, exception review, planning, and exercise time periods, and with the required levels of participation for the various components and resources of the program.

4.3 Assessing Risk Impacts in Technology Resilience

Just as in the case of introducing new business functions and processes into the Enterprise, it is imperative that all technology, infrastructures, or applications introduced into production operating environments provide the understanding and assessment of the inherent risk. As such, it is suggested that Applications and Technology Risk Assessments be required for all midrange-based server and mainframe applications; technology servicing software environments and acquired Technology utilities; and all key Technology infrastructure environments (e.g. network, middleware, security, etc.).

Technology and Application Resilience Risk Assessments:

The Technology and Application Resilience Risk Assessment (TARA) framework component process should capture essential technology data components as to the resources required to ensure technology availability to the Enterprise. The scope of this includes down-time incident analytical impacts, and planning for a worst-case disaster scenario that could impact the Enterprise's business strategies. This may include automatic identification from an IT Configuration Management Environment of applications and dependencies; integrated technology infrastructures and operational dependencies; hardware and network technology structures; database and storage requirements; data, file and database replication requirements. It should also include IT Third-Party processors. Figure 4.3 provides a conceptual flow for a suggested Technology and Application Risk Assessment processes.

Figure 4.3 Technology/Application Risk Assessment Process

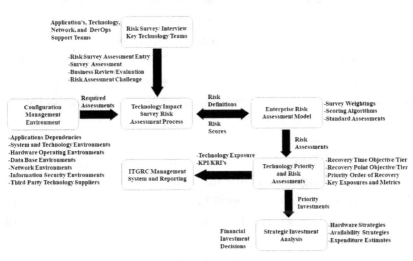

In this process, it is suggested that an automated federation or integration with IT Management Configuration environments be implemented to provide the base requirements of application and technology relationship targets for these risk assessments. The risk assessments should use an automated, objective level of risk weightings and scoring to ensure a standard assessment of the application and technology risk across the Enterprise. Final assessments should be reviewed with both the business stakeholders and technology teams. This can ensure collaboration and understanding of all stakeholders of the inherent technology risks to the Enterprise and the potential strategies to mitigate those risks.

Technology and Application Risk Assessment Component:

The Application and Risk Assessment processes should be used to understand and/or determine: Business impacts of application or utility outages; RTO's and RPO's for each application or technology environment; Key dependency business processes; DR Recovery Tiers for applications and technology environments, and Priority Order of Recovery (POR) for each technology within a DR Tier.

The TARA should address the impacts to the Enterprise from a Financial, Operational, Reputational, Customer, Legal, and Regulatory Risk exposure level for applications and technology Resilience, and recovery priority across the Enterprise. Figure 3.2 in Chapter Three, represents a demonstrated BCP Risk Assessment Tier Model that can be also used to represent the structure of the TARA process for Tiers assignments of these Enterprise technology.

This includes the designation of TARA Tier Recovery Categories for each of the technology and application environments, and the duration of time ranges for availability of each of the depicted Recovery Tiers. These TARA environmental Tiers can then assign the associated RTO, RPO, and Priority Order of Recovery, within each of the TARA categories. They are a key element in all TRDR frameworks throughout all industry business sectors and IT DR industry sectors. In some industries, the various frameworks for BCP may have the ability to align these RTO's with TRDR frameworks. However, it is common in many industries that the various frameworks and environments will define different criteria as to technology and business availability required hours and differentiations in Tier recovery standards and architectural strategies. This is due to the investment concepts and technology limitation strategies required to achieve the required availability of the business or technology and to meet the expected level required for business processes. Regardless of the frameworks it is important that the TARA process be conducted via an objective and systematic approach to ensure consistency of the risk assessment process.

Technology Resilience and Application Risk Survey Component:

The TARA uses a basic assessment process to define the various risks of technology availability in the Enterprise. A typical IT organizational approach is to use a survey process that identifies the key exposures of the technology and dependent business processes. Often the survey process is similar to the BCP BIA process and represents a series of risk exposure questions with analysis for the various applications and supporting technologies.

The survey often represents a standard questions and ranges of responses for those questions that are directed to the technology and applications support teams. The risk assessment survey can take the form of 10 - 15 key survey questions in a document form or spreadsheet type of reference to the technology support teams. In some Enterprises, it is known as a "Disaster Recovery Technology Assessment," "Application Technology Priority," or "Technology Criticality Assessment." However, in all cases it is designed to prioritize and classify the availability requirements and the recovery priority for the various technologies. It allows the Enterprise to determine the maximum allowable downtime for critical business technologies, recovery point objectives, target transaction level and replication data volumes, and the losses/costs associated with a technology outages and/or downtime.

As reviewed in Figure 4.3, it is recommended that the TARA process be automated via data capture that is driven by the IT Configuration

Management Environments (CMS) via a standard inventory for required TARA components. This should include the online capture of the survey responses with automated processing against a standard risk weights, algorithms/rules processing, and standard scoring. These standard assessment metrics can be provided in an automatic methodology from a Federated Enterprise Risk Assessment model.

Application and Technology Risk Assessment Determinations:

The essential focus in the TARA process is to assess technology to the standard guidelines and recovery or availability strategies for the Enterprise. Each of the Recovery Tier Categories requires specific Resilience strategy standards and investment strategies to support the various production, recovery technologies, and architectures for the specific recovery objectives of a Recovery Tier. Inherent risks to application and interactive technologies are associated to a direct correlation of the investments required by the Enterprise. These investments can ensure availability to customers and stakeholders of the various Enterprise technologies.

An example of this is the design and requirements for applications and the supporting database and infrastructures environments to ensure 99.999% availability of the services. This would include almost no loss of data for the application and business operations or services. Such environments are often defined as "High Availability" or "Continuous Operation" architecture designs and often use "Active-Active" architectures. They are considered some of the most expensive technology investments in the industry. This is due to the underlying technology infrastructures and resource investments used to ensure almost 100% availability to business and customers. Typically, these are complex design architectures and often utilize multiple Third-Party solutions. The environments are often reserved for the most critical of all application and technology environments, (e.g. in the financial industry (ATM and brokerage trading environments, online mobile banking environments, etc.); or in the airline industry (air traffic control, reservation systems, etc.); health care industry (hospital operating controls, etc.).

In fact, understanding the key availability and recovery requirements is a precedent to initiating and managing strategic investments for new product technologies, business processes, and innovative solutions. These requirements should be included in all product development projects to enable accurate investment requirements for technologies. It is often reflected in the specific application and technology Tier Categories, where 1x is a basic infrastructure/application cost expenditure concept with no or minimum recovery capabilities, and 3x to 5x, the costs for real-time application/infrastructure availability, active-active, or high redundant Technology environments.

Also, one of the key elements in understanding TARA is the exposure to an Enterprise from the potential loss of data. As such, the Risk Determination has a key component, RPO, to understand the Enterprise's appetite for loss of data, and drives risk based strategies for financial investments in data recovery strategies. This includes real-time replication technologies (*e.g.* data/operating system, *etc.)* and data protection used across the Enterprise, database and file back-up, and recovery environments.

Secondary Challenges to IT Risk Assessments:

Just as in the BCP BIA process, it is essential that the resulting TARAs and recovery strategies for applications and technologies that have been risk assessed be reviewed by the owning business lines. Collaboration is required to ensure understanding of the resulting determinations (*e.g.* RTO, RPO, and Process Priorities to the Enterprise, *etc.*).

It is suggested as a good practice that the area accountable for TARA activity review these with business lines, and also challenge, if necessary, the technology and business line areas on the findings. This process should maintain reasoning and challenge points in a documented, and if possible, automated repository to ensure consistent assessment diligence. This can support key corporate audit points and an iterative framework process methodology that can ensure a consistent evaluation review process. This can provide the ability for corporate accountability of the risk assessment baseline for other risk areas that depend upon specific applications and technologies, and a trusted quality control process.

4.4 Understanding Process and Technology Gaps

A key determination in understanding the risks associated with operational and business services delivery is to evaluate any gaps between the availability of technologies that are used by the various business processes, and their RTO requirements. This includes the business processes vs. their dependent technology. It is understood to be the Dependency Gap between the required technologies' availability required for the business process to conduct normal operations. It is important to understand these technology gaps, as the non-availability of the technologies could have a major impact to the delivery of the required operational services to customers or other stakeholders, and to downstream or upstream dependent business process.

Comparing the RTO's between business processes, technology/ applications, and Third-Party suppliers are a standard process in BCP and TRDR industry frameworks. While it is not required to use an automated gap analysis process to understand these gaps, it is a best practice, and one of several common concepts used by some large Enterprises. When this gap analysis is automated, it allows a rapid determination of processing gaps between the dependencies for business processes, technologies, Third-Party suppliers, and/or other target dependencies (e.g. potential key Production locations, or key Services within an Enterprise, etc.).

Figure 4.4 provides a concept for a generic Operational Business Process to Technology Gap Analysis model. It can be used to present an Enterprise risk profile of the gaps between all processes, MC processes, and all supporting dependent applications and technologies supporting those processes.

Figure 4.4 Process Dependency - Technology Gap Model

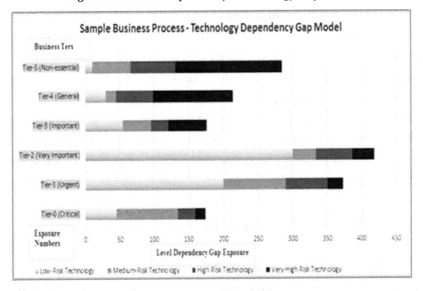

In this model, the operational business processes are inventoried and summarized by their defined availability Business Tiers. They are plotted against the various levels of Risk Exposure defined for the available Technology in an aggregate format for the Enterprise. Typically, the Enterprise will define specific rules and categories of risk (e.g. Very High Risk to Low Risk Exposure, etc.) and correlate levels of vulnerabilities, availability, and TRDR Tiers for the Applications and Technologies to be aligned into these various risk exposures. This is often a pattern seen in the identification of the Enterprise's most critical applications and business process tiers coupled with depiction of high or severe deficiencies in the Very High-Risk exposure level category. Also, in many Enterprises, depending upon investment strategies, a large number of gap exposures can be located in the lowest availability business and technology tiers, (e.g. within the non-essential business categories, etc.).

The targeted Risk Exposures are then aggregated into the over-all Dependency Model with the correlating Business Process Tiers to provide a full model of Dependency Technology Gap Risk. In an advanced-system and automation model there could also be an online drill-down, or point and click functionality, to identify and understand those business processes and the supporting technologies at risk. Mitigation must then be developed to develop increased automation capabilities or investment strategies to rectify the gaps and/or automation alternatives, and/or other process alternative considerations. The same type of modeling can be developed, and it is recommended to take place, for other RTO gaps, Third-Parties, key upstream process dependencies, and/or other defined dependencies.

4.5 Technology Recovery Planning for IT

While the TARA process is critical to understand the level of inherent risk to the Enterprise technology portfolio, it is also required to drive the planning for major technology outages and Data Center disasters. It can assist in the definition of technology recovery strategies that are critical to the Enterprise. The TRDR policy and framework of the Enterprise should define the guidance and strategy requirements for development of IT Recovery Plans. In some Enterprises, these are known as DR Plans, and/or Technology/Application Recovery Plans. In some organizations, it will follow the ITIL Service Management Life Cycle framework where recovery is defined as a Service Continuity Plan (SCP).

No matter what format or structure of the IT Life-Cycle concepts (e.g.: COBIT, ITIL, etc.) are used by the IT organization to manage technology environments, Recovery Plans should be required for all applications, technology structures, and supporting utilities and infrastructures, to plan for major outages and/or disaster scenarios, and system availability incidents.

Additionally, an overall governing control plan for Disaster Recovery should exist for the entire recovery of a Data Center due to catastrophic damage. Also, partial recovery plans due to intermediate service disruptions, and full cold restarts of Data Centers (*e.g.* In-Place Recover Plans, etc.) should be developed for defining step-by-step protocols during these recoveries.

Each of the governing recovery plans needs to identify the risks, vulnerabilities, and procedures for technology recovery when any of the following events impact Application and Technology services to the Enterprise:

- Failure of individual applications due to hardware or database failures or operating disruptions;
- Partial or Full Loss of Primary Data Center due to fire, floods, hurricane, tornado, or other natural hazards;
- Loss of Power due to the failure of power grid supply, failure of Backup Generators or UPS (Uninterruptible Power Batter Back-up Sources) equipment;
- Mechanical Data Center outages (*e.g.* HVAC, etc.) and/or major infrastructure failures;
- Impacts and/or unavailability of Replication Technology or Backup Technology components;
- Contaminations of facilities (man-made or natural events);
- Unavailability of dependent Third-Party supplier operating environments, and/or Cloud based applications and processing environments.

Technology and Application Recovery plan constructs, structures, and key components should be developed for the various types of Recovery Plans, especially for detailed recovery of Applications. At a minimum, these should include the following major plan components:

- Plan Overviews, describing the Application or Technology being recovered, and the overall purpose and target objectives for the plan;
- Recovery Plan Revision Control Tracking and Status of Plan Review (*e.g.* New Plans, Approved Plans, etc.);

- Dependent supporting Technology Environments, Technology Utilities, Databases, key Networks, and Operating System environments, and dependent RTO's;
- Identified Server, Hardware, and other key Configurations;
- Production and DR site and location information and alternative recovery locations;
- Service Interfaces and Process dependencies identifications and dependent Process RTO's;
- Virtual hardware and environmental layers, physical and logical;
- Data and database replication and resynchronization strategies;
- Special recovery requirements for outsourced operational processing sites, call centers, Co-location, and Hot sites;
- Plan Recovery and IT validation procedures for Full DR, extended Duration Outage recovery; and Cold Start with In-place recovery;
- Technology exercise procedures and validation procedures;
- Recovery team resources needed to recover IT and to continue operations;
- Return to Production Data Center Site procedures and Re-installing Production environments ("Return to Home").

4.6 Understanding IT Data Center Risk Exposures

Almost all Enterprises, inclusive of large Fortune 500 corporations, have developed formal criteria for secondary production and/or recovery sites, and in some cases the strategies are inclusive of tertiary data-processing site capabilities. The level of investment in Data Center Sites and Infrastructure Technology takes several forms dependent upon the size and complexity of the Enterprise. It is a major component of an Enterprise's strategic decision process and a major risk-focused mitigation strategy for most Enterprises.

Due to the significant costs and investment requirements for building standalone Data Centers, many Enterprises may outsource their Production or DR site management to one of the major DR Third-Party suppliers in the industry, e.g. Amazon, Google, IBM, Microsoft, or SunGard AS, etc., and/or co-locate their Data Center operations to a large multiple-tenant Data Center site. Also, new concepts have emerged because of Internet and Cloud-Based services offerings. These service offerings are now structured in the Cloud, as a Disaster Recovery-as-a-Service (DRaaS) option and are changing the way many Enterprises are managing the complexities of Data Center recovery planning. Enterprise decisions as to development and management of their own stand-alone sites, outsourcing Data Center operations, or utilizing Third-Party DRaS/Cloud solutions, are all major strategic IT decisions that require evaluation by the Enterprise. IT Data Center strategies should consider outsourcing decisions as to only their non-critical application vs. the full portfolio of critical and non-critical applications based upon their investment decisions and appetite for technology risk.

Data Center Basic Recovery Risk Strategies:

There are multiple concepts and strategies used in development of Data Center strategies, which determine the investment expenditures for the Enterprise. There are several strategic concepts for design and operations of Data Centers. Some of the key Data Center strategies used by many IT organizations are: Co-Location Sites, DR Hot Sites, Split-Operation Sites, and Cold Sites. These strategies are often intermingled to provide production and DR operational support structures for many Enterprises.

Co-Location Sites (Co-Lo), are data center sites that can be used to support various IT operations of an Enterprise. These are sites, where equipment, space, and network and data center infrastructure are available for lease to a corporation or IT organization. Ratings of these suppliers of space are specified in terms of their size, services, and redundancy capabilities. These centers can be used to support production or recovery sites.

Another type of center is a Hot Site. This is a secondary data center that is often one-hundred-percent configured with matching computer equipment at the Hot Site DR environment and Production center. These can be operational to recover the production site within several hours, or a few minutes, depending upon their architecture. In larger Enterprises, a significant investment can be expanded to store the required data from the production site to the Hot Site DR environment. It is achieved by use of High Speed data transmission, Virtualized hardware and storage layers, and often utilize Vendor management software products, data replication and operating environments. The level of investment can also be determined by the level of technologies implemented in this solution (e.g. Active-Active, Active-Passive, etc.). An Active-Passive environment provides a full redundant instance of each production environment that is brought online, when the primary production environment fails. In an Active-Active environment, processing and work-load distributions are level-loaded over the technology between multiple sites These environments typically utilize, "Synchronous" or "Asynchronous" communication architectures.

Some center sites may be structured as a Split Operational Production Sites. These can be a production site that uses identical split pod-based technology architectures and applications. These often will use an "Active-Active" or "Continuous Operations" network topology. Also, in some scenarios, they may use an "Active-Passive" topology, to avoid software licensing expenditures for dual environments. Each of these types of sites has the embedded logic architecture within the applications and/or use real-time replication that minimizes the loss between sites of data/systems.

Typically, Active-Active technology and Production sites can also require an in-region secondary data center. This is because, Active-Active sites, may have specific technology limitations related to the geographic distance between the sites (e.g. typical distance twenty to forty miles, *etc.*). It can be caused by potential impacts from "Network latency." These limitations are the result of a design of connections between sites that can experience data transmission delays and data synchronization issues due to network traffic loads and distances for data transmission.

Active-Active sites have the ability for active back-up of the other site, and to maintain production operational loads when the other site is lost. In most cases, there is minimum to no disruptive failover impacting customers and users of the services.

Many Enterprises use Cold Sites as a concept for Disaster Recovery. These locations are capable of recovery via the use of offline recovery techniques. They are sometimes known as "Quick Ship" sites, because this concept implies that in the event of a disaster at the Production site, hardware, equipment, and software would be provisioned, at the time of incident, via shipments to the recovery site. This option requires organizations to evaluate variables such as: equipment ordering time-frames, personnel transportation requirements, and configuration/installation time-frames, etc. The latter is often the least expensive strategy for DR, because it requires minimum upfront investments. This would include DR equipment, hardware, security, and network devices for the site, and contracted availability. This concept also may use a backup technology of tape, or delayed transmission of data via Virtual Tape Library transmissions, or offsite backup Third-Party suppliers (*e.g.* Iron Mountain, etc.).

Additionally, public Cloud-Based storage solutions have emerged for storage of recovery data in the Cloud, such as: Amazon S3, Google, HPE, IBM, Microsoft, Rackspace, Sungard AS, etc., as alternative recovery and analytical data-storage solutions. Each of these solutions requires the appropriate risk-based investment decision and accountability process. These offsite storage locations and co-location sites are also provisioned with the appropriate HVAC, electrical and network cabling, and raised floors. In many situations, these types of sites may also be contracted from a typical Data Center Recovery Third-Party Supplier.

Data Center Design and Operation Capacity Risks:

The design for the Operational Capacity of these Data Centers is a key risk assessment required for all types of Data Centers. Key elements include space and power requirements that are required to manage the specific loads required for the production and recovery data centers. How many applications? What types of applications? What types of capacity and equipment inventory for hardware and operational equipment? What are the operational hardware power requirements? What are the security requirements? Are there regulatory or physical space isolation requirements? What are the RTO's required for the specific applications and technologies? How much floor space is required and racks storage? These are all key determinants in assessing the capabilities required for understanding operational requirements for data centers, and investment considerations.

Redundancy Risks in Data Centers:

Additionally, a key requirement is to understand the level of Resilience or redundancy that is required to protect from a potential Data Center loss. The UpTime Institute has established several levels of Data Center Tier Fault Tolerance definitions for designing, building, and operating Data Centers throughout the world. These varying levels of construction and operation are defined based upon the level of building design, as determined by the needs and inherent risk appetite of the Enterprise.

The UpTime Institute levels of redundancy are defined based upon the major design, construction, and building of computer operational environments. It includes the standards and best practices for Data Center operations. Some of these standards include:

- Electrical and Power – Electrical distribution (dual paths) "N" number of building power line feeds and conduits, number and usage of diesel-powered backup generators, watts required per square foot, number and size of backup fuel tanks, UPS (number of and capabilities of Uninterruptible Power Supply battery banks), and the number of required PDU's (Power Distribution Units);

- HVAC Mechanical - Heating, ventilation, and air conditioning (location, distribution, and tonnage, heating and cooling/humidity controls, and air filtration);
- Raised Floor - Height and sizes of floor tiles and rack capacity, and spacing on the raised floor of hardware racks/cabinets;
- Fire protection, smoke detection, and sprinkler automation;
- Physical Security Control - External perimeter controls, access control and bio-med security, and surveillance/monitoring levels.

UpTime redundancy levels are defined in terms of "Tiers of Availability" or "Fault Tolerance" levels for the Data Centers. They assign a standards award level for Data Center service, such as Gold, Silver, or Bronze. This is for the overall level of Fault-Tolerance methodology implemented for a Data Center. The current Uptime Fault Tolerant Data Center levels are:

- Tier 4: Use multiple active power and cooling distribution paths; redundant mechanical and electrical components. Tier 4 is considered Fault Tolerant and has the potential downtime industry standard of less than 30 minutes annually;
- Tier 3: Multiple power and cooling distribution paths but with one path active, redundant mechanical and electrical components, and capable of concurrent maintenance with less than 1.6 hours' potential downtime annually;
- Tier 2: Uses a single or dual path for power and cooling distribution and has redundant mechanical components with less than 22 hours of potential downtime annually;
- Tier 1: Maintains a Single path for power and cooling distribution and has no redundant components and the potential

for less than almost 28.8 hours' downtime/year. The failure of one component can result in the various environments going offline to the IT organization and impacts to the Data Center or Enterprise.

4.7 IT Vulnerability and Operational Analysis

A key risk exposure in understanding Technology Resilience Risk management is that of Technology Vulnerabilities that could lead to technology availability issues, downtime, and overall Resilience for the Enterprise. Effective management and understanding of the vulnerabilities in the various technology environments of an Enterprise, and the priority remediation of those vulnerabilities are a major executive investment decision. These types of investment decision and vulnerability understandings are necessary as it relates to the risk exposure vs investment model for any Enterprise.

Types of Vulnerabilities for Resilience and Availability:

Some of the major Technology Vulnerabilities and Availability Threats that require management and monitoring of the exposure include the following:

- Technology Obsolescence - It includes applications software versions and patches, including licensing exposure, Operating System updates and patches, hardware, Data Center equipment/infrastructure, network infrastructures/equipment, and database;
- Data Center Redundancy - Tier levels of redundancy, configurations, and operational control in both construction and operation of Data Centers;
- Database, Operating System, and Hardware infrastructure configurations - Inconsistencies in configurations and organization in databases, hardware and OS environments to

include production vs DR configurations and sizing;

- Storage, Virtualized, Replication, and Backup - Issues with replication, virtual storage and hardware layers, and/or physical storage to include operational inconsistencies between production, virtual and replicated data copies and environments.

Technology Resilience Monitoring and Vulnerability Detection:

Typically, the level of technology infrastructure and operational monitoring of the major environments can be a major contributing factor to the level of maturity of Technology Resilience Risk Management. In large Enterprises, a well-structured and automated monitoring concept for technology environments is a key aspect in controlling the level of risk for the Enterprise. This is due to the size and complexity of large technology environments and IT organizations.

In most IT organizations, various monitoring environments will produce Operational Analytics about the various target environments. It is an essential IT risk control that these anomalies be escalated as needed to IT Executives and overall Enterprise risk management for both priority mitigation of issues and continual investment strategies. In many cases, these vulnerabilities may require immediate or some type of remediation that can't wait for executive decisions. They can require real-time automated notification of the vulnerability or issues to the appropriate infrastructure or application stakeholders. Figure 4.7 depicts a conceptual processing flow for a Technology Automated Management/Vulnerability Operating environment to assist in managing IT risk. A key element in ensuring a robust Technology Monitoring and Vulnerability management environment is the ability to automatically provide key IT system management data regarding various IT assets and infrastructure configurations.

Figure 4.7 IT Automated Management/Vulnerability Model

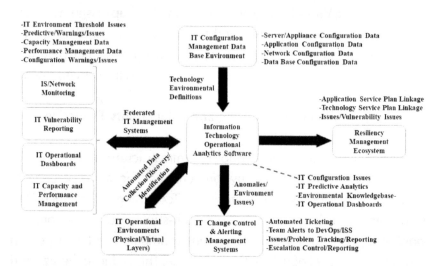

There are software products available to provide data as discussed in the model for IT Operational and Analytical software. This includes data regarding the IT assets, the types of assets, key configuration information of hardware servers, mainframe, network/security appliances, IP (Internet Protocol) address data, versions of application, operating system, and utility software and release data, replication, and virtual/physical hardware layer information.

In this conceptual model, the suggestion is to use one, or possibly more, Technology Operational System Management and/or Operational Analytical Software tools that are available in the IT marketplace. These software tools have proven invaluable to assist IT management in the automation of technology infrastructure workflows and ITSM/TRDR control management of the various technology environments. Many of these technologies have the ability and functionality to manage, monitor, and detect anomalies. They can provide key operational analytics reporting to IT management, application and infrastructure stakeholders, and the various target IT risk management environments. These IT management

130

environments include: Capacity and Performance Management Systems, Problem and Incident Reporting Systems, Security Vulnerabilities, Configuration Issues Management, and Resilience Management Systems. Many of the tools also provide advanced Operational Dashboards for oversight and in some cases KPI's reference their targeted monitoring and domain controls.

Technology Availability Management and Vulnerability Tools:

Some of the sample solutions available in the IT industry marketplace for support of IT Automated Management and Vulnerabilities detection include: BlueMedora Select Star; Continuity Software AvailabilityGuard; Data dog; DriveScale System; HPE OpenView; IBM APM/CRO; Ipswitch WhatsupGold; LogicMonitor; Virtual Instruments NAS Performance.

Each of the tools has specific target and native infrastructure environments and functionality, and the Enterprise can determine their requirements prior to selection of any of these management tools. As indicated, the IT environments can require more than one product type depending upon the complexity and size of the Enterprise IT environments. The tools range from Configuration Change and Optimization Analytics to Performance and Environmental Health Monitoring to Potential Infrastructure Failure Detection and Predictive Analytics.

The majority of these products use non-invasive computer scripts for collection of operational data automatically, and some products may use a key knowledge database of best practices to analyze target environments. They can detect inconsistencies that include identification of major anomalies and/or discrepancies, as measured against best-in-class industry standards for the technology environments. In some products, the software can provide automated ticket notification to enhance rapid stakeholder response to certain high-severity type issues detected by the management software.

Most of these products are available in a SaaS, Enterprise licensing, and/or hardware rental/subscription services.

4.8 Identification of IT Technology Dependencies

A major control in the management of IT Resilience risk is that of identification in the recovery planning process of key technology dependencies. This includes Infrastructure, Operating System, Application, Database and File, Security, Network, and Third-Party provider technology dependencies.

From a technology automation perspective, utilizing an automated federation or integration to an IT CMS environment can facilitate the identification of many of these technology dependencies. The CMS must be managed in an optimum manner by the IT organization, but there is no replacement for good IT recovery planning by the owners of the various technology recovery targets and to identify the dependent technologies.

Figure 4.8 provides a hierarchical concept for IT Dependency Processing that is recommended for automation within the overall IT recovery planning for all Enterprise technology Resilience. Development of the IT dependency mapping is critical for the full understanding of the potential impacts of key IT dependencies. Use of an IT Resilience Planning and Management tool that embeds automatic linkage of these dependencies in the planning process is a good way to simplify an upfront capture of the dependency information. It can be beneficial for development of key IT recovery strategies for these dependencies for the targeted TRDR environments.

Figure 4.8 TRDR Dependency Capture Model

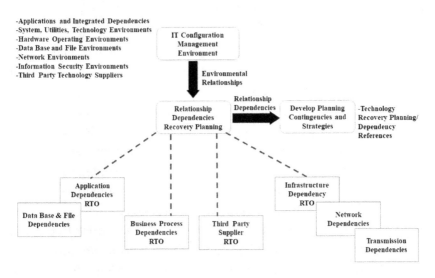

An example of this concept is the planning for the recovery of IT Application A; it allows the planners to select from CMDB federated database to ensure proper linkage to the correct Application A supporting databases; and file required environments, file transmission dependencies and time frames; infrastructure hardware, and network devices; and Third-Party provider technologies. Many of the technology applications used in most Enterprises provide federated links to external websites and/or systems hosted in the Cloud by Third-Party suppliers. It is an essential Resilience control to understand these dependency linkages for recovery planning during time-sensitive incidents, availability tracking, RTO understanding, and for testing these environments to ensure efficient interaction during an incident.

4.9 Technology Recovery - Demonstrated Exposure

Just as described in Chapter Three for BCP's, a rigorous testing program is one of the key risk management controls to ensure effective TRDR Planning and the ability to provide technology availability to the Enterprise. There are three major types of TRDR testing concepts that are consistent and best practices for demonstrating technology Resilience for the Enterprise. These include:

- Desk Checks - As in the BCP, this type of Recovery Plan Testing represents the basic concept for evaluating and demonstrating the recovery capabilities for each Technology Recovery Plan. It includes step-by-step reviews of the recovery components in the Application and Technology Recovery plans with the recovery planners, recovery managers, and technology resilience stakeholders. These testing strategies are used when new applications and/or technology environments are implemented into production environments, or combined releases to the production environments, and prior to technology implementation. Also, major changes to Recovery Plans and/or the technology environments can trigger further Desk Checks, once applications and technologies are propagated to production.

- Table-Top Testing - This is a more enhanced level of testing where the planning and recovery teams for both application and technology Infrastructure teams and observers meet at a scheduled time to test specific components of Technology Recovery plans. This is based upon a predefined threat or disruption testing scenario and scripts, and includes role-playing and simulated response; plan knowledge, team activities, and recovery team interaction; simulated responses and plan steps; and documentation of issues and addressing of detected plan gaps. This type of testing is conducive to those environments, where DR environments do not exist, e.g. (Quick Ship, etc.), and also where redundant Data Center Tier environments are unavailable to allow for simulated partial or fall-over testing of Technology Applications. It is often conducive for In-Place Recovery testing to demonstrate the ability to recover onsite where low-to-moderate site impacts are required, and/or Cold Re-Start Recovery Planning. It can be utilized where the Data Center environment is not designed for redundant system processing.

- Disaster Recovery Partial Fall-Over or Full-Scale Disaster Recovery Testing - In this type of testing, the entire Enterprise, including Application, Business, and Technology Recovery teams mobilizes and conducts all portions of the Technology and/or Application Recovery Plans and/or specific strategies by implementing processing of information, data, and transactions. They utilize DR Applications, DR/Backup Files/Databases, DR Technology infrastructures, and Third-Party technologies, as required by the Technology recovery plan. It requires physical fall-over of individual applications and/or full technology environments to include: network structures, servers and mainframes, appliances, data communication, and the use of key resilience copies of backup files and databases.

The types of testing and demonstrated activity conducted for the Enterprise as part of their TRDR program is often dependent upon the DR Data Center site strategies implemented by the Enterprise. However, it is recommended that at least an annual full-scale DR Testing be conducted to ensure at least full DR capabilities for the Enterprise. But for larger Enterprises, including those with high volumes of production and environmental changes and upgrades, it is recommended that these types of testing be conducted on a more frequent periodic schedule. Best practices Enterprise perform exercises more than 2X times or more per year. Also, it is imperative for good Data Center operational sustainability that key mechanical and electrical environments, e.g. diesel back-up generator initiation, UPS transfer, etc., testing also be conducted on low-impact and consistent periodic basis.

As in all planned simulations and testing, technology and application production environments should not be impacted from full site or partial fall-over testing. Additionally, the ability to record all technology issues discovered during testing needs to be documented and tracked where environmental anomalies are detected by the testing. Best-in-class industry activity drives a process requirement for actual Technology Change Control tracking, and updates that are performed to plans. These is required to mitigate issues uncovered during full scale and partial fall-over testing as potential incidents. Also, all other test issues discovered during Desk-Check and Table-Top testing require documentation and corrective actions.

As an overall Enterprise technology risk control, TRDR plan recovery testing is an absolute necessity to ensure the ability to demonstrate effective technology Resilience across the Enterprise. It requires that IT executive management and Enterprise senior business and risk executives be engaged to review the various levels of program testing and demonstrate the understanding of the technology Resilience of the Enterprise.

4.10 Evaluating Technology Concentration Risks

Risk management has several types of concentration risk exposure that require management and understanding from an overall perspective of Enterprise risk control. One type of major risk is that of concentrations of Data Center Technology Vulnerabilities, as discussed in the key vulnerabilities found in Section 4.7 of this chapter. A high concentration of vulnerabilities at a particular Data Center or in specific applications and technology areas can be a key exposure. These need to be reported and risk assessed for overall Enterprise risk control. An example of this could be a large exposure to some particular obsolete Operating System environments across multiple Applications and/or Database technology environments clustered in a particular Technology Resilience or DR Tier. These can be predictive of future technology availability issues. Also, a large number of production-to- DR inconsistent hardware/software configurations in a specific Recovery Tier environment could be indicative of major recovery issues for key applications/technologies.

Another Technology Resilience Concentration Risk is that of concentrated Third-Party technologies across multiple products and services provided by a single Third Party. A potential loss of one Third-Party provider technology environments could present a major exposure to one or more products and critical business functions when these technology services are concentrated with one Third-Party provider. Concentration Risk with a single Third Party could impact the availability of internal technology applications that are federated to the Third-Party technology provider.

Lastly, a high number of RTO Technology Dependency Gaps for individual applications and/or specific Technologies could present a major exposure to multiple business processes. It is important to understand these gaps for not just the supporting technologies, but in those cases where these dependent technologies are concentrated at a particular Data Center site or expose multiple levels of redundancy at these sites. This is reflected in Sections 4 and 6 of this chapter and can be predictive of potential availability exposures.

4.11 Technology Resilience Ecosystem Concepts

Technology Resilience Operational Automation Drivers:

The automation of IT Resilience and TRDR planning and management is suggested due to the speed and high volume of modifications in IT environments, and for the large volume of IT assets used in many Enterprise IT environments. This is true in large Enterprises where there are thousands of technology assets, infrastructures, and applications. The ITGRC Ecosystem is required to manage and monitor these large and complex Enterprise technology environments and is considered a best practice IT methodology. Just as in the BCP program, one of the key elements to maintaining a strong and effective TRDR Framework is the recommended integration and/or federation of key IT management environments and systems control components. This chapter section reviews Technology Resilience Management Ecosystems and key data concepts for these automation models.

The Technology Resilience Management (TRM) Ecosystem model is similar to the BCM Ecosystem and requires a clear linkage of technology recovery and BCP recovery to include business processes and supporting technologies. In many Enterprises, the Ecosystem technologies supporting these frameworks operates in a consolidated Ecosystem, and as such, are integrated into the overall frameworks technology. For purposes of this book, the management environments for BCP process and TRM are isolated to ensure a unique understanding of requirement for each framework. However, many of the supplier technologies discussed in this section can provide the base for the joint and linked Ecosystem in one BCP-TRM product. The various frameworks are then capable of leveraging many of the same data sources and technology integrations or federations and integrating the Resilience vision for business and technology.

Available Technology Resilience Software and Services:

A large number of the same BCM software suppliers listed in Chapter Three provide generic Resilience Management products that support both BCP and TRDR functionality. With a few exceptions, many provide the ability to develop and maintain Technology Recovery Plans, Risk Assess Technologies, Track and Test Recovery Plans, and Open/ Track Incident Recovery for Technologies and Data Centers. Most of these technology suppliers provide linkage of technology to embedded BCP's and business processes in their offerings. Some products are more configurable then others, but a key element of these products is having the ability to import and/or integrate or federate IT management environmental data, such as applications, servers, Operating System, databases, network devices and appliances, configuration data, file interfaces, and Third-Party technologies. These are all critical for effective TRDR planning and recovery and should be an essential component of any of the products selected for the Enterprise.

TRDR Trusted Data Sources and System Concepts:

Given the need for similar data sources and integration/federation sources between BCP and TRM planning, the same Trusted Data definitions and sources provided in Chapter Three are required for the TRM Ecosystem. As indicated in this section, introducing this concept is a primary driver for ensuring consistency and leveraging a management ecosystem that supports both frameworks, or one framework that includes, both BCP and TRM functions.

The Trusted Data sources include: Human Resource and Organizational Data, Risk Profile Data, Third-Party Supplier Data, Dependent Business Process and RTO's, Knowledge and Training Data with a focus on Technology Recovery, and IT Management environments. The additional TRM key management environments required for TRDR planning and recovery includes:

- IT Enterprise Configuration Management System data to include Application Inventories and Configurations, Application Security Profiles, Infrastructure Hardware Servers, Operating Systems, Network Equipment and Appliance Data, Database and File Data, IP Addresses Data, Licensing Data, Operating System version, configuration and deployment status;
- IT Incident Management and Problem Management data to include open and closed Incidents from technology incidents, remediation directions and status, severity levels and SLA requirements, problem and IT knowledgebase references, and linkages;
- IT Change and Release Management data for all Enterprise IT Changes, Status, and Linkage to all Applications, Database, Infrastructure, and Network Configurations, and Telecommunication Transmissions;
- IT Service Management data for all assigned Teams and linkage to requested Infrastructure and Application project impacts to IT assets;

- IT Operational Analytics data for all vulnerabilities and incidents detected by the IT Operational Analytics and Monitoring Technologies by the Enterprise.

Technology Resilience/DR Management Ecosystem:

Figure 4.11 depicts a conceptual flow for an Technology Resilience/DR Management Ecosystem. It provides an overview of the primary Technology Resilience automation concepts for managing the TRDR framework environment and processes. Included are the key Trusted Data sources discussed in the previous section and the required integration with the IT and Enterprise governance and risk management environments.

Figure 4.11 Technology Resilience/DR Management Ecosystem

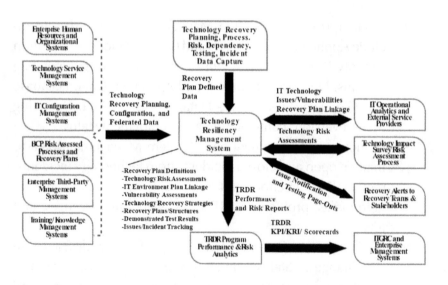

This conceptual model can provide IT Resilience analytics, KPI's, and KRI's that are discussed later in this chapter

A TRM software product is recommended for large Enterprises to support technology planning. Many of the available BCM software products provide generic components that are configurable and capable of integrating and/or importing key TRDR planning data from the targeted data sources. Additionally, the ability to alert and notify key technology support teams is critical to maintaining availability of all Enterprise applications and technologies. For smaller and mid-size enterprises many Third-parties can provide a Cloud based solution for this technology.

The TRM environment should be able to link the technology support and recovery teams to all Application and Technology Recovery Plans for immediate notification and tracking of recovery plan steps and status. As discussed, many of the available software technologies have the ability to directly execute notifications or embed APIs for linkage to NES products and services, or internal team paging and advice systems. Additionally, the TRM environment or selected tools should be capable of integrating alerts and issues with specific Technology Operational/Analytics environments. This is to allow linkage to specific environmental vulnerabilities to the TRDR Plans, and provide direct reporting of exposures of vulnerability risks for the associated applications and technologies

Another key component required of the TRM environment is the ability to engage and activate recovery plan structures for thousands of application and technologies during a major incident or DR event. The ability to engage and electronically manage all of the resources associated with complex infrastructure environments, systems, and application recovery is a formidable task for any Enterprise. It can be almost impossible to manage such environments, without the use of automated technologies that bring the entire recovery model into perspective during an incident, to include: application and technology recovery teams, applications, hardware, Operating Systems, network/security devices and appliances, business support teams, and Third-Party suppliers. Many of the technology supplier products suggested in this book provide the capabilities to automatically initiate planning recovery at an Enterprise level to engage and manage resources and environments.

4.12 Identifying TRDR Program Indicators

One of the major components of all TRDR Frameworks is the ability to explain the overall performance of the program to all business stakeholders senior Enterprise executives, and the Board of Directors. This chapter will define some of the most common TRDR program KPI's and KRI's that allow the Enterprise to better understand the compliance level and activity in their program. They will provide key risk exposure levels for decision and direction by Enterprise executive management. All TRDR frameworks must be capable of articulating Trusted KPI and KRI data to executive management along with key TRDR program escalations for proper governance of the program.

General Technology Resilience Program Performance:

A major program performance item is to be capable of providing KPI's as to basic framework construct and complexity of reporting TRDR inventory counts of plans, processes, and tests for the program. This will allow general profiling of the program and understanding of the program compliance level. An important characteristic of these indicators is to understand the performance level in the program of individual business technologies, but also the overall divisional or sub-corporate, and even Enterprise subsidiary levels of TRDR performance.

These indicators are suggested as a basic structure of key compliance constructs in the program and include:

- Technology Resilience Applications/Technologies in the Program - Number of target Applications/Technologies in TRDR program, to include work in-progress technology to the program;
- Technology Resilience Applications/Technologies in Program with Key Dependencies by RTO - Number of TRDR target Applications/Technologies with key dependences in the program by RTO (list of applications and technologies);

- Technology Recovery Plans in Program - Number of Technology Recovery Plans accepted into the TRDR program, and work in-process plans to program;
- Technology Recovery Applications/Technologies Risk Assessed or In-Process of Risk Assessment - Number of Applications and Technologies engaged in the Risk Assessments in program work in-process;
- Technology Recovery Plans by RTO within Technology Tier - Number of Technology Resilience Plans within Technology Tiers within RTO;
- Technology Recovery Plans and Applications/Technologies Compliant and Non-Compliant within TRDR Framework, including Late Compliance - Number of Technology Recovery Plans Applications and Technologies that are Compliant, and Non-Compliant to the TRDR Framework; with identification of Late Items and Days aged in program;
- Technology Recovery Plans and Applications/Technologies with Issues and/or Late Issue Resolution - Number of Technology Recovery Plans for Targeted Applications and Technologies with Issues, and those with Issues that are unresolved by their mitigation due date with days aged in program;
- Technology Recovery Plans and Application/Technology Issues Escalated for Management Action - Number of Technology Recovery Plans for Applications and Technologies with issues that have been escalated for management decisions and/or mitigation/resolution.

The importance of these indicators is that they provide an overall level of understanding for technology activity to senior executive management as to the size and complexity of the program. They provide a level of compliance and an indication as to TRDR program stability, quality, trending, and overall direction.

Program stability and trending are important in staff needs, just as in the BCP program, the TRDR program frameworks can be resource-intensive depending upon the level of program complexity and committed personnel resources. These are necessary metrics for understanding resources that are used for planning, testing, budgeting purposes, and for technology investment strategies. Therefore, it is essential to managing program frameworks for large Enterprise programs. KPI's also provides an overall direction of risk, where performance can be an overall predictive warning sign of potential risk, and exposure for operational risk management exposure.

Demonstrated Technology Resilience Testing Performance:

Another major KPI report set is for tracking the overall validation testing of the program. Demonstrating the efficiency and performance of the program is a major requirement in any TRDR framework and requires various levels of testing performance to ensure viable planning and risk management.

The major KPI's for understanding the overall performance of the TRDR program and compliance level require a complete set of metrics. Again, it is important to understand the levels of performance by both individual technology categories (e.g. applications, infrastructures, etc.,), and also by technology categories within the various subsidiary organizational levels.

Key Performance Indicators for TRDR Demonstrated Testing includes the following recommendations:

- Technology Recovery Plans Tested (Passed, Failed, and Incomplete) - Number of Technology Recovery Plans and Targeted Business Platforms tested;
- Applications/Technologies Tested - Indicates testing numbers as to testing Passed, Failed and/or Incomplete;
- Technology Resilience Applications/Technologies Testing Compliant with Framework Include Late Compliance (aging delays) - Number of Technology Recovery Plans and Targeted Business Applications/Technologies Tested within Framework

requirements, and number of Non-Compliant to Framework (Identify list of Plans, Applications, and Technologies) with aging of the Non-Compliant Plans/Applications/Technologies;

- Technology Recovery Plan and Business Processing Testing Categories - Defined number of testing conducted by category of testing (*e.g.* desk checks, functional, etc.);
- Dependent Processes, Third-Party Suppliers, and Technology Tested - Number of Identified Dependencies Tested within the Targeted Business Applications and Technologies;
- Technology Recovery Plans and Applications/Technologies with Testing Issues - Number of Technology Recovery Plans/ Targeted Business Applications and Technologies Tested with reported testing issues, and required to be mitigated per the Framework and within Framework Time-Frames;
- Technology Recovery Plans by Applications and Technologies with Testing Issues Escalated for Management Action - Technology Recovery Plans and Targeted Business Applications/Technologies with Testing Issues that have been escalated for further managerial action or mitigations;
- Technology Recovery Plans and Process with Testing Issues and/or Late Resolution (aging of delays) - Number of Technology Recovery Plans and Targeted Business Applications and Technologies with test issues and where issues are late in resolution, with aging of the Late Plans/ Applications/Technologies.

Depending upon defined thresholds in TRDR program framework, these indicators could be indicative of potential risk to the overall technology category, owning business lines, product areas, and the Enterprise. These KPI's could signal a negative trend of performance and compliance by specific IT areas and/or increased risk exposure to the Enterprise and require investment considerations that are based upon the discovered compliance and testing issues.

Key Technology Resilience Risk Indicators:

As an aggregation point for the Technology Resilience risk profile of the Enterprise, the TRDR KRI's allow the TRDR program owners to explain and drive the risk management profile for the program. The KRI's allow the program to measure the level of risk and sensitivity for particular technology and operational activities. It can provide an early warning and risk trending for potential IT technology disruptions and provide an overall Enterprise operational risk data component assessment. Therefore, TRDR KPI's measure how well the TRDR program and Enterprise are doing from a compliance perspective, and KRI's demonstrate and provide a view of potential inherent risk to the technologies and businesses, and the resulting residual risks of IT operational technologies.

Key Risk Indicators recommended as major risk measures for most TRDR Programs include:

- Technology Recovery Plans by Applications and Technologies with Recovery Strategy Issues (Within Threat Levels) - Number of Technology Recovery Plans and Targeted Business Applications and Technologies with Recovery Strategy Issues defined by the Targeted Threat Area and Threat Severity;
- Technology Recovery Plans and Business Process RTO Dependency Gaps (e.g. Process, Technology, Third-Party, etc.) - Defined number of Technology Recovery Plans, Targeted Applications and Technologies with RTO Gaps between Targeted Process Dependencies with Identification of the Targeted Dependency and Gap RTO's;
- Technology Recovery Plans and Process Testing Failures by RTO - Identification of the number of Technology Recovery Plans, Targeted Applications and Technologies with Testing Failures results and within group of RTOs with identification of Plans, Applications, and Technologies;

- Technology Recovery Plans and Process Testing RTO Misses - Identification of the number of Technology Recovery Plans, Targeted Applications and Technologies that missed recovery within the designated and risk assessed RTO, with identification of Plans, Applications and Technologies;
- Technology Resilience Process with RTO Testing Discrepancies - Number of Technology Resilience Targeted Applications and Technologies with RTO Testing Discrepancies;
- Business Process Detail Tracking of Testing RTO Failures and RTO Testing Misses Remediation - Continued Tracking of Targeted Applications and Technologies with RTO Failures and RTO Misses during testing, with aging of days and remediation target dates;
- Level of Risk Acceptance by Business Line Units (Defined Inherent Risk with no Remediation) - Number and identification of Technologies where Business Lines understand the threat remediation for their business, and for which executives have accepted the inherent risk.
- Technology Resilience Vulnerability Severity Levels - Identifies Targeted Applications and Technologies within various Vulnerability Categories and Issue Severity Levels;
- Technology Resilience Process Risk Concentration Levels - Identification of the Targeted Applications and Technologies with Risk Concentration Levels by Category of Risk, Severity of Risk, and Concentration Levels (at location, within Business Division, Mission Critical Technology Tier Groupings).

Utilizing standard KRI's for the TRDR program allows the Enterprise to better manage the complex IT risks of the Enterprise, and to demonstrate management of TRDR Risk. This can make it possible for business managers and executives to implement effective operational and strategic growth plans. Engaging and orienting senior Enterprise executives and the Board of Directors to the key program components can ensure that Technology Resilience is a component of the strategic planning process. It is recommended that all KPI's and KRI's be integrated into an IT and Enterprise governance and risk management environment that aggregates program risk metrics as key components of the IT risk profile of the Enterprise portfolio.

CHAPTER 5

IT Information Security

5.1 Introduction IT Information Security Risks

THE MOST FOCUSED level of IT and Enterprise risk management since the turn of the twenty-first century has been the risk associated with Information Security or Cyber Technologies. This is due to the explosion and proliferation of the internet, e-commerce, email, and ubiquitous mobile access to global social sites. Prior to the twenty-first century, the focus for IT risk management was on IT client-server distributed processing expansion into the 1990s. It then was dominated by a run-up and management focus on the "Year 2000 Bug (Y2K)" risk exposures and the advent of internet-based commerce sites.

During the last ten years, business have expanded sales and support services into the internet and cloud environments, concurrently with this exposure, security risks have increased exponentially with large volumes of high-profile cyberattacks and data breaches. This has focused the world's attention on IT security events in reference to data protection, encryption, privacy, and threat surveillance. Because of the increasing threat volumes and large numbers of data breaches and cyberattacks across many industries, Information Security (IS) and Cyber Management has risen to the top of the IT risk management pyramid for many Enterprises and senior executives.

Due to the IT industry growth, there are tremendous risk exposures and increased focus upon IT security expenditures. These expenditures are focused on Third-Party technology hardware, software, and resource services to manage and secure IT environments such as: hardware security modules, network devices, firewalls, email filtering and analysis, security appliances, authentication, encryption, vulnerability detection and analysis, security administration, cyber testing software and services, cyber and incident response technology, traffic and threat analysis, security risk assessments, and many other IT security products.

Therefore, it is imperative that IT organizations and Enterprises maintain appropriate and proven security governance and risk control processes over the environments. This is essential to protect the Enterprise from externally and internally sponsored cyber threats and potential data loss. This requires specific automation techniques to identify and for response to these threats. This chapter will focus on the key ITGRC controls to support integration of IT security practices and processes into IT and Enterprise risk programs. This will include a review of IS controls related to IS policies, governance, and standards; IS roles; identity and user data access; application risk assessment; system and data backups; production and system patches/changes; IT operational and environmental controls; Third-Party provider security; security testing; security automation concepts; and enterprise performance and risk indicators.

Organizational Accountability for Information Security Risk:

The IT organization has primary responsibility for control, oversight, and execution of the IS policy. The senior IT executives and Chief Information Security Officer (CISO) of the Enterprise are accountable for overall execution and oversight of the IS policy. However, each and every Enterprise executive, manager, and employee should also be held accountable for the IS policy components as they relate to each individual departmental activity within the Enterprise. This includes, but is not limited to, employee access to systems and other technology, securing confidential corporate and customer data/documents properly, and managing the daily messages and emails. As with other key Enterprise policies, such as BCP, the Board of Directors is accountable for corporate governance. This is true for overall oversight of the IS policy and the security framework of the Enterprise. The management and control of IS risks is an integral part of corporate governance and requires a key focus of the Enterprise risk organization.

5.2 IT Security Governance, Policy, and Standards

Information Security Governance:

IS governance is required for the assignment of responsibilities and specific role accountability. This requires establishment of Enterprise IS policies and compliance requirements; development of IS standards and procedures; allocation of IS and IT resources and other Enterprise resources; environmental monitoring; and risk exposure assessment practices. IT organizations and the overall Enterprise are required to ensure that all IS tasks are completed per the IS policies, standards, and are part of departmental oversight for security activities. These are essential for ensuring that security tasks are completed appropriately and that the appropriate risk management and inherent IS issues are mitigated via the accountable areas.

IS Policy and Standards:

The IS policy and program framework is by far one of the strongest controls for the enforcement of Enterprise IT Security Governance and Strategies for IT environments and technology usage. IT organizations should ensure that Enterprise IS policies are implemented and that compliance with the policies is maintained by all of the Enterprise organizations, stakeholders, employees, and Third Parties.

Additionally, it is suggested that the policy be enforced through use of automated system controls and system administration processes. This is often required where there are large numbers of personnel and IT assets across the Enterprise.

Effective IS policies and standards require a thorough understanding by all IT organizational resources. Also, these policies need to be communicated to all Enterprise employees and stakeholders. This communication can include effective IS-based training for all Enterprise stakeholders and employees. It requires introduction of key managerial approval hierarchies in the requirements for Security Policies; Types of Security Threats and Mitigations; Data Protection, Confidentiality and Data Sensitivity levels; System Access, Protection, and Specific Role Accountabilities; Physical and System Security Control concepts; and authorized computer and other device usage and procedures throughout the Enterprise.

Some key components of the IS policy and standards definitions can include: IS general responsibilities and IS roles; Enterprise employee responsibilities and roles; Definitions of adapted industry Standards (e.g. NIST, ISO, etc.); Network/Perimeter definitions and process requirements; Third-Party supplier requirements and risk definitions; Data classifications and authorized access zones; Environmental definitions and authorized usage; Access management and authorization privileges; Technology definitions and authorized usage (e.g. BYO devices, Smart Phone, PDA, USB drives, CD's, etc.); Crisis and Cyber event communication and response requirements; Employee training requirements; Reporting, Exception, and Escalation requirements.

In addition, the Enterprise IS policy may require approval of an Enterprise IS Steering Committee, an Executive Risk Committee, and the Board of Directors of the Enterprise. The IS policy needs to also be reviewed and approved at a minimum on an annual basis, or as conditions change within the Enterprise. This requires either annual and/or other periodic board approval requirements. The policy should be the subject of both external and/or internal audits to validate policy adherence by all stakeholders of the Enterprise and the results reported to both executive management and the Board of Directors. Security Standards and Best Practice Concepts:

The National Institute of Standards and Policies (NIST) is part of the US Department of Commerce. It is one of the oldest physical science laboratories in the US. It was established by Congress to develop key competitive measurement and standard structures. NIST has established IT Security Standards for protecting data, systems, and networks at government agencies, general IT services, and focused private sectors (e.g. utility, financial, etc.). The standards and guidance ranges across SP800 and SP1800 publication documents. The ISO 27000 standards are also a widely implemented frameworks published by the International Organization for Standards (ISO). They provide best practice standards and guidelines as an approach to IS management and allows organizations to be certified compliant to the standards. Figure 5.1 depicts a summary concept for IS best practice standards, principles, and concepts for implementation in an IS governance framework.

Figure 5.1 IS Best Practice Principles Framework

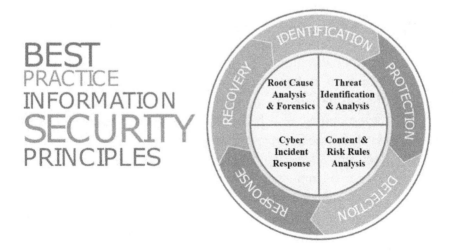

Each of these IS program standard framework concepts and many other published guidelines for IS management provide for specific methodology approaches to control IS risk. The focus in almost all cases is on establishing the following key fundamental IS principals:

- Identification - Ensures the identification of data, data usage, and business functions that are critical to the Enterprise and where, how, and what data is used in systems and processes by key business functions. Enterprises should ensure they can identify technologies, assess the risk of the various technologies, and risk assess and monitor technologies on a continuing basis, while ensuring appropriate training for all stakeholders and employees.

- Protection - Requires implementation of various data analysis controls, protection mechanisms, and testing methodologies (*e.g.* penetration testing, vulnerability identification, *etc.*) to maintain a robust IS framework for protection of the Enterprise and sensitive data, including customer data, throughout the Enterprise, and environmental/penetration testing.

- Detection - Establishing effective and rapid detection-control and filtering techniques to ensure the security of the Enterprise, and detect network attacks, malware, environmental anomalies, and vulnerabilities across the IT and Enterprise environment.

- Response - When IS protective measures and processes fail because of insufficient controls, or unauthorized access is detected or discovered, IT environments and confidential information are potentially compromised. At these times, a series of rapid response protocols and resources must be developed for responding to such events and mitigating the effects to such events for the Enterprise.

- Recovery - Developing recovery procedures and guidelines that can be implemented in a rapid and effective manner, manage prioritization of recovery for the Enterprise via the identification of critical assets, systems, and operating environments, and effective forensic and recovery controls.

In addition, an ITGRC management best practice is the establishment of Cyber Security Intelligence and Incident Response Team (CSIRT) structures. These teams operate in an integrated manner to evaluate, analyze, and monitor threats, vulnerabilities, and cyber risks to the IT environments. These teams can perform ongoing analysis of threat intelligence, analytics, network traffic, operational dashboards, and cyber threat sources (e.g. DHS, industry organizations, etc.), social media, manufacturer release guidance and patches, operational analytics/transaction logs and analytical tools, network pattern logs, and scanning technology and analysis. The teams assist in development of content rules for monitoring environments, respond to security and other events, perform root cause analysis, and support forensic analysis of intrusion events.

Another key IS program component to understand are approaches for communicating and managing the privacy of customer data. This is especially true as it relates to both United States and European Union certifications as to privacy rules and frameworks. This includes best-practices for addressing and reporting on the safe-guards to meet Federal standards for protection of customer information under the Gramm-Leach-Bliley Act (GLBA) of 1999. Additionally, the European Union introduced new General Data Protection Regulations (GDPR) in 2016 that Enterprises doing business in European Union countries must meet in 2nd Quarter 2018.

5.3 Assessing IS Risks in Technology Operations

Assessing the IS risk can assist in reduction of the overall level of risk associated with operational, legal, reputational, and strategic risks to the Enterprise. An effective IS assessment program can help limit the overall Enterprise risk exposure and vulnerability of intrusion attempts and attacks, minimize loss of customer confidence, and reduce stakeholder exposures. The IS risk assessments are used by Enterprises to identify and understand risks to the level of data confidentiality, data integrity, and the overall availability of

IT application systems and environments. The basis for the IS risk assessment requires, at a minimum, the identification and prioritization of Enterprise assets and resources. It also requires the ongoing analysis of the potential threats and vulnerabilities to those assets and resources.

This process is similar to the risk analysis performed in the BCP and TRDR frameworks to understand the critical assets and resources of the Enterprise. In many cases, IS risk assessments can piggyback onto the risk definitions and Enterprise priorities found in Chapters Three and Four of this book. However, in the case of IS risk assessments, it is also essential to understand the exposure levels of data, sensitivity of customer and confidential data, and the information processed by the IT assets and resources.

Information Security Technology Risk Assessments:

The IS program framework should require that all IT assets and key resources be assessed before the introduction to the various IT operational areas, Enterprise offices, and Data Center environments. It should also require ongoing risk assessments based upon the priority and level of exposure of assets for the Enterprise. This requires that the IS program framework develop a standard risk assessment methodology that is capable of ranking the assets and resources and assessing the level of vulnerability and exposure to these IT assets.

It is essential that IT organizations be able to identify all technology assets, to include network and perimeter assets, applications and systems, smartphones and other personal devices, telecommunication equipment, laptops and desktop computer hardware and servers, and physical equipment. Any asset should be included that can be used to access, store, transmit, and process Enterprise data and information. A combined IT Asset Inventory and Configuration Management repository should be current and maintained by the IT organization with cross-reference to the IT Assets Life-Cycle Framework. This is essential to ensure a complete and thorough IS risk assessment of all IT assets and resources.

After the Enterprise has identified their key IT assets and data sources, each of the assets needs to be assessed as to the potential level of security exposure identified for those resources. This requires evaluating the level of threats and vulnerabilities for these assets and assessment of the level of control effectiveness for the resources.

To ensure consistent IS Risk Assessment for these resources, each of the systems and technology should be rated via a standard IS Risk Assessment framework and methodology. The IS framework needs to categorize the levels of threats and risks to the IT assets and resources and the level of due diligence required to validate mitigation of those risks. To accomplish this, IS organizations often will use a IS Risk Tier Logic structure and methodology for IS risk assessments.

IS Risk Tier Methodology:

Typically, this IS risk assessment methodology considers the priority of the IT assets to the corporation. A good practice here is to use the IT TRDR priority or DR Tiers assessed for all IT systems and Technologies. It can be used to supplement this component of the IS Framework and allows for effective leverage of other ITGRC methodologies and processes for consistency and Trusted Data sources. These assets then need to be categorized based upon their data risk and sensitivity as to the class of data accessed, processed, and stored, (e.g. Customer Confidential, Employee Sensitive Data, Internal Business Confidential, Non-sensitive Enterprise data, etc.). In addition, the IS risk assessment methodology needs to evaluate the level of exposure to the Enterprise and the potential threat to the IT assets. This can include a Security Risk Profile that identifies the level of inherent risk posed to the Enterprise.

It requires the development of exposure classifications for the use of various technology methodologies and vulnerabilities to include:

- Technology Delivery Channels (e.g. web-based and/or mobile access by customers or employees, etc.);

- Types of technology products used by the Enterprise (*e.g.* Adobe, email systems, etc.); communication protocols and connection topology types (Secure HTTP, FTP, etc.);

- Potential external threats (*e.g.* Distributed Denial of Service (DDoS), malware/viruses, email and site phishing, ransomware, etc.);

- Third-Party Services and outsourced activities (*e.g.* Corporate Payments, Enterprise Critical Services such as: money movement, online banking, brokerage transactions, travel reservations, online shopping, etc.).

The inherent IS risk profile should also identify the volume, complexity, and type of operations, together with the exposure level of threats and vulnerabilities associated with the various Enterprise technologies. Figure 5.3 depicts a IS Risk Assessment model for automation of these concepts.

Figure 5.3 IS Technology Risk Assessment Concept

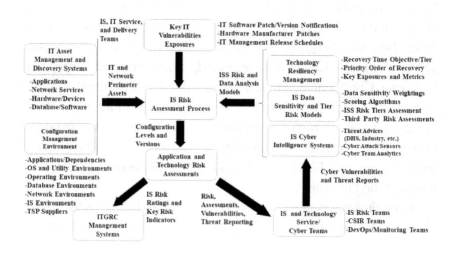

IS Threats and Vulnerabilities Identification:

Typically, the IS assessment of threats and vulnerabilities will endeavor to identify the threats to the confidentiality and/or availability of systems and data for the Enterprise. These events can be defined by the potential threats from cyber actors (e.g. national or state intelligence sponsored; organized crime members and associates; political or social activists; and internal or Third-Party personnel, etc.). They can exploit a vulnerability, and/or introduce computer malware or viruses into IT environments. These can alter or destroy data or information, invoke data theft and/or unauthorized use of data or data disclosures; introduce environmental performance degradation, or damage systems and IT environments.

These threats are intentional and may originate from any of the various sources indicated above. They can be triggered by vulnerabilities in technology that are control issues, man-made, and/or from natural events (e.g. fires, earthquakes, etc.). The IS vulnerabilities can arise from weaknesses in IS controls or gaps/issues in processes, and/or weaknesses in systems or technologies that can be exploited by one of the defined actors. System or control gaps exploitation could result in the unauthorized disclosure, misuse, alteration, or destruction of data and/or information systems.

The vulnerabilities can include but are not limited to: poor email or data controls, deficient patching of application software, hardware systems, technology obsolescence, inadequate access and password controls, deficient network rules, etc. Many vulnerabilities can be determined by testing the various environments and can be mitigated by the adequate response and investments by executive IT management to correct the deficiencies.

However, some vulnerabilities will not be ascertained until the vulnerabilities have been exploited by a defined actor, and then only after detection of the event and/or mitigation by IT Operational/Service or CSIRT teams. The level of potential exposure will depend upon the IS Risk Tier, Data Sensitivity, and the IS/IT department speed, and level of response to the cyber incident. This is why it is important to risk assess all IT assets and develop mitigation plans based upon the vulnerability and priority of the assets and resources, by understanding the level of threat, resulting potential inherent risk, and exposure level to the Enterprise.

Inherent Risk IS Assessments Modeling:

An IS framework should define as part of the methodology an Inherent Risk Tier model that assesses the inherent risks to IT assets and resources via categories of risk (e.g. Significant, High, Moderate, or Minimum Exposure, etc.). The inherent risk profile then helps management determine the level of exposure of the IS risks to the Enterprise. Executives may then outline mitigation activities and projects to fund and monitor for reduction of these risks to the Enterprise.

As business strategies expand, change, or new technology is introduced to the Enterprise, the IS program needs to continue to assess the risk profile for the Enterprise. Therefore, programs should assess the level of controls required to maintain the risk profile desired by the Enterprise executives and the Board of Directors. Additionally, the IS framework must allow for ongoing evaluation of new and/or expanded threats from new types of actors and/or new technology introduction to the Enterprise.

Most corporations have structured CSIRT teams to assist in development of threat intelligence data and response processes. These CSIRT teams work in partnership with Enterprise BCP/TRDR, Crisis Management, and IT Operational Monitoring/Support Teams. Key to the protection of the Enterprise is understanding the priorities of IT assets, level of cyber risks to those assets, the vulnerabilities and threats to those assets, and the level of mitigation and response required for a particular cyber incident.

5.4 Identity Access and Authentication Management

Identity Access and Authentication Management is the component of the IS framework that enables authorized individuals to access the appropriate system, network, and technology resources for the correct reasons. Identification of the correct personnel and their activities or role requirements is a key defensive strategy for the protection of Enterprise assets, data, and resources. From an IS framework perspective, it is a mission-critical requirement to ensure the administration and identification of personnel authorized to access systems, data, and the various IT environments.

Identity and Access governance should be controlled by the Enterprise IS policy. It requires administrative automation due to the large number of system and network access rights, and variations of the security permissions associated with these access rights. Key functionalities in administration of these access rights are: Fulfillment of access rights by individuals with appropriate hierarchical approval levels, password management, entitlements to appropriate roles, certifications of roles, and overall process workflows over system and environmental access. Authentication and entitlements of the authorized users is also a major component of the IS framework and the associated guidance required to ensure and validate that authorized users have access to the correct system and can access technology environments.

Authentication Security Operational Processes:

The authentication of users and granting of entitlements is a key IS governance component for users to gain access to any system or technology environment. A user is afforded an opportunity to present their credentials (e.g. user or account name, etc.) for granting access to the various Enterprise environments. The most typical credential used throughout the IT global footprint for system access is a single password assigned to that particular user for access to the environments. In many large Enterprises, the capability for assigning "Single

Sign-on" passwords have been automated through "Self-Service" enabled technologies. They are often administered by the IT operational departments with oversight by both IT network and IS departments.

Also, various operating environments have been enabled via Third-Party "Single Sign-on" environments that use a common security protocol for controlling access to multiple environments of the Enterprise with the same credentials. It is used to grant access and validate the user password and credentials against common access control environments. Multiple security protocols exist for "Single Sign-On" access in the IS and IT industry for maintaining access rights to the various network and operating environments. Some of these are: IBM, Microsoft, Oracle, and Unix environments. Also, typical manufacturers of Single-Sign-on products includes: IBM Enterprise Manager/Tivoli, Oracle Identity Manager, Microsoft Active Director/ Account Manager and NetIQ Access Manager to name a few.

Also, additional authentication can be introduced based upon the level of risk and data sensitivity for specific environments, and specific types of sensitive and network transactions. These are identified during the IS Security Risk Assessment process (see Section 5.3). Many IS organizations will identify multiple layers of validation, to increase security access protection for the specific risk identified environments and transactions. This protection is known as, "Two-Factor Authentication," or "Multi-Factor Authentication." There are various forms of authentication methodology used to conduct additional validations for ensuring user identity and some include: Key word or image validations, Pins or Security Tokens (Hard or software based), Smart-Cards, and Biometrics (e.g.: finger-print, retinal or facial scans, etc.).

From a technology perspective, it is imperative that no matter what authentication methodology is used, the IS organization maintain oversight over the administration and validation of these environments, as well as, the software technology for maintaining access to the various systems and environments. IS should set the level of control, types, and reset frequency for passwords and is accountable for inventories of multi-factor identification software and devices, and the governance over the support environments for these multi-factor environments.

Access Permission and Administration Management:

In addition to ensuring the authentication and verification of the users, it is just as important for IS to identify what applications, systems, technologies, and environments a user is authorized to access. Known as "Access Permissions or Entitlements Rights," this component of the IS framework is also essential for ensuring the protection of the assets and data of the Enterprise.

The administration of these rights can be a labor-intensive process for both IS organizations and an overall challenge for many business organizations. It can require significant automation and ongoing maintenance to ensure the right people are authorized to access the appropriate systems and data required for their role in the organization. The IS organization must define and maintain the level of access rights to all systems and technologies of the Enterprise with the input of the accountable business areas.

Access right levels are often maintained in hundreds and thousands of applications and systems used throughout an Enterprise. These are often managed through the various user and system administrator areas for these application environments. However, the IS Access management environment should administer the overall authorized access control to the various network, environments, and application environments. Application environments must coordinate with IS for a clear technology handoff of access to these applications and key data by users. It is also essential for IS to maintain the appropriate hierarchical approval levels and certifications as to what users have access to what systems and the varying levels of authorized access to those systems. This includes the various technology environments that includes production servers, databases, and network devices, etc.

Identity Access and Administration Technology:

The automation of the Identity Access, Governance, and Administration (IAGAM) Management Life-Cycle has become a major IS technology sub-sector within the IT industry. It includes provisioning to access governance functions and maintenance of administrative rights for the various systems, access technologies, and other major IS functionalities, which includes automated assignment of user accounts to multiple environments; fulfillment of access requests to include self-service protocols; password management/maintenance; target system access and certification protocols and administration; IAGAM workflow technology and approval certification administration; risk assessment of user access rights; administrative role definitions; organizational group inheritance; and special IAGAM analytics.

This IAGAM technology software sub-sector includes Enterprise level, SaaS, and Cloud solution suppliers such as: Alert Enterprise, ATOS Identity/Access Management, Avatier Identity Management, Computer Associates Identity Suite, Courion Access Assurance, Dell/EMC-RSA Identity Management and Governance, Hitachi ID Systems, IBM Security ID Governance and Administration, Oracle Identity Governance Suite, Pulse Secure, and Microsoft Conditional Access.

5.5 Application Security Assessment Process Controls

As defined in Section 5.3 of this chapter, assessing the business priority and criticality of applications to the Enterprise is of paramount importance for protecting these assets of the organization. Understanding the overall risk profile of applications in the Enterprise requires understanding the exposure and threats to all applications and systems data. The thousands of web-based, intranet, desktop, and mid-range/mainframe applications operational throughout many Enterprises require the use of a systematic approach to prioritize and assess the security risk to applications in the environments. To accomplish this, it is essential to maintain a central and current inventory of all assets applications, hardware, and databases (physical and logical) that are operational in the Enterprise for IS analysis. Given the speed of software time to market implementations and the overall rate of product introductions, this has become a major automation task for most Enterprises. It is recommended as a core base for any IS Risk Assessment process.

IS Assessments Controls Methodology:

Utilizing a methodology to secure Enterprise applications depends upon the accuracy, due diligence, and frequency of the IS Risk Assessment process. Once Enterprise applications have been risk assessed, the IS framework must define the approach and priority for evaluating security vulnerabilities and threats to those applications selected for risk profile activities. In many large organizations, the level of applications inventory can be anywhere, from 2,500 to 5,000 applications, and most organizations have limited resources to perform continual application vulnerability evaluations and inspections on each application. This is why business priority and risk assessment processes are defined in the IS framework to dictate the level of frequency and evaluation level of applications for risk mitigation based upon the overall defined Risk Tier. In most IS frameworks, the most extensive and highest frequency assessments are reserved for applications with the most critical business priorities, significant data sensitivity, and more severe vulnerability and threats.

Application Code Assessments Controls:

The IS organizations can often use multiple strategies and best-practice techniques for assessing applications. In order to test for security issues, a potential large number of target security cases must be checked for each application and software interface. As a result, the development of security test cases can be resource-intensive. Therefore, automated security test tools and software can be used to evaluate software applications. Many tools use industry knowledge-based rules databases. This can result in efficient security testing, more effective results, and consistent security vulnerability reporting. There are many commercial and open-source products available that can be evaluated for appropriateness for this IS process. Additionally, the IS organization should partner with and ensure that the internal IT development organizations use key Life-Cycle development processes that include Application assessment testing.

One of the primary detection mechanisms for performing security assessments for vulnerabilities is the use of Automated Source Code scanning tools for detecting anomalies in purchased and internal developed IT code for the Enterprise. These software tools are used to evaluate the programming code for discovery and reporting of items such as: program code use and violations, scripting errors, code constructs and violations, open source/third product software calls, authentication and password issues, parsing logic, data sensitivity exposure, overflow logic failures, and data variable inconsistencies. Many resulting code issues can create security vulnerabilities that can expose an application to multiple attack threats and/or identify poor coding techniques used by Enterprise developers.

Some of the key technology suppliers providing Application Security Testing software products includes firms such as: Aspect Security, Checkmarx, HPE, IBM, Qualys Veracode, and White Hat Security. In addition, there are solution firms such as: Accenture, Cognizant, CSC, IBM, TATA, WiPro and other key solution test service suppliers. These later can provide both on-premises and off-premises solutions for evaluating and assessing applications for their clients. Additionally, these services are available to clients as a SaaS or Cloud-Based offering from many of the solution and software suppliers.

Application Penetration Testing Controls:

Another IS framework control component for detecting weaknesses and/or vulnerabilities in applications or operating environments is the use of Penetration Testing ("Pen-Tests'). A "Pen-Test" is a testing approach to attempt access to an application or computer environment. They check for security weaknesses in the application by trying to gain access to the operating features or data. An Application "Pen-Test" process often identifies a target application and/or system environment to meet a particular objective (e.g. capture data to databases, transfer control to federated environments, etc.). The results of the testing are then reviewed by a team of IS specialists to better understand vulnerabilities of the application or operating environments. A "Pen-Test" can assist in determining whether a system is vulnerable to attack, or if the security defenses are sufficient to fend off attacks, and which defenses (if any) in the test are defeated in the "Pen-Test." These types of tests are conducted on a periodic basis, and once all vulnerabilities have been mitigated for an application. This is useful when new technology or functions are introduced into the technology environments.

Security issues and vulnerabilities detected during a penetration test should be reported as part of the overall vulnerabilities reported for specific application assessments. The goals of a "Pen-Test" will vary depending on the type of approved activity for any given project. It has a primary objective to detect vulnerabilities that can be exploited by one of the various actors defined in section 5.3 of this chapter. These tests can be performed by a team from the Enterprise Testing group, development teams, operational support teams, and/ or by IS personnel.

A "Pen-Test" may also involve the use of automated tools and workflow processes. Additionally, full network penetration testing is employed across multiple application environments. But the focus is on the test planners and team personnel, objectives of the "Pen-Test," skills and knowledge of the testing teams, and the ability to achieve the attack against the applications or environments. Many of the software suppliers and firms reviewed in this section provide "Pen-Test" technology software, and/or services to their clients, and in some cases, will bundle application and penetration testing services in their offerings to clients.

5.6 Security Controls for Data Backup and Recovery

One of the key security controls for effective risk management is the protection of the Enterprise key databases and file archives. In addition to the major threat from data theft, another key threat is the introduction of destructive malware into production systems or environments. The introduction of malware to alter or destroy Enterprise data presents a major threat to daily operations and business continuity. It has the ability to impact confidentiality, integrity, and availability of data. It can also threaten an Enterprise's ability to recover from an attack. Enterprise of all sizes must review their existing strategies to protect critical assets from distributive malware attacks and ability to recover from data corruption events. They must ensure continuity of operations and that countermeasures exist to respond to operational introduction and data impacts from data corruption events that are manifested by destructive malware.

Database and File Backup Process IS Controls:

Many IT Organizations maintain database and file data backup capabilities. Typically, many large Enterprises maintain key sophisticated backup technologies to protect them from any natural or man-made incident. This often requires the use of data mirroring and/or replication methodologies for the production data and operating environments to an offsite or secondary operating environment, or DR site. These environments provide both a physical and logical segregation of production systems and databases and the backup or DR environments for systems and data. In some Enterprises, additional offsite tape (magnetic and virtual "disk" tape) environments are maintained, either as a primary backup, or alternate recovery medium at a tertiary site.

In many large IT environments, high-speed data replication technologies are used to move large blocks of data updates and changes over long distances to the backup or DR sites. These environments employ sophisticated Third-Party hardware and operating environments that require significant IT investments and monitoring. Such resilience strategies often provide a buffer between production systems and the backups. They can provide the rapid ability to recover data corrupted by introduced malware or other corruptions (e.g. logic or programming events, etc.). However, it is also recommended that application-centric and environmental recovery plans be developed for managing the recovery of interim processing files and databases journals for rapid recovery of corrupted databases and file environments. This should be part of a full data control framework. Just as in BCP/TRDR testing, it is critical that Data Recovery plans be tested on a regular basis to ensure the ability exists to recover from operational data corruptions regardless of root cause (internal or external causes). The plans should demonstrate the capability to reconstruct in-process transactions or full/partial database recovery.

Data Protection with Data Snaps and Safe Harbors:

High-speed replication technology is a widespread recovery strategy for many IT organizations and Enterprises. However, it presents a unique security vulnerability that can be exploited by unidentified malware introductions to the IT operating environments. The same effective high-speed replication ensuring backup capabilities can propagate destructive malware in a rapid manner from production to the recovery or backup environments. As such, it can reduce the ability to effectively recover from such events and can be a high risk. As recovery in such situations is potentially problematic and complex, high-speed data replication can also extend the potential outage times of such events based upon the length of time before discovery of the data corruption event.

It is suggested then that technology processing controls be introduced to increase the frequency of data back-ups and that data snaps be used to ensure a faster response time to such incidents. Data-snap technology takes a time-based data cut at frequent intervals. It can increase the response capability for such events by utilizing an automated backup process control taken at specific intervals of various data changes and modifications. The frequencies of such snaps are an IT technology resilience decision and require specific Enterprise investment for storage that should be based on the Enterprise appetite for data loss These can be evaluated as to the volume, type, and data criticality correlated to backup strategies.

A Safe-Harbor data protection concept, known as a "Data Vault," can also be used to secure data. This is a centralized data and risk management control strategy that can provide offline or off-network preservation of key critical Enterprise data required to sustain Enterprise operations. It is often defined as last line of defense against data corruption events to assist Enterprises in the recovery of key data impacted by large-scale program errors or cyber events caused by the introduction of external malware or internal manifested corruptions (e.g. programming errors, file truncations, etc.). It is a fail-safe concept to store key data offsite from primary production or recovery facilities, and in a segregated network environment and/or offsite storage environment. Due to the required data frequencies and storage requirements, such techniques are used for critical financial or other such Enterprises where a complete data loss could be both a major financial or public impacting crisis event.

5.7 IT Security Controls for Technology Changes

One IT Security Control area that has become a major focus for security compliance and operating resources is the effective control of applications and technology changes introduced into production. In fact, failed or inconsistent security and operational releases are one of the major causes of system outages in many IT organizations. This is a direct result of the potential high volume of existing vulnerabilities introduced from previous releases into production and the identification and the correction of existing problems in those releases.

It is reflective of the large number of security and operating environmental releases and updates, often known as "patches," or version upgrades for the various IT environments. The additional introduction of multiple heterogeneous hardware and infrastructure environments proliferate complexities for change throughout most Enterprise IT organizations. More and more operating failures and incidents have been identified via root cause with a basis in flawed, untested, or inconsistent patches of hardware and software production operating environments.

Effective Security Patch and Release Control:

The establishment of well controlled and routine patching and release process routines is an important component control for IT Security. It requires an ongoing process and set procedures be created as part of the overall ITSM Control environment (see Chapter Two). It requires adherence to a centralized IT Release and Patch management process and key security procedures as part of this control process.

Efficient IT processes for patch control define a specific time frame for identification and scheduling specific security-required checkpoint patch timeframes. Often these are defined in terms of the level of vulnerability update exposure required based upon the criticality of the security upgrade or patch (e.g. Extreme Critical Risk through Very-Low Risk Levels, etc.). Additionally, a key part of the release or patch process requires that the patches or version upgrades to hardware infrastructures, operating software, and/or applications are well communicated to all changes, and the dependent processing and configuration changes to the updated environments.

Environment Control and Patch Change Monitoring:

Just as in the overall ITSM Life-Cycle process, the size of the environments, the complexity of monitoring and managing security patches, and operating component upgrades are essential for effective management control. It is recommended that automated monitoring systems and tools be used to manage and evaluate the patch and version upgrade process. There are several commercial tools available to provide this type of functionality for monitoring these patches and release environments.

Typical considerations include the level of adaptability to the IT operating environment platforms and technologies, the ease of deployment and management, and the ability to develop operating metrics, automated alerting, and trend identification in the operating environments. Additionally, as described in Chapter Two, Operational Analytics automation tools can be a key security risk management control for identification of potential issues from production security patches and other operating environment updates within the production and DR environments.

5.8 Monitoring Controls - Prevention and Detection

Operational Analytics tools can then assist in monitoring both the IT release and operational management environments for Security and Operational patches/upgrade, identification of vulnerabilities, and isolating core operational environment gaps and technology exposures.

Some of the most common used IT security risk prevention and detection controls that are best practices include:

- Security gateways, firewalls, load balancing, and security appliances - Used to monitor web services and network traffic, manage network traffic, emails, and perform other content filtering and data screening;
- Application access and Transaction Security Controls - Administer application access by users and monitor transactions completed through their access;
- Malware and Virus Scanning Tools - Provides identification of potential security problems, detection, and removal of malicious agents and software from emails and operating libraries;

- Anti-tamper techniques and automated tools for systems - Used in order to prevent tampering, deter system reverse engineering, and masking the intent of programming code to intruders;
- Forensic transaction log and network log analytic tools - To evaluate network traffic and other security logs to capture and analyze mass amounts of data, and for evaluation of data logs and libraries for security anomalies;
- Server and host-based integrity verification tools - To perform scanning and ensuring the integrity of network, storage, security appliances, infrastructure hardware and operating components, and detecting anomalies in these environments.

Just as it is important to maintain upgrades and patches to operating and application environments, IS departments must ensure protection and detection systems are current and configured to the correct versions for secure operations. This requires that anti-virus and anti-malware protection software be maintained at the most current levels, because new threats are identified daily. These types of threats are known as "Zero Day Threats," until remediation is provided by an anti-virus software, hardware, or software suppliers.

Additionally, firewall rules and other security appliance hardware must be accurate and reflect the most current IS policy requirements and rules, and all intrusion protection systems should be maintained at the current level of system release.

Consistent monitoring of IT Operational Analytics and IT Security Monitoring for systems and logs is a key preventive control for ensuring the protection of all network and infrastructure operating environments. Establishing and understanding the baseline operating environments for these IT assets provides the IT organization with the ability to detect anomalies in network traffic and other IT operational behaviors. IT organizations that establish CSIRT teams can monitor automated system real-time alerts and dashboards; identify, prevent, and contain attack attempts from actors; and analyze web, network, and email traffic anomalies.

The IT supplier market for IS environmental protection, detection, analysis, and remediation is a large and crowded industry sector. Several Third-Party suppliers provide vertical and horizontal integrated platforms to create a complete holistic IS portfolio solution for their clients, and some provide Security Threat Intelligence services. However, this includes some niche IS suppliers that focus on security monitoring and threat detection, identification of "Zero Day Threats", email filtering, and/or virus detection. Almost all provide proprietary security hardware appliances and/or software in their product mix.

Many of the IS preventive technology supplier products are purpose-built appliances for securing enterprise corporate networks, but some are designed as regional- and/or branch-distributed sites for appropriate scaling of networks across the Enterprise. These products support single Enterprise or site deployments and/or large complex network deployments with complex network and distributed environments, and multi-tiered demilitarized zones (DMZs) for controlling network isolation and segmentation.

Overall, most of the industry IS suppliers are focused on the protection from external network attacks and securing and protection of data. The level of protection varies from use of Firewall, Network Endpoint Protection, Email Filtering, Virus Detection, Security Intelligence, and Data analytics/reporting. A partial list of these various suppliers includes: Cisco, Clear swift, Checkpoint Software Technology, Dell, F5, Fortinet, HPE, IBM, Juniper Networks, Mcafee, Microsoft, Palo Alto Networks, Proofpoint, SilverSky, Sophos, Splunk, Symantec, TrustWave, Tripwire, WatchGuard Technologies, and Websense.

5.9 Managing Third-Party Supplier IT Security Risk

Just as in the other core ITGRC management domains, risk management of Third-Party IS activities is required to assess the supplier's use of technology and resources. It requires controls to ensure that adequate measures are taken to secure Enterprise customer and corporate information. Based on the sensitivity and volume of the data maintained by the supplier, the IS policy and program should determine the required level of pre-contract due diligence and ongoing monitoring of the supplier's technology activities and security profile. Any control weaknesses identified under the IS program should be required to be risk assessed and reported within the Enterprise Risk Program.

Evaluating Third-Party IS Policy and Security Activity:

Additionally, a Third-Party supplier should commit to treating the Enterprise information and systems as confidential and maintain the accuracy and integrity of the Enterprise's information and systems in a manner consistent with the Enterprise's defined IS policies, standards, and practices. Periodic evaluations should be conducted of the Enterprise's Third Parties. This should be based on the priority and importance of the Third-Party services and products, and the overall risk classification of those services or products to the Enterprise. It is a best-practice that in the cases of large-volume Enterprise use of Third Parties, that a continuous risk categorization of suppliers be conducted by the IS organization. IT should be based upon the exposure to the activities of the Third Party. This categorization is similar to the process described in chapter section 5.3.

Required Third-Party Testing and Environmental Monitoring:

The Enterprise IS framework should provide for ensuring that the Third Party perform periodic network vulnerability scans, identify the time periods for such evaluations, and if changes are performed to the Third Party's networks and environments. The program should stipulate mitigation requirements when vulnerabilities are detected by Third Parties or external auditors. The IS framework must also identify to the Third Party, when and how vulnerabilities are to be reported to the Enterprise, and when the Enterprise IS department teams can inspect the results of these activities.

It should also specify the requirements and types of security, penetration, application, and network testing to be conducted of Third-Party environments, and the specific time period for conducting these types of testing (often annually). The Enterprise should specify how such results are to be reported, and review frequency by the Enterprise's IS teams. Additionally, it is recommended that Third Parties be required to engage and perform independent Third-Party penetration testing exercises and results reported to the Enterprise. Additional information can be found on Third-Party governance and risk exposure in Chapter Six of this book.

5.10 Emerging Information Security IT Risks

Cloud-Based Federated Technology Risk Controls:

As discussed in the majority of the book chapters and also a focus for IT Security is the expansion and emerging usage of Cloud-Based technologies by almost all Enterprises. This business strategy, coupled with the concept of technology federations of security, is a primary risk for IT. Just as this book promotes the concepts of internal Enterprise federated applications and technology usage within the ITGRC Ecosystems, a Cloud service introduction of federated architectures is an expanding and growing challenge for all IT IS organizations.

Federated Cloud architectures (public and private) use architectural concepts of integrating systematic mechanisms across multiple layers of technology that consist of connecting the various layers of applications, infrastructures, networks, and security into a seamless environment. A prime example of this is the expanded usage of Cloud-Based social media within employee productivity solutions being implemented by many organizations, coupled with individual Cloud-Based email solutions.

However, the challenge for IS organizations is that they must interweave security mechanism controls across the various platforms and environments outside of their operational control, just as in the IS protection of individual in-house IT applications within isolated layers of traditional IT network and perimeter controls. Therefore, it is even more difficult with virtual Cloud-Based solutions and when integrating multiple Cloud-Based suppliers. This is because Cloud-Based solution suppliers must provide access to multiple users, clients, and customers. Also, Public Cloud environments have a much broader IS attack footprint than that which exists within dedicated Enterprise applications with their structured security layers controlled with internal IS measures. The risk to the Enterprise then is exponentially increased by the fact that other Cloud-Based client users could introduce malicious download attacks against the various web-based applications integrated in the Cloud and available to the general public, just as exists in generic Cloud-Based email environments. Email environments in general are one of the primary delivery vehicles for introducing malicious activity and given external usage by many other non-Enterprise users, it puts all of the Cloud-Based users at risk, regardless of the standard Enterprise controls.

Cloud-Based suppliers often create environments and hosting operations that outsource some operations to co-location and data center operational suppliers. This can include even their operational and security monitoring of hosting activities. This introduces additional layers of risk exposure to the Enterprise, as these suppliers are sub-contracting the Enterprise's security protection to another group of IT suppliers. This is often unknown to the Cloud-Based subscribing Enterprise.

Therefore, the IT organization and Enterprise's key defense in this area is to be proactive and ensure they are linked into the various security monitoring controls and reporting of the Cloud-Based environments, and that each has access to alerts, logs, and incidents within these Cloud environments. Additionally, it is even more important to provide for the overall effective management of these IT suppliers and their subcontractors. For these high-risk service suppliers, more frequent vetting is required with validation of the supplier's IT security practices.

Big Data Technology IS Risk Controls:

With the introduction of less-expensive data storage technologies and the explosive number of Cloud-Based data repositories, Enterprises are using new "Big Data" technologies to store and analyze petabytes of data. This includes millions and billions of data points and records in web-based logs, audit logs, and other transaction data stores. These are used by many Enterprises to gain behavioral insights into key customer activity, backgrounds, and preferences, and for aggregating customer issues or requests.

Therefore, the level of security concerns for these new technologies is a primary concern, as these are target rich environments for all criminal and nation attack actors. This is due to the volume of information captured in these data stores. As pointed out in this chapter, many IT organizations already struggle with control of basic control access, data categorization and encryption, and the protection of individual applications and data environments. Big Data technology usage raises the level of control requirements and complicates the management of access privileges and data risk.

IT organizations should provide the standard environmental security and resilience protections as described in this chapter but must also introduce new controls and potentially data governance policies to classify data, regulate access, and provide encryption for data sensitive attributes within all data structures. Given the lack of Big Data expertise in the industry, many organizations are turning to Big Data suppliers to implement these solutions. This further complicates the management of these risks, as a Third-Party supplier relationship introduces an additional risk component.

It is also suggested that IS departments ramp up their security portfolio to expand the management of the Big Data environments for data attribute access control and build upon their existing security access administrations, data classifications, and categorizations. They can expand their ability to integrate security event log aggregations and security event monitoring.

Additionally, given the expansion of e-commerce activity and the size of the data banks being created, IT organizations should recognize the need for inclusion of fraud detection, fraud prevention and monitoring, and investigative analytics into these Big Data operations. For monetary transactions, it is important for inclusion of specific real-time monitoring, scoring rules, and fraud protection methodologies. These are essential control system environments that can be included to manage the risk and understand transaction patterns and financial fraud activity within e-commerce environments.

5.11 Information Security Ecosystem Concepts

Information Security Management Automation Drivers:

It is essential for the IT organizations to automate the IS Management Ecosystem with the required tools, software, and automated real-time processes. The increased volume/speed of internet and mobile network transactions, and the large amount of identifiable personal and customer information available on the internet has driven the need for automating IS management environments.

Additionally, Enterprises are required by many regulatory and industry agencies to implement appropriate detective and preventive controls to safeguard their environments from attacks, destructive malware, and provide the ability to respond and recover from successful cyber events. The IS organizations are also required to implement appropriate automation controls and management practices, to limit, manage and control user access permissions for job functions, and monitor network activity.

IT organizations can implement appropriate detection and preventive controls to minimize the likelihood of attacks, to detect and prevent malware from intrusion into the network environment and systems, monitor and manage the effectiveness of scanning technology, and perform appropriate vulnerability assessments and testing of IT asset environments.

Information Security Management Ecosystem:

Figure 5.11 provides a sample IT Information Security Management Ecosystem that builds upon a fundamental IS Risk Assessment process, and incorporates key IS principles and use of best practice concepts in the automation of the IS Management Ecosystem. It also includes: Identity and Access Control Management; and Cyber Monitoring and Intelligence Management systems. The later can ensure consistent evaluation, analysis, and awareness of all IT perimeter, network, and system security profiles and states. Many IT suppliers already discussed in this chapter provide various products in these IS product sectors that would integrate within the IS Management Ecosystem. However, several IT supplier vendors are focused on providing full or intelligence Security Operational Management software. There are multiple suppliers in this IS software market sector, some of these include: CISCO, EMC/RSA, Fortinet, HPE, IBM. LogRythm Security, MicroFocus, Splunk, etc.

Figure 5.11 IS Management Ecosystem

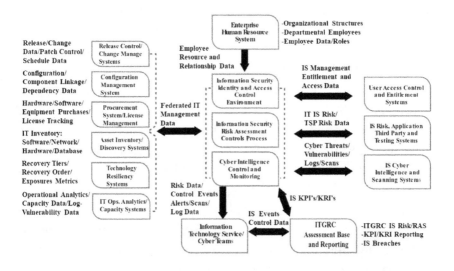

Security Management Trusted Data Sources and Concepts:

As with all of the ITGRC Ecosystems exhibited in this book, it is a primary requirement for efficient IT operations to ensure consistent and standard trusted data sources. Those data sources include: Human Resource and Organizational Data, Risk Profile Data, Third-Party Supplier Data, Dependent Business Process and RTO's, Knowledge and Training Data with a focus on Enterprise security curriculums, and IT Asset management environments. Human Resource and organizational data are key to understanding and controlling user access and role definitions for the IS Management Ecosystem components.

IT Enterprise Configuration Management System data, as previously defined, is essential to understand full security operational perimeter assets and the physical layers of hardware and network appliances, operating hardware and software environments, and applications. It is important to understand the varying layers of application operational and federated technology layers, IP addresses, and communication port configurations.

Incident Management and Problem Management data is required for efficient IT and Security operations to report and track open and closed Security and Operational Incidents from Technology; remediation directions, status, severity levels and SLA requirements; and problem and IT knowledgebase references, and linkages.

Change and Release Management data for all Enterprise IT Changes, Status, and Linkage to all Applications, Database, Infrastructures, and Network Configurations, and Telecommunication Transmissions, are essential for understanding, scheduling, and controlling version upgrades and patches to all hardware and appliances, application, and system operating environments.

ITSM management data for all assigned teams and linkage to the requested infrastructure hardware, network, security firewalls and appliances, and application impacts to IT and Network perimeter assets required to be evaluated, tested and scanned.

Operational Analytics data for evaluating all vulnerabilities, threats, and incidents with automatic detection of technology gaps identified by the IT Operational Analytics and Monitoring Technologies, to include all environmental processing, security, and network monitoring logs.

5.12 Information Security Key Indicators

IS Operational Performance and Risk Drivers:

As discussed throughout this chapter, the frequency, severity, and sophistication of cyber-attacks have increased over the last ten years. It illustrates the high inherent risk that security poses to the Enterprise from attacks by the various defined actors, increases in internet site phishing, and the exploitation of computer vulnerabilities, together with expansion of high target ecommerce attacks, and the increased usage of Third-Party Cloud suppliers by Enterprises. It requires an effective IS Operational and Risk management reporting program that is automated and that provides real-time KPI's and KRI's.

The risks to Enterprise operations and organizational assets because of the potential for unauthorized access, use, disclosure, disruption, or destruction of information or systems is focused on data loss and disruptive cyber-security attacks. These associated risks can cause serious losses or damage to the Enterprise reputation.

IS Key Performance Indicators:

Key IS Program Performance Indicators and metrics suggested for inclusion in the core IT Security Management and Enterprise Risk programs include:

- Monitored Network End-points - Number of Network End points monitored as a percentage of total End-points in the IT Operating Network (number and percentage);
- Monitored Applications Critical and Non-Critical - Number of Applications that are monitored for IS Risks (number and percentage), isolates the Critical/Non-Critical Applications, and Levels of Priority to the Enterprise;
- Servers Monitored - Number of Hardware Servers monitored within the IT environment (number and percentage), isolates by device all of the various operating environments monitored;
- Network Devices Monitored - Number of Security Devices, Network Appliances, and other IT Network assets that are monitored within the IT environments number and percentage), isolation by type of devices monitored;
- End User Devices Monitored - Number of Personal Devices (PDA's, mobile devices, smartphones, laptops, PC's, other devices) assets monitored within the Enterprise (number and percentage), isolation by type of devices monitored;
- Databases Inspected and Monitored - Number of Enterprise Databases monitored (number and percentage), isolate by database structures (e.g. Oracle, Microsoft SQL-Server, etc.);

- Outbound Data Packets inspected - Number of Outbound data transmission inspected across the networks (number and percentage);
- Security Environments Tested - Number of network, application, servers and other environments tested via Penetration and Vulnerability conducted (Critical and Non-Critical and levels of priority to the Enterprise), isolation by type of IT environment (number and percentage);
- Identity and Access Management Users and Roles Maintained - Number and Percentage of users and assigned roles updated, deleted, and added to Operational Systems; Detail isolation by system categories (internet, intranet, mainframe, etc.), and category of user roles (administration, read/write privileged, etc.);
- Security Policy and User Reviews Conducted - Tracking of Security Policy exceptions and approvals (number and percentage); User Roles and Exception requests reviewed and approved (number and percentage);
- Total Third Parties Monitored and Risk Assessed - Number and Percentage of Third Parties Monitored and Risk Assessed for IS Security evaluation, isolated and categorized by Third-Party priority and risk level to the Enterprise;
- Employee Training and Knowledge Level - Identifies the level of training by curriculum and courses required and taken by Enterprise employees and other personnel (number and percentage) by various course levels.

IS Key Risk Indicators:

As with other IT Operational Risk components, a major factor in identification of security risks is understanding where risk mitigation controls are ineffective, and where employees do not adhere to the IT organization and Enterprise policies. The adherence to the IS risk controls thresholds established within the IS framework provides for understanding where cyber risk vulnerabilities and potential exposures exist in the Enterprise. The level and percentage of control issues and abnormal levels above IS thresholds are indicative of increasing security risks and/or focused mitigation and review required by IT and Enterprise management.

KRI's recommended for inclusion for the core IT Security Management and Enterprise Risk programs include:

- Network End-points Monitoring and Vulnerabilities -Network End-points not monitored (number and percentage), and Network end-points with vulnerabilities detected due to late patching, testing, and/or detected security validations (with issue categorizations);
- Applications not Monitored and with Vulnerabilities - Applications isolated by category and level of priority and risk to the Enterprise that are not monitored; Applications by category with security vulnerabilities, including security violations, obsolete patches or updates, and code/penetration testing security issues detected (number and percentage);
- Servers not Monitored and with Vulnerabilities - Servers isolated by criticality category and risk servers not monitored (number and percentage), Isolates by critical category server vulnerabilities in security processes/controls (number and percentage) - includes software updates, data encryption, configuration, access, anti-virus protection, etc.;
- End User Devices Not Monitored and with Security Vulnerabilities - End-User Devices not monitored (number and percentage); End-User Device vulnerabilities that present either security (integrity, confidentiality, or functionality) and availability, or test issues (number and percentage);
- Databases not Inspected or with Vulnerabilities - Isolate by criticality Enterprise Databases not inspected or monitored (number and percentage) - Isolate by database environment; and databases with vulnerabilities (number and percentage)

including delayed software patches, security violations, or tested/detected vulnerabilities;

- Outbound Data Packets not inspected - Number of Outbound data transmission across the Enterprise not inspected (number and percentage);
- Detail Security Vulnerabilities by Criticality - Detail identification of Applications, Networks End-points, Technologies, and Servers by type of vulnerability and criticality (numbers and percentage by category and vulnerability);
- Security Policy Exceptions - Provides by key Security Policy any exceptions granted (Number and Exception Business);
- Level of Security User Roles not managed - Isolates by Security Policy and Rule exception requests that are not managed and/ or not approved by Management (number and percentage);
- Employee Training and Knowledge Level - Identifies the level of training by curriculum and courses required and taken by employees and other personnel (number and percentage) by course level;
- Detail Security Vulnerabilities by Criticality - Detail identification of Applications, Network End-points, and Servers by type of vulnerability and criticality (numbers and percentage by category and vulnerability);
- Third Parties Not Monitored or with Risk - Third Parties Not Monitored for Security (Number and Percentage) - Isolate by Enterprise Criticality; Third Parties with security risks or policy violations (number and percentage); Isolate by Enterprise criticality and level of security risk.

In addition to these recommend KPI's/KRI's, it is also important to understand subjective levels of IT security risk that may be difficult to quantify in KPI's or KRI's, but which require in-depth understanding by IT and Enterprise executive management. These additional focus areas by management for IT Security include:

- Understanding the velocity of changes and level of quality control and testing of IT production application and environmental changes;
- Level of production control and release management over End-user devices introduced into production environments, and level of security patching conducted in relation to volume of changes implemented into IT environments;
- Quality and sophistication of asset control and inventory for the IT organization and Enterprise, and for perimeter network assets;
- Extent of penetration and performance testing conducted, and simulations of cyber-attack testing and other vulnerability detection techniques;
- Sophistication of IT monitoring of networks, security, and operational environments and level of response to incidents and service levels;
- Extent of monitoring of Third-Party applications and Cloud environments, level of Third-Party access to confidential and customer sensitive data, and quality of Third-Party program evaluations;
- Level of employee knowledge and understanding of security policies and use of email, end-user devices, and mobile devices.

As data and information are key assets of any Enterprise, protection of these assets is required in order to continue to maintain the trust of the Enterprise customers, stakeholders, employees, and regulatory entities. It is required to maintain compliance with laws, regulations, and the reputation of the Enterprise.

The security of the Enterprise's systems and information is then essential to the viability of the Enterprise, and the risk posed to the Enterprise. Effective management of an IS program, and ability for the Enterprise to respond to new and changing threats, technologies, and business strategies requires a fundamental and tested ITGRC security program component. The program requires proactive and ongoing monitoring by IT and Enterprise executive management of key IT performance approaches, security risk indicators, and automation of the IS Management Ecosystem.

CHAPTER 6

Third-Party IT Supplier Management

6.1 Introduction to IT Third-Party Risk Exposures

ONE OTHER MAJOR risk that Enterprises are exposed to is the use of external IT service suppliers, product and software suppliers, and outsourced Third-Party technology services. With the increased use of Cloud services and the proliferation in outsourcing of IT services to external environmental hosting suppliers (e.g. Amazon, Google, IBM, and Salesforce.Com, etc.), Enterprises have in many situations transferred the IT operational accountability, processing, and in some cases the servicing of customers and businesses to these external service agents.

Also, over the last several years, there has been a proliferation of regulatory directives and increased oversight of Third-Party suppliers. While the increased scrutiny has been across several industries including health care, energy, and transportation, the financial industry has seen an expanded level of focus by the various Federal regulatory agencies. This chapter will focus on the controls, approaches, and automation techniques for management of IT Third-Party supplier governance and risk.

Enterprise Third-Party Supplier Exposure Control:

A key component in managing the Enterprise and IT Risk Portfolio is the understanding and organizational accountability required to manage the risk posed by these external service suppliers. Typically, Third-Party supplier risk in many Enterprises is managed by a contract negotiations area in a procurement or a legal department. In some cases, it is part of the Enterprise risk or Financial organizations, although IT divisions will often operate their own internal IT supplier management program that is aligned with an overall Enterprise structure. However, these IT functions can operate somewhat autonomously, due to the unique nature of IT service suppliers and IT cultures.

Increasingly, many organizations are realigning Third-Party supplier risk management to be included in an overall Enterprise risk management program, often under the governance and accountability of a Chief Risk Officer or Chief Financial Officer. But regardless of the organizational division alignment, there are clear accountabilities that are required to be executed and managed over Third-Party supplier risks. These requirements necessitate a best practice Enterprise approach and alignment of the IT supplier management activities to an overall Enterprise Third-Party management program and policy.

With the aforementioned transfer of IT activities to Third-Party suppliers have come an increased focus and responsibility for managing the underlying key risks associated with supplier IT services, dependencies, infrastructures, resiliency, security, and processing by these suppliers. All of this requires a clear delineation of responsibilities and deliverables for the Enterprise organizations for the suppliers. Accountability for monitoring the risks of these key IT service activities falls not to the supplier, but to the contracting business organization. They must ensure the products are supplied, their customers serviced, and/or the ultimate delivery of the contracted technology processes and activities. The risk to the overall organization becomes even greater with this transfer of full service delivery to the supplier and increases the contracting organization's responsibility for oversight and accountability of the supplier inherent risks.

For example, data breaches at a Third-Party supplier can often impact customers and product delivery, but there is also an overall general liability for the Enterprise. Failure of Third-Party supplier technologies or processes to deliver the services or product contracted by the organization can impact Enterprise customers and organizations; as such, contracted IT Third-Party supplier risk demands the same level of risk and service profiling of all key technology and operational domains. In many organizations, the accountability and process for evaluating Third-Party supplier risk is often reduced to a simple questionnaire format or general validations of supplier information service. However, an increased due diligence focus is required to ensure a comprehensive understanding and evaluation of the true risk and exposure from the use of IT Third-Party suppliers.

Third-Party Supplier Organizational Accountability:

The CEO, CRO, and CIO, or equivalent level in IT, along with the Board of Directors, are accountable for the organization's IT risk profile regardless of where the technology, systems, and/or processes reside (internal or external). As such, a holistic approach by management at an Enterprise program level is required for the risks posed from IT service suppliers and for outsourced IT activities. Therefore, the IT supplier management should be an essential component of the overall Enterprise risk management portfolio. For the purposes of this book, IT Third-Party management is described in terms of IT supplier management as a component deliverable of the overall corporate Third-Party Supplier (TSP) management program.

6.2 Requirement for Third-Party IT Supplier Controls

Over the last ten years, the rise of business-enabling services, such as Cloud-Based DR Recovery Service suppliers and the expansion of

Application Service Providers (ASP), has led to a proliferation of start-up ASP suppliers and organizations. Often, the key essential controls for infrastructures and organizational risk structures are afterthoughts by these suppliers, including IT governance and control. Additionally, many Enterprises, in a rush to enable their organizations for these services, may have sided-stepped key ITGRC structures and control over these suppliers.

Third-Party Supplier Management Market Drivers:

Due to the proliferation of ASP, Cloud-Based services, and Cloud recovery service suppliers, there have emerged some key market drivers for many organizations to increase awareness of, and refocus, the IT governance over the risk posed by these suppliers. These are specific to the focus as it relates to IT suppliers and many of these market drivers include the following:

- Increasing reliance upon Third Parties in outsourcing of sensitive functions to these Third Parties;
- Lack of a centralized control over all sourcing decisions and understanding of Third-Party provider risk exposure, and full Enterprise due diligence;
- Insufficient service inventories for Third-Party services, and/or those processing sensitive data components and structures;
- Lack of alignment with an Enterprise-wide Third-Party supplier program frameworks;
- Increasing focus on Third-Party cyber security issues and exposures, due to data breaches;
- Escalating regulatory scrutiny in the utility, transportation, financial, and healthcare industry sectors;
- Inconsistent compliance and risk assessment across Enterprise organizations and Third-Party issue resolution processes;
- Board-level scrutiny and focus on Third-Party service suppliers risks.

Third-Party Supplier Program Framework Direction:

Organizations that lack a structured TSP program and disciplined approach to dealing with the risk posed by Third-Party suppliers omit a major component in overall management of the Enterprise risk. IT Third-Party suppliers require a supplier risk discipline and more due diligence because of the nature of the services and dependent processes being provided that can result in IT risk exposures. It is suggested that IT TSP processes build upon and align with an organizational Enterprise approach to management of Third-Party suppliers and the associated risks regardless of the services and supplier categories.

Key risks exposures to understand as it relates to Third-Party servicers include: Strategic, Financial, Reputational, Operational, Geopolitical, Compliance, and Regulatory Risks. Each of these risk categories must be understood and monitored as a result of the Enterprise conducting business with an external Third-Party. IT exposures as identified in this chapter can be more prolific due to the nature and volume of potential transaction and business exposures. Therefore, all supplier types need to be categorized and their risk assessed based upon these key risk exposure categories.

The risk categorizations for suppliers is essential in order to identify and understand the overall risk to the organization. They require a prioritization sequence be developed to manage the suppliers' due diligence. This is a necessity in vary large Fortune 500-type organizations in order for them to align the level of resources required to manage the volume and types of suppliers across the organization. These companies can ensure that sufficient resources are available to validate high-risk-sensitive suppliers and IT outsourced environments.

6.3 Approaches to IT Supplier Management

Regardless of the organizational framework used for managing Third-Party supplier risk, a holistic approach to Third-Party supplier management is required to ensure consistent risk modeling and reporting to senior executive management and the Board of Directors. Therefore, it is also recommended that a standard TSP policy exist and also that the Enterprise use standard contract templates. These can be developed by the Enterprise legal department and vetted by specific IT organizational evaluations that demonstrate the discipline to ensure IT supplier due diligence. Using a decentralized approach to TSP management will produce varying risk quantifications that are difficult to align for executive management. A holistic approach to managing these suppliers will provide a consistent view of the TSP risk to the organization, including specific categorization of these suppliers, key risk variables and components, and standard processes for both pre-assessment and continuing assessment of suppliers.

A key factor in understanding the overall risk of the services or products provided by the Third-Party suppliers is to develop a risk categorization and priority scheme for supplier evaluation. Often, major Enterprises will engage thousands of suppliers and vendors to provide IT and other services. In fact, many of the largest Fortune 500 corporations maintain as many as thirty to forty thousand various suppliers. Many of these are IT and global based suppliers.

Third-Party Risk Exposure Categories:

Because of the high volume of suppliers used across the Enterprise, most Enterprises need to develop a methodology to understand and categorize each of their suppliers into specific risk categories by the type of service level or products provided, and risk exposure level. Typically, Enterprises will then develop an assessment scheme for preliminary stratification of these vendors based upon key assessment criteria for the specific risk area of concern and/or key domain of risk (e.g., IS, Credit, BCP, TRDR, Operations, Legal, etc.). Later in this chapter, these will be discussed in further detail and a concept provided for development of such assessment criteria and risk modeling.

Once preliminarily assessed, Enterprises can assign the specific framework of the Enterprise policy for managing risk associated with the Third-Party suppliers. It can perform further due diligence and assessment of the various suppliers within the specific risk categories. Many organizations will use some type of pre-assessment questionnaire that can filter the various categories of supplier, and assess the risk of these suppliers, for more detailed evaluation by key areas of accountability, or Subject-Matter-Experts (SME).

Regardless of the approach taken by the Enterprise, IT organizations should build upon the Enterprise TSP framework that exists and supplement it with more detailed assessments and due diligence requirements to ensure a consistent level of risk scrutiny of IT assets, operations, systems, and resources.

6.4 IT Third-Party Supplier Management Frameworks

Many organizations will develop a key TSP management service program that has overall guidance and accountability for managing the due diligence and program risks associated with using Third-Party service suppliers. The program will often develop a TSP policy and key procedures for ensuring pre-contract, post-contract, and ongoing due diligence evaluations of all Enterprise Third-Party suppliers, including software and outsourced services to the corporation.

Framework for Third-Party Subject Matter Experts:

The TSP program should develop a clear set of process assessments, supporting organizational procedures, and accountabilities. The program has the overarching responsibility of ensuring key SME's engage in the evaluation all Third-Parties. An SME should have the discipline and knowledge to evaluate the key areas of risk exposures for a Third Party.

Figure 6.4 depicts a conceptual framework for TSP framework management, to include key IT supplier functionality and validation.

The framework often includes a Pre-Contract Evaluation process that engages the key SME's supporting the Third-Party framework, with a periodic process for evaluating the quality and services provided by the Third-Party supplier. The SME areas will include key individuals from the corporate finance or credit organization, IS, Physical Security, BCP, TRDR, Technology Operations, Software Assurance, Corporate Procurement, Legal, Transportation and Operations, and the Enterprise risk management organizations

Figure 6.4 TSP Management Framework Process

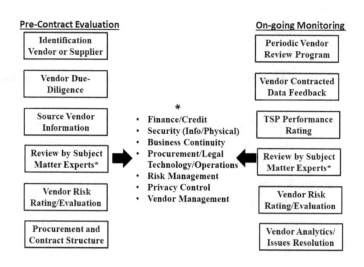

(*A high priority in Healthcare, Consumer Financial and Financial Services, and High security clearance industries.)

Each of the assigned SME areas should then perform evaluations based upon their discipline areas' predefined requirements for various service provider categories. They can then perform an ongoing analysis of the Enterprise or IT organizational suppliers on a periodic basis. This ensures the supplier meets the prerequisites for doing business with the key operational areas of the Enterprise and also provides for an ongoing and continuous evaluation of the various risks posed by the targeted supplier categories. This can ensure that key contract requirements for the SME-focused area continue to be met by the selected Third-Party suppliers.

Third-Party Supplier Program Policy:

The requirements for evaluating Third Parties should be developed and structured into a standard TSP policy. The policy can enumerate the specific key framework process accountabilities of the various SME areas, requirements for the suppliers to address, periodic supplier reporting based upon specific Third-Party risk exposure to the corporation, and the required reporting data and the periodic data requirements.

Enterprises that develop and enforce use of standard corporate templates for engaging Third Parties can ensure effective supplier due diligence. These templates should be structured to have a basis in the key corporate TSP requirements and SME required criteria. They are an essential program tool in negotiating with a Third Parties for any services and/or products. Contract templates can assist in ensuring requirements of the Enterprise TSP program are incorporated into final contracts by the corporate procurement and the legal departments of the Enterprise

Third-Party Framework Structures and Processes:

The majority of standard Enterprise TSP frameworks will establish specific ongoing monitoring of their key suppliers. They will also develop specific criteria for evaluating the suppliers based upon specific SME requirements for standard supplier reporting of specific information and data about their operations. This may include: financial statements, to include P&L-balance sheets; public financial statement disclosures; employee background validations; operational statistics and reporting elements; key audit statements about specific operating areas, such as the results of technology, security, and business continuity and DR operations and testing; evaluations; critiques of operational issues, SLA's, and anomalies encountered in support of the service or product delivery; copies of various types of IS and BCP/DR test results; and other such due diligence to ensure consistency with the contract services.

Third-Party Supplier Periodic Evaluations:

Initially, during the pre-contract evaluation period, an operational or service area defines their needs and often identifies a specific Third-Party entity to facilitate their service or product. They will then engage the Enterprise TSP evaluation process for the Enterprise. The supplier can provide the required data for pre-analysis review. The program will then assess and categorize the exposure of services or products. These contribute to the overall risk rating and evaluation of the service provider.

Once the supplier has been evaluated and assessed by the Third-Party initial SME specific pre-assessment criteria, the initiation can be started to support the contracting process and identification of any deviations from the overall TSP requirements program. Typically, the TSP program will identify key risk ratings for specific categories of suppliers that is based upon a risk rating (see section 6.7) to determine the requirements for further initial and ongoing assessment and monitoring of the service provider.

6.5 Standard Third-Party Assessment Practices

Pre-Assessment Process Methodology:

Enterprise TSP programs use a multitude of assessment practices to evaluate and understand the risks associated with doing business with a particular Third-Party supplier. Key among the assessment practices is the ability to pre-assess suppliers and vendors based upon a particular risk categorization. This can identify the supplier for further due diligence to assess and rate the level of risk associated with doing business with the particular supplier.

As indicated, due to the large number of suppliers to be evaluated in any TSP program and the larger subset of IT suppliers, a mechanism that is often used for an initial TSP analysis is a Pre-assessment, or Supplier Questionnaire. These initial questionnaires are useful in high-volume supplier environments where extensive due diligence can be a major resource drain on key SME's.

Assessment Rules-Based Processing:

Many large Enterprises will use some automated rules for the categorization and selection of target vendors for advanced risk and resource review by key SME areas. Typically, this involves utilizing some type of system of record TSP inventory and/or supplier prequalification system. Also, the use of forms-based technology for assessing the supplier within a TSP environment can be a supplier product e.g. RSA's Archer, IBM, Metric Stream, *etc*. These types of systems will allow suppliers to complete key information about their operations and can trigger automatic detailed information requests.

Standard Third-Party Assessment Concepts:

Some Enterprises accept, a Standard Information Gathering Questionnaire (SIG), for an initial assessment of specific IT, security, privacy, and business continuity profiles. It is often developed by the Third-Party supplier to respond to specific requests from their customers about their IT and other GRC programs. However, these are often insufficient for large Enterprises, as they lack the level of detail for qualifying and understanding the risks associated with high-risk suppliers specifically, complex IT suppliers, such as ASP's and DR recovery suppliers to Enterprises, and those that house sensitive customer data and corporate information.

Additionally, a SIG Lite concept has been developed for dealing with the resource-intensive evaluations; however, in the author's opinion, this will not deliver the level of risk due diligence and the appropriate detail for all areas of assessment required for proper supplier evaluation.

In addition, many organizations, in a move to reduce the resource loads for periodic reviews and even some pre-qualifications, have been opting to use SOC-2 and SOC-1 reports from suppliers. The SOC-1 report is focused on organization and financial report controls; SOC-2 is focused on IT Operational and Information Security supplier controls. These documents are based upon Financial Report Audit Control standards as developed for the suppliers for ongoing audit evaluation by the supplier. While these may support the overall evaluation process, these reports in many cases are too generic for sufficient due diligence of IT suppliers. They may be beneficial for initial supplier assessment or a general TSP qualification category.

As indicated, some organizations can use a series of assessment concepts for both the pre-assessment and ongoing TSP evaluation process. Many of the discussed and other program sampling concepts and approaches are depicted in Figure 6.5.

Figure 6.5 Standard Assessment Practices

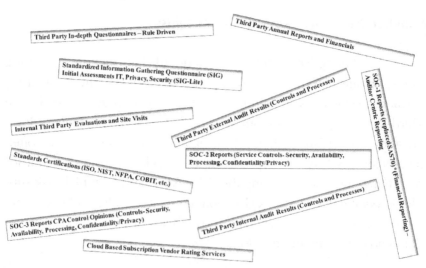

Third-Party Program Standards Usage:

Many suppliers, including IT suppliers, have opted to obtain specific certifications to a standard from external standard certification organizations and/or consulting/audit firms. These are based upon specific standards such as: ISO, NIST, NFPA, COBIT and ITIL etc., to support their IT organizations. While these may be beneficial for some organizations, these should not be used for evaluations by organizations for mission critical, IT essential, and any high-risk suppliers.

For these high-risk supplier categorizations, it is suggested that organizations develop a specific core requirement and process for high-risk suppliers to submit periodic reports of specific IT audits of IS, BCP, TRDR, IT project delivery, and technology, copies of specific types of security and continuity exercises, key technology plans, and operational metrics.

Other Assessment Capabilities:

With the advent of the Cloud-Based ASP's, key IT supplier data aggregation subscription service sites are available for use by clients from Cloud-Based data aggregators. These aggregation sites can collect data and information about public corporations, such as Dow Jones, but some firms can aggregate data about specific IT domains for certain types of IT suppliers (e.g. network and equipment suppliers, etc.). This can include IS and infrastructure data collected by various supplier manufacturer and industry sites. They can also be used to pre-assess and qualify suppliers but also used for ongoing evaluations of IT suppliers.

Additionally, it is suggested that organizations conduct specific onsite inspections, participate in detailed IS, BCP, TRDR, and Crisis Management exercises with the suppliers, and complete evaluations of IT operations and environments for the Enterprise for all high-risk profile suppliers to the organization.

Standard Third-Party Contract Templates:

One of the key components of any IT and overall Enterprise TSP programs is to ensure that a set of standard contract templates is defined for the organization for the various services and contract products to be supplied by the Third Parties. Many IT and procurement organizations will often use a Master Service or Software License Agreement (MSA). It spells out the required service or software product requirements being delivered by the Third Party to the Enterprise. These contract templates are enumerated in structured and boilerplate-type contracts between the service provider and the contracting organization.

Third-Party suppliers will attempt to drive the supplier relationship with a contracting organization via their own MSA standard template or licensing contract paper. However, often these supplier templates are structured to focus on the suppliers' SLA and costs for the contracted service to the contracting organization and do not spell out the overall risks of delivery to the Enterprise for the contracting organization. The supplier and contract organization will then "redline" or modify the contract to the specific agreeable terms of the supplier for the customer relationship. This is conducted via a joint collaboration of the contract organization, legal, and corporate procurement environments. It often may not engage the specific SME's of the key areas accountable for evaluating the suppliers. The latter should be required, both on an initial and on an ongoing basis. Therefore, one of the major components of a solid TSP or IT supplier program is to ensure that the Enterprise-specific contract templates are established to support the program and are approved by the Enterprise SME's.

In all cases, regardless of the contract type agreement, Third-Party supplied or Enterprise standard, the specific SME clauses should be tracked in any redline review of the service agreement or license between the supplier and Enterprises. Negotiations based upon these standard structures should invoke a standard adoption of requirements for all targeted suppliers and assist in ensuring that the Enterprise TSP policy and framework requirements are sustained through any negotiations.

Third-Party Contract Exceptions:

In all cases, exceptions to the Enterprise standard SME clauses and TSP frameworks should be approved and reviewed by a specific organizational area responsible for ongoing monitoring of the supplier risk discipline areas. Some organizations allow key operational or service accountable areas to conduct primary negotiations with the supplier for their services or products. However, often these stakeholders lack the detail knowledge for all areas of the TSP policy, let alone the consistent technology for specific IT requirements. They often require training and more important, the support of the required SME areas for effective supplier due diligence.

Key TSP Contractual Processes:

It is incumbent on the Enterprise TSP framework and the IT organization to ensure that key contractual processes exist and include:

- Ensures the usage of standard contract templates for MSA's, and approved legal contract verbiage;
- Provides for exception processes for Third-Party contractual template usage;
- Contract structures include form and content for key contract domains (e.g. IS, finance, credit, BCP, TRDR, technology, operations, etc.);
- TSP processes include SME's in evaluations of contract variances from MSA templates;
- Develop specific timeframes for key supplier contract review periods based upon standards established by supplier risk categorizations;
- Establish processes and controls for tracking, reporting, and escalation of standard contract and material deviations from template verbiage.

Third-Party Supplier/Organizational Accountabilities:

Some of the generic responsibilities associated with suppliers and the contract organization in the negotiation process for closing on the contracted services or products include the following organizational accountabilities.

- Negotiating Business Line - Time to market and visibility to contract due diligence, responsible for Third-Party relationships, performance, risk and compliance, and SME engagement;
- Third-Party Supplier- Negotiates in good faith, executes per contract, shares assessment results, and provides relationship evidence due-diligence support;
- Procurement and Legal - Enables the contract process, identifies contract risks, and ensures defensible verbiage and compliance requirements;
- Risk, Compliance, and TSP Management - Maintains overall supplier relationship TSP process, key TSP policies, enables review processes, monitors risk, compliance and reporting, and Third-Party issue escalations;
- Subject Matter Experts - Ensures contract SME template requirements, participates in contract exception process, and conducts relationship domain activity review and SME due diligence of Third-Party suppliers.

IT Domain Third-Party Accountabilities:

Specific to IT organizations and their accountabilities, two key areas of concern are service availability and data security, and as such, these require even further detailed due diligence. From an IS requirements perspective, the contract base should include at a minimum the following concepts related to security consideration risks:

- Requirements for the Third Party to maintain a complete set of IS policies, standards, and practices.
- Adherence to industry and regulatory best practices without limitation, as it relates to IS areas (e.g. network and perimeter defenses, resilience technology, monitoring and protection, authentication and administration, data protection, intrusion detection, data encryption, network structures and protocols, malware detection and virus protection, patching, security testing, countermeasures and incident response, and asset structures, etc.).
- Notification by Third Party of specific material changes of IS policies, standards or practices, and specific notification time frames for such modifications.
- Identification and disclosure of all embedded or linked/integrated user and open source code licensed in contracted services and products.
- Ability for periodic review of the Third-Party policies, standards, practices, and standards adherence, and ability to perform site inspection visits.
- Immediate notification requirements of actual or suspected security breaches, and immediate coordination to remedy and investigate all breaches, and notification of performance impacts to the contracting organization.
- Right to review all security controls (physical access and data), security testing results, internal and external audits of testing results, and specific IS program audits, and allowed periodic review time frames.

As it relates to the risks of service availability and for business continuity of services and technology resilience, the contract base should include at a minimum the following recommended concepts:

- Business resumption, crisis, and contingency plans, and policies of the Third Parties, and adherence to specific industry standards, and notification requirements for changes to these documents;

- Provisions for ensuring continuation of services in the event of operational impacts from natural or man-made disasters, intentional or malicious attacks, system breakdowns, and operational issues;
- Specifics as to back-up requirements, offsite and data vault storage, and specifications for protecting programs, data, and equipment;
- Details regarding periodic Third-Party plans maintenance (e.g. BCP, TR/DR, and CM plans, etc.) and specific as to RTOs, RPOs, and other SLAs for the services provided to the Enterprise, and because of processing delays and/or disasters, and resumption of service requirements;
- Need for periodic or annual review requirements of Third-Party BCP, TR/DR, and CM Plans; internal and external program audits, and demonstrated exercise results for technology and services;
- Requirement for alternate work-area recovery, technology, and secondary process locations, and specific requirements for alternate recovery site specifications;
- Periodic ability for site validation visits and the ability for active participation in multiple scenario exercise concepts (e.g. DR to Prod, Prod to DR, CM Communication, Joint-Cyber, IS Intrusion response, etc.);

6.7 Stratification of Third-Party IT Suppliers

Third-Party Supplier Stratification in High Volume Enterprise:

When dealing with large volume of suppliers, it has been indicated that some review structure is required for prioritization and stratification of vendors into key assessment categories and levels of risk. The contracting organization may have the ability to enter key information about the supplier's products/services and key questions about the supplier's operations, systems, and technology into an automated TSP inventory system. However, it is essential that all Enterprises maintain a detailed and centralized inventory for all of their Third-Party suppliers, TSP risk categorizations, and performance reviews. These assist in the appropriate due diligence and understanding of all supplier risk.

Framework Assessment and Advanced Filtering Scope:

The purpose of the initial definition in Enterprise TSP frameworks is to assess for further analysis and evaluation those service suppliers that present some enhanced exposure to the organization. As indicated, these TSP assessments are often automated with key SME rules that have been predefined to select variables entered about the supplier's operations or products. These can then trigger more detailed evaluations and assessments of the supplier's operations or products.

Advanced filtering information can be initiated about supplier financials, credit; data exposures; IS; BCP; TRDR; Technology; geopolitical/location and governmental information (e.g. for off-shore third parties, etc.); MC process designators; strategic information about the use of these suppliers; and the support from key areas of SME discipline. These can result in final assessments by each of the required SME domain areas.

Once the Advanced Filter (as needed) is completed, a Risk Sensitivity ranking or prioritization can be applied that further rates the supplier as to their potential exposure and can also determine any follow-on due diligence required by SME's. Also, based upon the established TSP policy the level of ongoing review and monitoring can be established as it relates to the level of risk sensitivity.

6.8 Third-Party Compliance and Risks Controls

In order to ensure appropriate compliance and risk management for organizations the TSP program and framework requires specific TSP Life-Cycle controls to be implemented, to provide the appropriate oversight for the supplier program and support executive management governance. Key accountabilities and controls for these compliance controls require definition in the TSP program policy and framework, along with the supporting processes and system automation for these controls.

Some of the key controls required from a TSP policy perspective include, but are not limited to:

- Creating point-in-time TSP Life-Cycle status and control of Third-Party contracts content, exceptions to contract template tracking, contract mitigation and escalation of contract issues, and contract expiration and review periods.
- Providing the ability to determine issues with SME review of Third Parties, tracking both SME contract issues and overall issues with Third Parties, TSP assessment, and issues resolution of SME findings.
- Develop Contract SLA performance levels for all Third Parties based upon their Risk Categorization and Assessments; Enterprise should develop TSP Scorecards to include service complaints, resolution of complaints, and SLA contract and financial performance levels.
- Ensure there is appropriate Secondary and Tertiary Supplier performance measurements and tracking where Third-Parties use subordinate suppliers and/or outsource specific activities and the appropriate escalation of past-due compliance issues, and significant contract anomalies.

- Determine requirements and ability to house and support Third-Party Compliance evidentiary documents and ensure quality control and assurance processes.
- Develop TSP KPI's for executive analytics risk controls.

As it relates to risk monitoring, some of the key controls to be implemented for understanding the exposure of use of Third-Party suppliers include the following:

- Determine Third-Party Relationship Risks - Inherent Risk Definitions to include: level of Monetary Contract Value; Reputational Risk from Risk Data Breach; Threats from Security Violations; Potential Operational Disruptions and Availability exposure; Level of Regulator or Contractual Exposure; Geopolitical Concentration Risk.
- Ensure controls exist for the determination of the impact of Third-Party Assessments Controls and Mitigation Solutions.
- Assess Third-Party Operating Profile Risk - Define Third-Party Risk Levels and Residual Third-Party Risk definitions the organization based upon the level of controls and processes in the TSP program.
- Complete periodic compliance and risk control validations and evidence review, dependent upon compliance and risk tier assessments.
- Provide KRI's, Risk Control Metrics, define and establish a Risk Appetite threshold for the TSP program.
- Ensure annual audits of the TSP program by an external audit firm or Internal Audit departments.
- Develop and automate executive reports and analytics, and escalation of program anomalies to senior executive management and the Board of Directors.

6.9 TSP Management Ecosystem and Data Concepts

Requirement for Centralized Third-Party Inventories:

As with all environments, a key to understanding and supporting a TSP program is to maintain a centralized inventory of all Third-Party suppliers and the services they provide. This should be coupled with a complete TSP Life-Cycle control process. A TSP Life-Cycle process should be a suspense-based tracking environment that provides for the understanding of specific deliverables and accountable issues associated with the Third Party. It should include the status of all contractual, SME reviews, and due diligence results.

There are multiple generic GRC inventory type suppliers available in the IT software space at an Enterprise level, to include: Dell-EMC/RSA, IBM, Metric Stream, Prevalent, SAP, Oracle, etc., and also boutique supplier management software that can support a Centralized Inventory and TSP Life-Cycle process.

TSP Supplier Management Ecosystem:

As indicated, a centralized inventory of suppliers is recommended to be maintained for all suppliers with the accountability for such inventory within one organization. It is the authors opinion that all of the core TSP Life-Cycle Data (e.g. status, issues, performance, documents, etc.) can be maintained within one physical system. Point of fact, that many organizations maintain multiple management systems for many of the key data structures needed to support a TSP Life-Cycle Process. For example, the Legal Department may maintain an automated base of contracts and contract amendments, procurement can maintain contract and procurement Supplier inventories, and the IT Departments will often maintain operational control data in Technology Resilience, BCP, Cyber/Security, and ITSM Management systems with the required TSP Life Cycle Process data components. These can be federated sources, but as defined in the book thesis, the data should be a single source and/or a Trusted Data source, with accountability by one accountable area for maintenance of the data sources.

For the purposes of this book's concepts, a suggested federated system concept is provided for automation of the full TSP Management Life Cycle. Much of the TSP core data can be maintained within a key Enterprise-level product supported by many of the Enterprise GRC software supplier firms. But a federated or Enterprise level integration is essential to maintain and ensure data integrity and control data among the various TSP Life-Cycle data source Ecosystem. It should include key alignment of supplier control data, with unique identifiers, such as, a Supplier Management ID.

At a minimum, the IT Ecosystem data configurations require supporting data as to the Hardware, Applications, IS, and Management Information System configurations and data structures for supporting Third-Party service activity. This may include the results of integrated BCP, IS, and TRDR internal systems testing with Third Parties, and recovery plans by the target organization with the supplier, and overall cyber and IS key references and risk assessment detail analysis

Figure 6.9 provides a conceptual TSP Life-Cycle Management Ecosystem for managing a TSP Process.

Figure 6.9 Third-Party Supplier Management Ecosystem

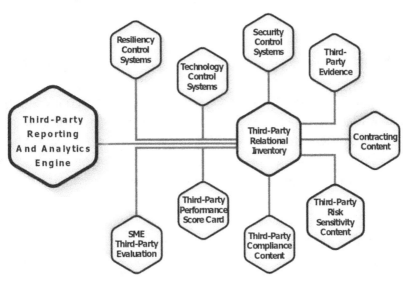

TSP Contract, Evidence, and Performance:

It is also important that all supplier contracts versions to include: Final, Red-Line and In-process contract versions, and amendments, statements of work, special support contract document versions, and all material contract issues be maintained in a centralized repository. The actual documents can be maintenance in a centralized TSP repository that also stores SME and other stake-holder's due diligence data/reports. Also, Enterprises can consider the centralized maintenance of evidentiary results and documents from the Third Parties for all SME reviews, to include: Financial Statements, Financial Audits, and Specific Technology, Technology and Operational Contract support, Cyber Configurations and Responses. BCP, TRDR, Crisis Plans and individual program test results.

A TSP Performance Tracking and Monitoring data component is suggested to track the status of the Third-Party supplier assessments; assessment issues; suspense date tracking (e.g. contract renewals/ expirations dates, review dates, etc.), as required for controlling the assessment and review process; escalation key trigger rules for SME review status; TSP life cycle status, and other key monitoring data components for ensuring TSP program control.

TSP Performance and Data Aggregation:

It is also important that the TSP Life-Cycle Management Ecosystem maintain the ability to score the performance of all suppliers on a periodic basis. The results of these performance scores require storage in a centralized repository that contains feedback from the various operational engagement areas utilizing the suppliers. This data should include supplier overall performance, SLA obtainments, contractual and performance issues, expenditures, and resolution of performance issues.

The Ecosystem should have the ability to aggregate all of the TSP Life-Cycle performance, compliance, and risk data variables. This should be available for delivery of periodic operational reporting for all SME and stakeholder areas, Enterprise executives, and the Board of Directors reporting. As part of providing data aggregation, it is a key component in either a federated Ecosystem or full Enterprise centralized solution for Trusted Data sources to be defined for operational control. These are needed for the integrity of the various data source environments. The key to a Centralized Inventory and Service environment identification is the use of a consistent Supplier Identification (Supplier ID) in all environments. This Supplier ID requires referential integrity be maintained for these key program key data variables.

TSP Trusted Data Repositories and Analytics:

As suggested, a single trusted Enterprise repository of supplier responses and due diligence documents be maintained that enables access and update by each of the key stake-holders and SME's that support the TSP Life Cycle. An internal and external Hybrid-access TSP environment is also beneficial to reduce processing overhead. The suppliers can then be enabled to access and update the TSP documents library from a secure Extranet site. This allows them to provide their responses to the SMEs, contract program requirements, communications, and SME evaluations/feedback for each of the supplier due diligence reviews.

Any databases or system environments used in federated or integrated Enterprise solution need to ensure use of integrated and quality-controlled data points. The data and technologies need to align to the TSP Life-Cycle workflow and include key SLA attainment of SME's and Third Parties within the required process for any integrated technologies. KPI, KRI and advanced analytics/trend analysis should be automated wherever possible and are essential in large TSP populations. In such environments, it is important to provide internal stakeholders with reporting, and where possible, real-time access to Trusted Data information and metrics, and to provide isolated external and internal data segmentation.

IT TSP Operational Control Environments:

One of the key concepts in understanding and controlling TSP supplier risk is the overall operational control environments for the IT organization. A key Third-Party TSP relationship linkage exists and is suggested, to the IS, BCP and TRDR operational environments, for support of the Enterprise in the event of a system, natural disaster, or cyber outage. Therefore, IT operational controls management systems (e.g. BCP, TRDR, ITSM, and IS, etc.) should be integrated or federated with the key TSP Management environments. Having a relationship of planning and data federation assists in mitigating the risks and reducing the potential impacts of Third-Party events.

This allows maintenance within a Trusted System of record to validate the results from exercises, planning, and IS risks, and reduces the level of resource impacts for managing data and manual handling of the results of these components. It also ensures a solid base for auditors and external agencies seeking to evaluate the Enterprise's efforts to ensure compliance to regulatory requirements and internal risk management in the TSP framework and activities.

6.10 Approaches to Managing IT Suppliers

Third-Party Supplier Partnership:

It is important to realize that no Enterprise enters into a contract with a Third Party in order to end up in a situation of litigation or operational disruptions for their customers. In many cases, significant time is spent in completing the supplier contract due diligence process with significant back-and-forth communications and documentation between the various parties. It is important that a strong working partnership exist between the Enterprise and their Third-Party suppliers to ensure a win-win situation exist for the contracting entities. However, it cannot be overstated that the resulting exposure from the transfer of activity to provide technology services or products to your organization or your customer should not result in the transfer of risk management of the Enterprise to the supplier. The ultimate responsibility for the risks associated with this transfer of activity remains with the contract business organization, and as such, should be managed by the organization regardless of how strong the partnership between the supplier and the Enterprise.

Consistent Communication Resources:

A key organizational requirement structure for ensuring continued and consistent communication between the Third-Party Supplier and the Contracting Organization is the designation of essential TSP Resource Supplier Manager. This resource should be accountable for all interaction between the Third-Party Supplier and the contracting business organizations. This includes understanding and explaining the requirements of the contracting organizations TSP policy and Life-Cycle process; contract discussions, negotiations and exception follow-through; working with SME's, and other stakeholders to ensure appropriate compliance and risk assessments are conducted correctly and contract variances resolved; facilitate communications with the supplier and all internal departments; and ensure that all required due-diligence artifacts and documents are provided by the supplier. Resource managers should also meet with the supplier on a periodic basis, review the results of all performance activity reports, and advise of any program issues with the suppliers.

Enterprise Third-Party Communication Contacts:

Additionally, all contracts should establish a specific operational and legal contact who is accountable for working with the Resource Manager of the business organization, along with alternate contacts, if the primary contact is unavailable for notification. This is needed during specific operational availability and crisis situations. Also, a process needs to be defined with the supplier to identify, report, and mitigate material contract variances from the key contract templates and final operational contracts. Internal to the Enterprise, the Resource Manager should understand they are accountable for contract variance ownership, mitigating controls, and review of contract variances with legal and procurement areas, and as required with the SME's accountable for the specific areas.

A Cross-Domain TSP Steering Committee can also be established that can review all material contract variances and ensure escalation points are established to escalate to senior executives, and as needed to the CEO, and Board of Directors. The Steering Committee should be comprised of members of the Legal and Procurement Departments, Risk organization, and key SME representatives. The committee would have overall accountability for Third-Party supplier relationships, exceptions, and issue resolution.

Third-Party Supplier Contract Exit Strategies:

Each new Third-Party supplier relationship requires the establishment of clear and realistic exit strategies for divestiture of the supplier and Enterprise relationship, due to specific default or extraneous conditions. This also requires internal decision points for managing Third-Party financial failures, consistent SLA failures, major cyber and operational incidents, and/or major contract breaches. Waiting until a major data breach or operational failure event occurs and the resulting fallout is not conducive to appropriate TSP risk management and planning.

The legal department will manage the resulting impacts and contract-based litigation required from a supplier exit situation. However, the Enterprise needs to be able to continue business operations and service to its customers. Therefore, exit strategies need to be realistic, identify and engage the appropriate internal Enterprise processing departments, and understand the impacted system environments and areas. It requires timelines and plans for migration of operations and/ or systems, internal development plans, and the required funding for ongoing operations, and workaround processes in the event of a major Third-Party issue.

For exit strategies that identify an alternative Third-Party Supplier usage, the strategy should identify the various realistic time-frames and migration processes to contracting with and working with the alternate Third-Party suppliers. It may include plans for integrating, as needed with internal systems and processes, and interim workaround processes until full exit strategy implementation.

IT Third-Party Supplier Requirements:

Another key element in developing a working relationship with IT suppliers and other risk-sensitive suppliers is the understanding of the requirements for conducting TR/DR, BCP, and cyber joint exercises between the supplier and the organization.

Key attributes of effective IT Supplier management are to include the following exercise concepts in an ongoing supplier due diligence management and process:

- Periodic exercises with usage of internal Third-Party recovery plans with bi-directional communication to Third Parties;
- Conducting applications and system technology testing with Third-Party technology systems during the Third-Party DR Exercises;
- Ensure that the Enterprise BCP processes execute recovery and use of Third-Party technology and processing environments during Enterprise BC Plan exercises;
- Organizations need active participation and joint tests with Third Parties of their technology during their own Enterprise DR exercises;
- Enhanced testing with high-risk-sensitive Third Parties service suppliers as defined by the risk management program;
- Engage and test with Third Parties during Industry-wide Table-Top and active Industry Sector Exercises.

6.11 Federal Regulator Third-Party Scrutiny

Key Federal Regulatory Market Drivers:

As discussed in this chapter introduction, Federal regulatory scrutiny has significantly increased over the last ten years. The key market drivers for the increase of federal regulatory oversight in the Financial industry (FI) includes:

- Increasing level of outsourcing by financial institutions to Third-Party suppliers and/or Fin-Tech provider partnerships;
- Emerging natures of Third-Party relationships products and services being offered to Financial institutions including the use of complex Cloud-service-based application provider services and full federation with Financial internal systems;
- Increasing concentration risk exposure to financial institutions resulting from Fin-Tech Industry consolidations and integration activities of these suppliers;
- Daily mass-media focus and the volume of Third-Party Service cyber-attacks, data breaches and service outages, and the expanding public exposure to such events;
- Increasing compliance scrutiny due to Dodd-Frank regulations and the Consumer Financial Protection Board, including Third-Party servicing of FI customers.

Financial Services Regulatory TSP Focus:

In 1st Quarter 2015, the Federal Financial Examination Council (FFIEC), issued new standards and guidelines for supervision of financial institutions with reference to management of Third-Party suppliers to financial institutions. The FFIEC is a centralized committee representing several federal regulatory organizations. The new guidelines are known as "Appendix J," to the industry. These guidelines redefine and expand the requirements for financial institutions to address managements responsibility to control the business continuity and cyber risk associated with utilizing Outsourced Technology services for critical business functions.

Recent Financial Industry TSP Guidance:

The recent guidance objectives of Appendix J that are impactful to financial institutions and all technology firms servicing the financial industry include:

- Ensuring Third-Party management of suppliers addresses a financial institution's risk management of Third Parties and their subcontractors;
- Financial institutions demonstrate the ability to keep critical processes functioning during a Third-Party or Enterprise service disruption;
- Requires the financial institution to develop recovery procedures for a disruption when services become available from the Third Party;
- Validates the Third-Party supplier service continuity capability and capacity through robust testing program of technologies and cyber events;
- Provides for continuous monitoring and reporting of KPI and KRI along with gaps and risk mitigation of Third Parties.

Third-Party Supplier Industry Regulation:

The key understanding here is that management of Third-Party IT supplier risk should be included as a component of an overall TSP management program for Enterprises. The key regulatory agencies expect a consistent approach to Third-Party supplier management across the Enterprise. Also, there is an increasing focus on the management in particular of Third-Party IT outsource Cloud-Based service suppliers. Over the last five years there has been some twenty-five-plus

regulatory laws and published directives that are focused and/or relates to IT service suppliers in the banking, brokerage, savings and
loan, and also health care Industries.

6.12 IT Third-Party Supplier Key Program Indicators

Typically, many organizations will use a level of TSP performance
as a KRI for a TSP program, but this may miss the overall risk associated with the exposure from use of key vendors. While KPI's described
in this chapter section can lead to a risk exposure from use of certain
supplier types, or where compliance levels are performing outside
of the norm, they may not be true indicators of risk to the Enterprise.

For example, many organizations will track the level of compliance to the framework of the organization and the overall response to
the organization's query results from the suppliers as KRI's. However,
these are basic levels of compliance and delays in response by suppliers that are indicative of overall performance of the TSP program.
They can often be a potential lead indicator for an overall increase
in residual risk because of non-compliance, but these often may not
consider the key TSP inherent risk exposures.

While TSP performance could manifest a level of performance
for these suppliers and signal a risk to the corporation, they are a basic performance KPI. They track the numbers and types of suppliers,
types of vendors, number of supplier responses, cycle response time-
liness, cycle past-due reviews, SME activity, and evaluation results.
However, they may or may not present inherent risk to the corporation. This requires a judgment review by auditors, senior executives, or the Board to understand if there is a real inherent risk that
could be manifested because of a poor performing IT supplier, or TSP
Management Program, or group of suppliers.

Inherent TSP IT Risks:

Real inherent TSP IT risk manifests itself to a corporation by the
actual activities and types of services provided by the Third-Party

suppliers, and the actual level of SME controls and performance management of the various inherent risk controls presented to the Enterprise from the use of certain types of suppliers. As indicated, one of the greatest risks to an organization is the outsourcing of technology activities and application services for the Enterprise. Key inherent risks then are to understand these types of supplier issues correlated to the key ITGRC indicators. Also, a major item to understand is which suppliers are providing critical services or products to the Enterprise.

Key TSP Risk Indicators:

One of the many common variables used by many organizations to understand their key suppliers is the aggregation and level of expenditures for these suppliers. However, this element on its own could incorrectly measure a level of risk to the organizations. What is needed is a real understanding of what services and products are being provided by these suppliers and even more important, what Mission- Critical processes are supported by these suppliers, along with other types of supplier exposure. These are similar to the internal understanding in IT departments as to what Mission-Critical services are supported by critical applications within the IT internal portfolio. Once understood, the organization can perform the required due diligence to understand the inherent risk exposure from use of these suppliers.

Key TSP Risk Metrics:

After the Enterprise has filtered through its supplier centralized list, it can identify through key linkage of suppliers to the various IT control systems of the IT organization. Key elements to understand, and effective measures then, are the level of IT controls and governance of the suppliers related to the internal organizational processes and systems; the level of supplier standard ITSM controls; exposure of the customer data of the Enterprise processed and housed by the supplier and the supplier data controls, and IS protection mechanisms and controls; all testing conducted by the supplier over the various systems; key operational availability planning and recovery of business and validation of continuity, disaster recovery planning and testing of various plans and environmental fall-over.

Standard Enterprise understanding of the overall level of financial performance and liability exposure for these suppliers is also a key element to understand any financial and credit exposure from suppliers. As such, the inherent risk of exposure from any supplier is the ultimate Key Risk Indicator that should be assessed by the primary assigned SME's. That is to understand the nature of risk posed by the initial and ongoing usage of various IT and other suppliers to the organization.

Another KRI to understand is the overall Concentration Risk associated with use of a particular supplier. It is just as important as the concentration of services in some locations or at operational sites. Concentration Risk, often a term associated with a financial credit portfolio, is an emerging as a key indicator in terms of the impact on operational risks exposure for an Enterprise.

TSP concentration risk results from a large aggregation of a particular level of services to customers, types of services, level of product usage, and component aggregation in Enterprise products or services with a single supplier. Also, this risk can result from potential industry concentrations between suppliers, and/or concentrations of exposure from political, geographic, or natural hazards for a particular supplier. Often, SME's can be the best judge of the level of concentration risk for a supplier. It is recommended that these considerations be included in understanding the overall inherent risk in use of IT Suppliers.

Regardless of the risks, the management of Third-Party IT service suppliers and other critical Enterprise suppliers has emerged as a major ITGRC and Enterprise GRC component that requires an Enterprise risk-based approach with key IT organizational support.

CHAPTER 7

ITGRC Executive Oversight

7.1 Introduction to ITGRC Executive Oversight

DUE TO THE expanding complexities in the delivery of IT services and operations for Enterprises throughout the world, IT Governance, Risk, and Compliance (ITGRC) has become one of the many major challenges for IT executives. Execution of the most effective strategic risk decisions and implementing ITGRC framework controls, processes, technologies, and reporting are at the core of the oversight requirements for all IT executive managers. As the introduction of more complex technologies continues to expand the focus and pressure of IT risk management, executives require an expanded focus on active identification, monitoring, and management of IT emerging threats and vulnerabilities.

Also, a key challenge in the development of an effective ITGRC program strategy is to validate the alignment of the ITGRC frameworks to the overall governance and operational risk management framework of the Enterprise. For an effective Enterprise risk program, the IT framework, processes, functions, and supporting technology of IT domain programs should provide consistency and standardization across the entire Enterprise. Establishing a standard ITGRC framework environment can assist IT executives and Enterprise management in more effective oversight of IT risk. It can increase the alignment of the IT directions and strategies to risk-based investment decisions. Additionally, it can support regulatory direction and satisfaction of Enterprise audit and risk requirements.

7.2 IT Risk Oversight Organizational Responsibilities

The overall responsibility for ITGRC management strategies and oversight rests with the Board of Directors and the CEO/President of the Enterprise. However, implementation and execution of the ITGRC program and the tactical and strategical accountability rests with the most senior IT executive officers of the Enterprise. This often includes the CIO, CTO, or a designated Senior IT executive. More and more IT organizations, including those in the financial industry sectors and other industries, are introducing an accountable IT Chief Risk Officer (CRO). The IT CRO helps set risk strategies, IT control management, and oversight of day-to-day ITGRC management activities. The senior IT executives and IT CRO are accountable for:

- Ensuring IT risk management technologies, processes, and controls align with new Enterprise business strategies and changes.
- Controls development and maintenance of key ITGRC frameworks, policies, controls, compliance, and risk assessments.
- Monitoring regulatory and audit directions and compliance changes that can impact IT strategies and risk programs.
- Ensuring ITGRC domain standards, processes, and roles are communicated to the IT and Enterprise personnel.
- Developing and maintaining ITGRC-appropriate committee charters, risk control inventory, control testing programs, and oversight committee due diligence.
- Providing for the capturing and tracking of ITGRC program issues, incidents, threats, and program deficiencies, and implementation of corrective and/or mitigation activity.

- Enabling and maintaining appropriate IT risk training, issue tracking systems, risk data structures, and compliance and risk reporting environments for control and management of ITGRC activities.
- Providing efficient and consistent communication, and coordination with Enterprise Risk and Compliance management departments, regulators, and auditors.

7.3 Management Framework for ITGRC Activities

The development, maintenance, implementation, and communication of the required IT risk framework, component policies, and oversight committees (e.g. Project/Portfolio, ITSM, BCP, TRDR, and IS Controls etc.) are essential to establishing a good ITGRC framework. The enforcement and compliance of these policies are paramount to ensure that IT risks are managed and communicated throughout the Enterprise.

IT executive management need to ensure that compliance with these policies is continuous with monitoring and maintenance, and that standard processes established to control IT risk are executed throughout the Enterprise. Exceptions to the controls must be understood and reported to senior Enterprise executives. It is essential that senior IT executive articulate and set the strategy for management and development of the ITGRC framework. Many organizations have focused their ITGRC frameworks around the ISO31000 risk management framework and/or use the NIST, ITIL, or COBIT standards to assist in establishing a basis for their ITGRC frameworks.

ITGRC Management Framework Drivers:

ITGRC management can be difficult and complex to manage across the Enterprises where IT execution is distributed in organizational lines of business (e.g. sales/marketing, finance, distribution, and other operational units, etc.), or where multiple IT organizations exist within subsidiary corporations, as opposed to a centralized IT organization. In many cases, it is just as challenging for Enterprises where IT is centralized under a senior IT executive and in large global organizations. The larger the organizations, the more difficult it is to monitor the organizations and the Enterprise's compliance with the required IT program policies. As such, it is recommended that an overall ITGRC framework policy be established for governance of ITGRC throughout the Enterprise, all operating divisions, and subsidiaries of the Enterprise.

Additionally, the regulators in several industries (e.g. financial services, insurance, etc.) have provided direction to the monitoring of IT corporate governance and increased their scrutiny of the Board of Directors in the areas of IT governance, corporate audit activities, and overall IT investment strategies.

ITGRC Framework Process Oversight:

To ensure that the ITGRC framework is established and managed correctly, the ITGRC framework policy should establish criteria based upon an Enterprise's risk base standards. This includes the requirements to develop, approve, issue, and set rules for governance and oversight of IT activities. To ensure appropriate oversight and participation in ITGRC management, it is recommended that the ITGRC frameworks designate an appropriate ITGRC senior executive committee. The committee can be chaired by the senior accountable IT executive and authorized by the Enterprise Board of Directors or an Executive Risk Committee. The ITGRC committee participants include chairs of ITGRC sub-committees that are accountable for implementing and management of the associated ITGRC governance policies. The participants work together with key Enterprise risk and business senior executives in validate the ITGRC process.

The IT framework should also authorize the establishment of the appropriate ITGRC charters and approve the various ITGRC governing charters. These operating committees can then establish the policies that are authoritative documents that provide clear and actionable requirements for the programs and describe the strategies and expectations for oversight and management.

7.4 Oversight Accountability for ITGRC Activities

In many large IT organizations, the typical key ITGRC oversight sub-committees and policies includes the following IT program areas and policy domains:

- Asset and Configuration Management Program and Policy - Develops, manages, and sets requirements to manage IT hardware, software, databases, and other physical asset attributes and operational information.
- Architecture, Data, and Standards Governance Programs and Policies - Develops and sets requirements to manage the IT analysis, design, planning, and implementation of Enterprise IT architecture principles, data standards, and practices.
- BCP and TRDR Policies - Develops, manages, and sets requirements to manage oversight of Enterprise BCP, crisis management, TRDR recovery planning, operations, and testing.
- ITSM Change and Release Management Policy - Develops and sets requirements to manage IT software, application, databases, system, network, and infrastructure changes and releases to the production environment.
- IS Program and Policy - Develops, manages, and sets requirements to manage and protect Enterprise assets and information from unauthorized access, loss, and/or damage.
- PPM Program and Policy - Develops, manages, and sets requirements to manage the delivery of IT projects and assets environments, and the demand request portfolio for requesting IT resources *(interacts with standard Enterprise Capital Expenditure financial policies).

- QA Testing Program and Policy - Develops, manages, and sets requirements to manage the assurance and testing of the quality of IT software and products delivered into IT environments.
- Third-Party Risk Management Program and Policy - Develops, manages, and sets requirements to manage Enterprise IT Third-Party relationships, services, and activities provided to the Enterprise.

Each of these ITGRC program sub-committees and policies should be required to establish the required policy scope, owners, and stakeholder participants in the IT sub-committee. The roles of the various ITGRC sub-committees are to:

- Approve policies within the scope of their IT domain responsibilities and oversee ongoing compliance of those domains.
- Establish a comprehensive body of policies and standards for over IT domain operations and oversight.
- Perform annual policy reviews, updates, approvals, and amendments to documents.
- Provide oversight of policy compliance, primary action through metrics monitoring, and risk reporting to the senior ITGRC Operating Committees.
- Evaluate and review of ITGRC programs KPI and KRI, Policy exceptions, and trending performance and risk issues.
- Monitor Risk QA Testing Control activities conducted by the various risk quality assurance and audit organizations within IT and the Enterprise.

7.5 ITGRC Risk Assessment Controls and Monitoring

ITGRC Control Environments:

Another element within the IT framework is the establishment of ITGRC management controls and the inventory of these ITGRC controls via a centralized IT risk administrative organization. This can be often facilitated by an IT CRO or Enterprise risk organization. An administrative control organization has the primary objective for the maintenance of an inventory of all IT framework committee policies, charters, and standards. Additionally, the requirements exist to maintain a complete inventory of all IT compliance and risk program controls to facilitate management, reporting, and audit activities. Each of the IT risk oversight sub-committees is accountable to work with the individual stakeholders of the ITGRC domain control areas. These areas should conduct activities, to develop and support the creation and monitoring of these domain controls and interact with the IT risk control and other administrative teams.

It is recommended that the IT compliance and risk controls be maintained in a standard IT and/or Enterprise risk control repository or database library component. They should be monitored with automated mechanisms to control the level of compliance and associated resulting risk assessments. Figure 7.5 depicts a concept for supporting the automation of IT Risk Control and Assessment environments.

Figure 7.5 ITGRC Controls Assessment and Automation Concepts

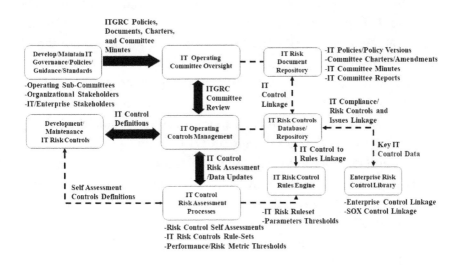

The IT controls inventory repository should at a minimum provide definition of the following major data components:

- Control definition and purpose with Unique identifiers;
- Inherent IT risk classifications and exposures;
- Descriptions (e.g. alerts reports, processes, testing, etc.);
- Organizational owner and dependent organizations;
- Indicators as to the Primary or Secondary nature of the control (e.g. Essential Controls, SOX*, etc.);
- Associated and dependent IT control references;
- KPI and KRI reference to the Control classification;
- Controls status and linkage to other key IT/Enterprise and Regulatory controls, issues tracking, and Sarbanes Oxley *(SOX) Enterprise key controls.

IT Compliance and Risk Control Assessments:

Once a complete inventory of ITGRC controls is approved by the committees, then IT-accountable program and sub-committee areas are required to maintain the IT controls and the associated reporting of these controls to a centralized IT or risk management area. The IT controls can be associated to the primary inherent domain risks and evaluated by the IT domain stakeholders, together with the IT risk control areas. They need to understand the level of effectiveness of the controls to mitigate the inherent risk. Each control should determine the level of residual risk remaining after application of the controls. Also, the ITGRC areas can establish the required reporting and monitoring of risks for the specific IT domain.

A standard corporate risk methodology often used throughout many industries is an RCSA (Risk Control Self-Assessment) process. This is often used to evaluate performance and risk controls of various risk domains. These can be captured and evaluated within the ITGRC control environments for preliminary and ongoing self-check evaluations. They provide a benchmark for future reference in risk reporting.

However, as the base theory defined in this book, such evaluations are often qualitative evaluations of controls and associated risks for input to an initial decision process. They should be coupled with and supported by key quantitative performance and risk metrics associated to the various IT risk domains.

Additionally, it is recommended that these ITGRC metrics be developed and aligned to an ongoing automated rules base. This rules base should be in the form of an automated analytics engine to conduct procedural evaluations and conditional threshold range testing levels. These can be used to provide a baseline and trending directions for each of the various control areas and domain risks, as depicted in Figure 7.5.

The rules can be automated and stored into a repository rule set and provide the flexibility for adjustment by the various target IT domains stakeholders. The rules require the appropriate oversight by ITGRC committees or domain area SME's. Rules control thresholds can then be structured to trigger key control breaches or performance levels in associated parameter high and low ranges. They can be structured to a standard and consistent definition of compliance and risk trending directions. More important these standard risk definitions should be set as values against a standard Enterprise risk framework of risk classifications and definitions (e.g. Very High, High, Medium, and Low risk, etc.) and with specific tolerance levels that create exposure for the Enterprise. Also, these should be based upon quantitative parameters that are defined risk exposures from the Enterprise risk areas and understood and evaluated by the ITGRC committee.

IT Governance, Compliance and Risk Control Monitoring:

ITGRC monitoring requires that the supporting IT environments be capable of providing the information and data for IT and Enterprise executives. A primary mechanism then for supporting these objectives is for the effective maintenance and reporting of the key controls on a time sensitive basis to the senior IT risk management executive committee and other IT domain oversight committees. It is suggested that periodic meetings (e.g. monthly, etc.) of the senior ITGRC operating committees take place to review and evaluate all pertinent compliance and risk controls for the ITGRC. These should be defined in the IT risk framework along with other pertinent IT compliance and risk information. Each of subject ITGRC domain areas and other pertinent activities are described in Section 7.9 of this chapter.

The defined IT framework sub-committees should also meet on a periodic basis to review the same governance components for their respective areas. Each sub-committee meeting should be aligned with the ITGRC structures. Also, sub-committees need to perform escalations to the senior ITGRC executive committee to ensure the appropriate senior IT executive and Enterprise oversight of IT issues, compliance, and risk status.

Standard and explicit meeting minutes should be maintained and stored for future regulatory and audit review by the various committees to include reporting and decisions. These should be maintained in a standard ITGRC risk document repository. along with all amendments and versions of all committee documents. Specific KPI's and KRI's starting points for each of the key ITGRC domain areas have been described in each chapter of this book.

7.6 Trusted Data Integration and Aggregation

It is suggested that the specific ITGRC domain performance activities and metrics for each of the key primary and secondary controls be generated by a specific system of record or domain system environments. They can be automatically integrated to the ITGRC reporting environments. Also, limiting the number of times that performance and risk data can be manipulated on a manual basis by stakeholders and/or by other systems can be important to ensuring that a uniform and transparent reporting framework exists from multiple ITGRC domain areas. This allows for consistent data inputs and reporting formats that follow a standard reporting methodology on a real-time and periodic basis.

An integrated ITGRC technology solution allows IT executives to administer the entire ITGRC program from a central library of compliance and risk controls. It can enhance Executive oversight to manage, monitor, and report risk through a centralized management prism. A unified and standard ITGRC framework with centralized controls and reporting can also be better aligned to an Enterprise risk program

ITGRC Trusted Data Integration:

Senior ITGRC and other sub-committee members can then use aggregated and integrated data to manage IT exposures of the Enterprise and perform more effective risk-based investment decisions. Utilizing trusted and integrated data support applications with a common set of principles, uniform metrics, and consistent verbiage can facilitate communication and understanding between ITGRC and Enterprise risk stakeholders.

As IT metrics are applied to an ITGRC program, it can be challenging, given the large array and volume of IT operating indicators, to maintain and report data in spreadsheets to senior executives. Therefore, ITGRC programs should consider a systematic approach to capture and process this data within an ITGRC Ecosystem. They can then use aggregation technology and data to interface with any EGRC environment.

This type of IT automation, data integration, and logical data aggregation can be a cost-effective investment for many IT and Enterprise organizations. This is due to the fact that it removes multiple and manual touchpoints of data and relies on standard formats. It also can be a complete transparent operation, which uses trusted systems of data, to remove any potential conflicts of interest and can be supported by auditors and regulators across almost all industries.

ITGRC Data Aggregation and Rules Processing:

Important to understanding the various ITGRC domains are the ability to aggregate data across the Enterprise by divisions and sub-divisions, and for domestic and global-based subsidiaries. This allows for effective understanding of specific performance, as well as reporting control breaches within specific business divisions and geographic areas. It can provide the ability to respond in a rapid manner to various US federal and global national stakeholder queries for understanding and reporting ITGRC activities for these entities.

It requires a flexible control rule set environment that is automated and that can be used to examine several hundred IT metrics. This often will require real-time evaluations and should support version control and organizational rule sets. These are required to address various organizational and other Enterprise reporting structures and to provide the ability to selective view data aggregation reference point data for each of the organizational entities.

There are several IT technology software suppliers that provide general rule-based software products that can be used to evaluate the many rules required to analyze all of the ITGRC data. These suppliers provide rule-based authoring platforms, to develop selection, filtering, and rule logic, for real-time evaluation of transactional and aggregated ITGRC data. The suppliers provide Enterprise onsite and Cloud-Based solutions that can be integrated or federated to ITGRC domain processing and reporting environments. They can be embedded into the ITGRC Ecosystem and database environments.

A sample of market software suppliers includes: Corticon/Progress Software, IBM/Decision Manager, InRule Technology, and Oracle Software/Business Rules. Additionally, Business Intelligence type software has emerged to provide business analytics and processing that can also be used in this process. Some of the suppliers in this market include: Qlik, IBM, Microsoft, SAS, and Tableau.

Metrics and Data Anomaly Processing:

Automated system integration and programmable data can often reflect data anomalies due to programming issues and/or changing business conditions. This can necessitate potential adjustments metrics data. As such, it is important in any IT performance or risk automated data integration to have the ability to perform controlled data modifications. These modifications must be auditable and actionable for correction of any data anomalies. They should allow the flexibility to ensure business decisions based upon data that is capable of being adapted to certain exception conditions and environments. In many instances, rules may also have to be adjusted to ensure that the correct ranges and thresholds can be calibrated to standard baselines, and due to other errors. Such corrections must be documented and noted as part of the change process for effective transparency and risk reporting. Additionally, some software suppliers provide cognitive-based software tools for evaluating data. These can enable the expansion from pure Boolean-based rules sets to a learning/knowledge-based evaluation environment. These types of systems are capable of detecting anomalies in data used to assess ITGRC performance and risk analysis.

7.7 ITGRC Management Ecosystem Concepts

Since data is key for ITGRC domain areas, Trusted Systems of Record can be the core foundation as data for the ITGRC Trusted Data aggregation and reporting process. The data provided from these sources can federate or integrate directly into an ITGRC risk data repository, via standard interfaces of file sources, or linkage with the target ITGRC domain and database environments.

Trusted System Data Sources:

The primary ITGRC Trusted domain sources that can be integrated and/or federated with the ITGRC Management environments includes:

- Asset and Configuration Management Systems - Physical IT Asset and Configuration Management environments;

- BCM and TRDR Systems - Business Continuity and Technology Resilience/DR Management, Business Risk Assessment/ Priorities, Resilience Performance Management Analytics, and Reporting environments;
- IT Service Management Systems - IT Service Management, Change Control, Release Management, and Problem Management environments';
- IS Operational Systems - Identity and Access Management Control, Cyber Intelligence and Vulnerability, Threat Analytics, Cyber Event Management, Security Risk Assessment and Reporting environments;
- IT Project and QA Management Systems - Project and Portfolio Management, Project Life Cycle, and Quality Assurance/ Testing environments;
- IT Operational Analytics Systems - IT Operations Monitoring, Operational Analytics, Auto-Discovery, and Configuration Management environments;
- Third-Party Risk Management Systems - Enterprise and IT Third-Party Management environments and inventories';
- Human Resources/Organizational System - Human Resource employee association and Enterprise organizational layer environments

Figure 7.7 provides a concept for an integrated and/or federated ITGRC Management Ecosystem environment. The management environments focus on automating and integrating key ITGRC data sources. This can provide real-time and periodic updates, to a consolidated repository of ITGRC data metrics from these Trusted systems.

Figure 7.7 ITGRC Management Ecosystem

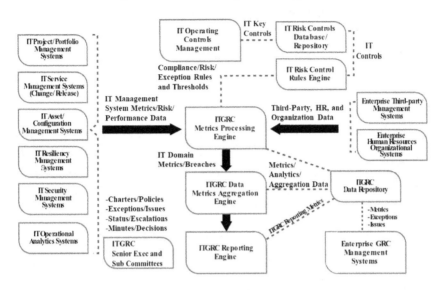

ITGRC Management Ecosystem Processing Components:

One of the major logical processing components of the ITGRC Management Ecosystem is the maintenance of the ITGRC controls, rules management repositories, and document libraries. These components are the primary mechanisms for analyzing and evaluating the key IT domain data points and metrics processed from the key Trusted Data sources.

The ITGRC Trusted Data sources can be processed via direct file integrations or federations of the required metric data from the defined ITGRC sources. The data can then be processed through a metrics processing engine against the key controls and rulesets developed as part of the ITRGC controls processing environment. An ITGRC metrics processing engine can then select the key metrics and data points. The data can be evaluated and tested against predefined rulesets for the targeted IT domain area.

Anomalies can be identified, performance measured, and variances, exceptions, or violations captured against the defined thresholds for rulesets. The selected data points and results can then be processed against the required ITGRC domain structures, business relationships, any special rule sets and data aggregated into ITGRC repositories. The results of the aggregation process is to consolidate the metrics into the appropriate domain and risk categories for reporting to the ITGRC, and integration with Enterprise risk management environments.

ITGRC standard report engines can then be used to provide the reporting that is required for the Senior ITGRC committee, and ITGRC sub-committees for risk management, and if required, provide real-time alerts to stakeholders. The reporting repository and data can be audited for consistent control effectiveness. It can also provide a historical audit and regulatory reporting environment and create a baseline vs trending performance data for the various ITGRC committees.

ITGRC Ecosystem Solution Suppliers:

Several IT solution suppliers have developed standard GRC authoring, management, and reporting platforms and toolsets. Many support the general management of Enterprise ITGRC requirements. They provide basic products, and in some cases some advanced GRC capabilities (full GRC template sets, graphical dashboards, etc.), for overall generic Enterprise GRC business requirements. Also, these solutions may include SOX control and/or financial control reporting needs with software flexibility that can be adapted to ITGRC.

These GRC products support major corporations and government agency frameworks throughout the United States, and internationally. The various software solutions provide functionalities that can store GRC documents and manage reporting content; support control definition, tracking, and analysis of GRC workflows; perform compliance and risk analysis; maintain policy data; manage GRC audit data; automate tracking and monitoring of GRC controls; issues management tracking and controls linkage; and various capabilities for reporting and risk data analytics. Some of the key vendors providing both Enterprise and Cloud-Based solutions in the this sector includes: Dell/EMC/RSA-Archer, IBM, Metric Stream, Modulo, Oracle, SAP, SAS, Servicenow, Software AG, and Wolters Kluwer.

7.8 ITGRC Management Reporting and Analytics

A major objective in automation and integration of the key ITGRC data into a centralized management environment is to enable ITGRC oversight, transparency, and consistent reporting activity from Trusted Data source. This is a required for optimization of compliance and risk analytical activity. In order to accomplish this objective, ITGRC strategies should define the key IT risk and controls, and indicators in response to a defined ITGRC framework. This should also be aligned with an Enterprise risk framework.

Development of a standard risk taxonomy construct for IT compliance and risk domain reporting categories is a key process in development of ITGRC reporting and analytical structures (see Chapter Eight for Enterprise Operational Risk Taxonomies). These categories can be aligned to an Enterprise risk program taxonomy of risk classifications.

ITGRC Reporting Categories:

Once the controls and key performance indicators have been defined and linkage established to the Enterprise reporting categories, it is important to develop standardized reporting structures for each of the key ITGRC reporting domains. This should include defining the periodic reporting from these IT domains (e.g. real-time events, anomalies, daily, weekly, monthly, etc.), and structured to the level of exposure and performance relevant to the data metrics provided by these IT domains.

A suggested categorization for reporting of ITGRC performance and risk metrics is to organize the reporting based upon the key IT Domain areas defined in this book. Each of the key chapters of this book has suggested Key Compliance/Performance and Risk indicators that can be captured and reported against a defined rule set. These can then identify anomalies in the control reporting elements. The reporting should highlight those KPI and KRI metric breaches for the thresholds established for the specific data controls and be capable of identification of these breaches.

ITGRC Performance and Risk Analytics:

Often, ITGRC and Enterprise governance organizations use a standard compliance and risk classification that monitors the performance level and risk heatmaps. These are often conveyed via a multi-color identification or "Stoplight Reporting" (e.g. red, yellow, green, etc.) to indicate the level of performance or risk for the particular IT metric reporting elements. However, it requires understanding the baseline and historical trend analysis of a particular metric performance level. This is important, as a threshold breach may occur on a particular periodic report. So, it is just as important and appropriate for ITGRC senior executives and other operating committees to understand the positive and negative trend direction for this range of elements.

Executive understanding of continuous trends can be key to managing the particular area of performance and risk. It can provide executive insight into mitigation strategies for resolution of issues represented in the reporting metrics. Utilizing standard performance metrics, trends, and analytics then are key elements in the delivery of ITGRC reporting activities.

7.9 ITGRC Committee Meeting Structures

The senior ITGRC committee and sub-committees should review the overall level of exposure for the IT domain environments within the IT framework. Each committee should have an executive stakeholder who is defined in the committee charter and who acts as the primary chairperson. The chairperson should have the ability to delegate to an alternate chairperson. They should develop an agenda for each meeting and solicit input from other committee stakeholders for consideration of other subjects. Committee members should approve committee charter and policy modifications and amendments.

ITGRC committee briefing materials and packages should be provided by IT administrative support teams to committee stakeholders with advanced communication to afford stakeholders sufficient time to review the materials prior to meetings. In addition to reviewing previous meeting minutes and conducting stakeholder roll calls, an executive review of the overall status of the key and most important IT domain risks should be reviewed by the committee chairperson. Also, outstanding program performance, audit, and regulatory issues should be reviewed as to updates on all major project statuses and mitigation to resolve the various program issues. Each of the key IT domain KPI and KRI metrics can then be reviewed in relation to threshold breaches and/or primary exception metric areas. The committee then needs to define and escalate key compliance and risk items to the overall Enterprise risk committee and then to the Board of Directions.

ITGRC management is a major component of an Enterprise's GRC management process. This has been exacerbated by the recent major threats of cyber and technology outage events. It is front and center for all IT and Enterprise senior executives and Board members. As a result, the ITGRC committee stakeholders' role in these committee meetings is to oversee the overall performance of the ITGRC controls and domain activity and the level of IT risk sustained in the delivery of IT strategies. ITGRC stakeholders need to ensure the implementation of an effective ITGRC framework that has a complete management oversight of all IT assets, resources, and system operations, and for evaluation all Enterprise IT investments and risk mitigations.

CHAPTER 8

ITGRC Enterprise Management

8.1 Introduction ITGRC Enterprise Management

OPERATIONAL RISKS ARE inherent to almost all services and products offerings, business activities, and technology provided by any Enterprise. This is due to the prevalence of threats and inherent risk in delivery of business technology and other operations. Therefore, efficient corporate governance requires that a standard Enterprise risk- management approach is applied for coordination and communication among all executives, divisions, and support functions. There is also a requirement at the Enterprise level for an independent and integrated management of operational risk across the Enterprise. This is required to enable the transparent identification and management of operational risks.

As it relates to IT activity, this includes the engagement of all organizations for adherence to the ITGRC frameworks and processes within an Enterprise and Operational Risk Management (ORM) program framework. Typically, operational risks include the risk of loss resulting from inadequate or failed internal processes, people, systems, and/or from external events. Also, operational risk will often include legal risks. Additionally, losses that occur because of operational risk can also be impacted due to the lack of program compliance. or when the loss is a result of an operational event. Examples of IT Operational failures that can cause such losses include, but are not limited to, IT product or service execution or delivery failures, systems disruptions, data breaches and/or security attacks, damage to physical assets, service performance issues, and/or Thirty-Party operational service failures.

At the Enterprise level, an operational framework to manage operational risk structures sets specific standards and governance across the Enterprise for all types of operational risks; identifies key operational risk categories and taxonomies for the Enterprise; provides overall policy creation frameworks and compliance tracking/reporting; manages operational risk loss limits and risk scenario testing; and manages Enterprise compliance to legal and regulatory requirements.

Three Lines of Defense Framework Concept:

Many Enterprises are now utilizing a "Three Lines of Defense" (3LD) oversight framework approach for the management of risk across the entire Enterprise. This includes both Enterprise operational and ITGRC management environments. This approach provides for a collaborative operating model between the Enterprise and subordinate operating divisions, including the IT organization. It also assists in the identification and coordination of roles and responsibilities across the Enterprise, related to the 3LD framework and IT operational risk management activities.

8.2 Enterprise GRC Framework Concepts

In a 3LD Enterprise governance model, the First Line of Defense (FLOD), for any Enterprise is the actual operational and IT business lines. These business lines are accountable and responsible for identifying, managing, and controlling their division's operational risks. This includes the IT domain organizations that are accountable for their various IT operations execution, risk outcomes, and adherence to the various ITGRC policies.

The Enterprise's operational risk management function, organizations, and ITGRC control areas (e.g. PPM, ITSM, BCP, TRDR, ISS, TPS, etc.) are responsible for the development and maintenance of the governance programs. These organizations provide oversight, monitoring, and reporting for the various IT activities conducted by all IT FLOD organizations. These IT control functions are defined as Enterprise Second Line of Defense (SLOD) organizations and ensure that the key ITRGC framework principles and standards are integrated across all Enterprise business lines, operational work, and strategic activities. They ensure that FLOD IT and other business organizations adhere to the ITGRC framework and policies. This is accomplished through the key ITGRC oversight, monitoring, and reporting, with strong participation by Enterprise operational risk organizations. ITGRC as a separate operating governance structure partners with the overall Enterprise level on operational risk and governance activities. They provide a comprehensive review and oversight of the GRC activities within the IT domains and Enterprise environments,

The Third Line of Defense (TLOD) in the 3LD model is accountable for independent verification, assurance, and testing of the effectiveness of the ITGRC program(s) controls, and provides additional oversight of the various GRC programs by the Enterprise. This function is often the responsibility of the internal enterprise auditors or corporate auditors, and/or external Third-Party audit firms.

8.3 GRC Policies and Accountabilities

Just as in the governance of IT organizational activities and the ITGRC framework policies, Enterprises need to define the Enterprise GRC Management framework. This includes oversight and other governance of the various stakeholder roles and responsibilities, key operating committees, and risk framework processes. The framework is designed to assist the Enterprise in operating in a safe and sound

manner and to manage all risks of the Enterprise. including operational risks. In public corporations, the Board of Directors, is the most senior independent oversight level for the Enterprise, should approve the Enterprise-level policies so that they are applicable to all organizations, divisions, and subsidiaries of the Enterprise.
Operational GRC Frameworks and Policies:

As they relate to operational risks, including IT risks, the Enterprise risk framework and policies should:

- Define the objectives and approach for Enterprise operational risk management;
- Outline specific roles and accountabilities for the various operational risk committees, ITGRC committees, and the accountabilities for the various risk stakeholders;
- Specify the various approval requirements for policies and other risk oversight control documents;
- Manage the Enterprise risk appetite statements that define the acceptable and unacceptable operational risk threshold levels of the Enterprise, inclusive of IT risks;
- Create the Risk reporting levels for operational risks and controls;
- Define standard and exception risk reporting and escalation requirements.

These Enterprise policies should also define and outline requirements for various other area risk levels and definitions for the Enterprise and pertinent industry, but for purposes of this subject, the book's focus is upon operational ITGRC domain activity. In addition to the overall Enterprise risk framework policy, the GRC framework should be established for structuring consistent periodic reviews and framework maintenance across the Enterprise of all GRC policies and charters. It should include the reporting that is to be used for oversight of Enterprise risks, to include the senior ITGRC and ITGRC domain sub-committees.

EGRC Operational Risk Organizations:

In some Enterprises, and often in the financial service sector, the framework will employ the use of both senior Operating Risk Committees and Executive risk committee levels. These may include participation by the CEO, COO, CFO, CRO, Senior Legal officers, and other Senior business executive officers. They should review all risks prior to any Board of Directors updates or evaluations of these risks. These committees may direct specific actions to be taken to mitigate operational IT risk, monitor the Enterprise-wide risk management performance, review regular reports, and approve key risk management policies, including the ITGRC framework policy. However, this depends upon the oversight structure defined within the Enterprise risk framework.

Technology oversight and risk management are, as suggested, a coordinated effort between the Enterprise IT organizations, the senior ITGRC committees, the ITGRC domain sub-committees, and the Enterprise operational risk management committees. However, IT personnel or officer engagement is required on these committees due to the detailed and highly specialized technology nature of IT, rapid industry changes, and alignment to IT strategies for risk mitigation. The Enterprise framework policy can establish the key roles and responsibilities of all 3LD methodology entities as part of the accountabilities, and for the participation in ITGRC. It will also define the key reporting and monitoring requirements for domain risks. The senior ITRGC committee in some organizations may be subordinate to either a senior executive risk committee and/or report directly into the CEO or Board of Directors. This is often dependent upon the requirements of the Enterprise, organizational culture/politics, and specified organizational governance frameworks.

8.4 Developing IT Risk Appetite Statements

Driver for Risk Appetite Statements (RAS):

Enterprises and IT organizations can develop and execute against Risk Appetite Statements (RAS). These statements express the level and types of risks defined by an Enterprise's Board of Directors. It authorizes Enterprise management to undertake some risks in their pursuit of the Enterprise business objectives but within the boundaries set for its business strategy. These statements should also be included as part of the Enterprise risk management framework. RAS definitions should be approved by the Enterprise's Board of Directors and the senior executives that manage the Enterprise and ITGRC areas.

Each of the various risk operational committees, including the senior ITGRC and IT domain sub-committees, need to develop and maintain operational and compliance risk tolerances and limits for the ITGRC domains. These operational metrics and ranges should reflect the level of operational risk required to operate safely in the various IT environments and that are required to support the Enterprise's customers and stakeholders.

Defining Risk Appetite Structures:

The Enterprise and IT organizations' RAS for operational losses and risks should specify the acceptable level and exposures for operational losses, if any, and the resulting impacts to the Enterprise. It can be defined based upon historical, current estimates, and impacts from any such previous IT operational experiences. These statements are to be reflective of the various ITGRC domains services and associated potential impacts from operations within the defined IT domains. They are qualitative in nature but require an associated definition of key controls and quantitative metric thresholds for tracking operational activity against the RAS for the Enterprise.

The RAS should be communicated by the Enterprise risk and ITGRC committees to other organizational employees and stakeholders as to their objectives and expectations for ITGRC requirements. The ITGRC RAS need to be evaluated based upon their performance against such objectives. Also, the IT organizations and Enterprise need to demonstrate and adhere to consistent standards, limits, and measures defined within the ITGRC risk appetite framework. They should assure that stakeholders have the necessary experience and knowledge to execute that framework through training, certification, communication, and reporting. A good practice is to use internal IT domain websites and newsletters to communicate and explain these objectives.

The ITGRC domain areas need to establish and link to the overall Enterprise operational RAS,. They can use metrics thresholds and ranges to allow for executive understanding of the impact from RAS breaches for ITGRC control areas. Also, they can provide forward-looking metrics and trends analysis. These can enable IT and Enterprise executives to gauge the impacts of associated risk events and pressures on the various ITGRC operational limits.

The IT domain areas should develop and review risk monitoring dashboards reporting for KPI / KRI performance against thresholds, tolerances, and provide reporting measures and trends that are approaching threshold and/or breach levels. They also need to advise stakeholder committees on problem and issue root causes and provide mitigation directions and recommendations for preventing breaches and/or risk-limiting strategies.

8.5 Standard ITGRC Operational Risk Taxonomies

Many Enterprises and IT risk organizations will often categorize many of IT risks within standard taxonomies of Enterprise operational risks. These operational risk categories have been established by several standard groups across several industries and often include risk classifications as to: Actions of Personnel or Employees (Errors/Omissions and Intentional/Deliberate), System or Technology Failures, Failed Processes or Controls, and External events.

The Operational risk categories may also contain key sections for ITGRC risk taxonomies that may include the following major potential impacts and losses for the Enterprise:

- Asset Destruction and Damage - External and internal events Natural disasters, Cyber Attacks, Third-Party Suppliers, and/or other man-made events;

- Transactional and Customer Delivery Failures - Failed or delayed internal process controls and/or system processes that can cause losses or customer impacts;
- Operational Disruptions - Technology and system failures triggered by hardware, software, system design, testing issues, performance cyber-attacks, IT control failures and/or delivery change/release impacts;
- Security and Data Breaches - Security release setting and configuration issues, virus and malware events, ransom and fraud events, and data loss events or recovery impacts.

Depending upon the level of reporting data taxonomies and structures defined for ITGRC, the reporting categories should be aligned to provide impacts to these specific general sub-categories of operational risk for the Enterprise. These should align to specific standards for the Enterprise, industry, or regulators. Many of the IT industry standards (*e.g.* ISO, COBIT, NIST, etc.) discussed in this book define the various key categories and sub-categories associated with operational risk.

8.6 Enterprise GRC Program Indicator Structures

A complete suite of KPI's and KRI's should be defined and maintained by all key GRC control areas that need to be monitored as to the performance and risk exposure associated with the various operational risks. This includes all of the IT domains discussed in this book, and that represents the ITGRC oversight areas. These indicators should be developed into Enterprise-wide Compliance and Risk Dashboards or Scorecards that reflect the level of current control and trending of performance and risk for the various ITGRC domain areas.

ITGRC domain and all other dashboards/scorecard metric indicators should be practical variables that have a direct link to the target ITGRC domain area being measured; indicate the level of performance or risk for the area; provide quantifiable data in percentages, amounts, number counts, and/or ratios; provide predictive future performance and/or trending risk direction; and allow monitoring and auditing by the various performance and risk stakeholders within the TLD framework.

Enterprise Oversight Indicators:

Key Performance or Compliance Indicators ("KPI's") are used to measures the performance of a given control for ITGRC domain areas. KPI's also measure how well operational or compliance levels are being managed by the ITGRC domain areas.

Key Risk Indicators ("KRI's") provide data about the level of exposure to a particular ITGRC domain operational risk area. KRI's should have an explicit relationship with a particular IT domain risk exposure. A change in risk direction of a KRI should signal a change in risk for exposure that it represents to the Enterprise.

KPI/KRI's may also identify "Leading Metrics Indicators," that can signal expected or emerging future issues or changes in performance or risk direction for ITGRC domain areas, or "Lagging Metrics Indicators," can identify past performance or continuing ITGRC issues. All KPI and KRI indicators should provide a current snapshot of compliance/performance and risk for the ITGRC domain areas and for the targeted reporting periods. Additionally, it is important to establish guidelines on how the metrics data is to be interpreted, and for establishment of benchmark management limits. Comparing data metrics to key IT industry benchmarks can also be beneficial to the level of understanding by the Board of Directors and senior IT/Enterprise management, as it relates to ITGRC domain performance areas. However, this understanding should be rationalized to the specific risk appetite limits that are established and approved by the Board of Directors.

KPI/KRI's Accountability and Control Quality Assurance:

Each of the ITGRC domain owners are responsible for the development and maintenance of their respective KPI/KRI's and for the development and delivery of their data to the ITGRC committees. This should be done in coordination with the Enterprise ORM areas. The various ITGRC domain category owners are also responsible for establishing and maintaining processes and controls to ensure the accuracy of the underlying data and metrics within their respective performance dashboards and scorecards.

These controls should be documented and tested on a periodic basis to ensure they are working as designed. RCSA's should be performed to provide a qualitative assessment of the metrics' performance. In some organizations, it may be effective to perform special QA control testing from a centralized IT control testing organization or Enterprise-level organization. This can provide additional transparency for evaluating the performance data metrics. Additionally, the IT controls should be evaluated and audited by the framework TLOD and the results reviewed with the Board of Directors and senior risk committees.

Ongoing Data Metrics Monitoring and Reporting:

The most effective means to ensure transparent and trusted quantitative metrics in all dashboards and scorecards is to ensure that the data metrics are programmatic and created by the system of record. This data can then be integrated and/or federated to the ITGRC environments of the Enterprise.

Each of the ITGRC domains should review their respective dashboards/scorecards metrics during their periodic meetings and governance review committee sessions. Also, the quality of the dashboard and scorecard metrics should be reviewed during these sessions and any issues and concerns highlighted for management action. This should include any metrics breaches or notable trends that require escalation to the ITGRC committees or as appropriate to the various risk senior executive committees or Board of Directors.

8.7 Standards for ITGRC Risk Categories

One of the most important characteristics of good governance and for standardize risk management across the Enterprise is to ensure consistency in performance and risk evaluations. It is therefore a key requirement to outline the Enterprise level of inherent and residual risk ratings and guidance for risk exposures across the Enterprise. This entails the engagement of the key Enterprise risk organizations accountable for operational risk areas including IT domains to assist in the definition of the risk exposure classification.

Many organizations can define several standard levels of inherent and residual risk exposure categories for their Enterprises. This often take the form of risk level categories, such as: Very High Risk, High Risk, Moderate Risk, or Low-Risk categories of risk. Often these categories of risk will be specified in a color rating scheme (e.g. Orange, Red, Yellow, or Green. Etc.). This is also typical of a stoplight- type structure that appears in most Compliance and Risk Heatmaps, Controls, Dashboard/Scorecards, and/or Trending reports. The later often expressed with colored directional arrows for trending directions.

It is important for consistent risk management and communication that the level of associated risk for these risk categories is communicated and understood by all ITGRC domain areas that report compliance and risk. This is especially true when these are reported directly to ITGRC, Senior executive risk committees, or the Board of Directors.

Standard Risk Rating Category Qualifications:

Often these risk category definitions will be expressed in terms of the impact and exposure to the Enterprise in financial terms and/

or potential qualitative impacts. Also, these categories can be expressed as to the of level of exposure from a resulting operational event, impacts, or level of control failures. These defined categories can include:

- Impacts to Enterprise revenue at specific financial and/or sales revenues levels*;
- Results in varying levels of operational financial losses at specific financial loss ranges*;
- Cause impacting events that generate potential regulator fines and/or legal expenses at specific financial ranges*;
- Impacts to shareholder equity value or Enterprise capital structures*;
- Generate levels of quantifiable impacts to customers, operational service levels to customers, and/or internal stakeholders;
- Results in Enterprise reputational impacts or detrimental social-media exposure;
- Impacts to external entities, environment, and/or internal business process execution.

(* Represented in High and Low financial ranges)

The important consideration here is that all ITGRC and other Enterprise programs can use standard classifications to articulate qualitative risk definitions for their various areas.

8.8 Enterprise GRC Ecosystem and Data Concepts

An Enterprise GRC Ecosystem can provide a uniform and coordinated environment that will allow the Enterprise to assess, validate, manage, monitor, and report program compliance and aggregate risk to the Board of Directors. It should include the technology ecosystems to support the various 3LD levels (See section 8.2) of accountability to support the various governance management initiatives and required levels of document and other GRC artifact controls.

The question arises as to the level of data to be enabled and stored within the overall Enterprise GRC environment. Many Enterprises use a single GRC environment for storage and retention of all data, metrics, and documents to support GRC for all risk areas, including ITGRC data. Still others use multi-layered and staged ITGRC data and aggregation environments within various domains with multiple systems of record. This is similar to the recommended ITGRC environment that requires a tight level of control integration or federation with the key IT domain systems of record.

In some large and global Enterprises, it can be more beneficial to allow the key target risk domains to maintain their own GRC detail data that can be either federated or integrated into the Enterprise GRC environments. This can provide for specific aggregated data to be maintained for the key GRC RAS levels. It is an important decision for executives, in the development of any Enterprise GRC and ITGRC strategies. The decision may depend upon the level of complexity, internal Enterprise governance trends, corporate resources, and strategic financial investments for the required integration technologies with multiple systems of record.

Key GRC Data Sources and Integration:

Technology enablement from the federation of data to the key GRC environments is an effective methodology to control the Trusted Data interfaces and required data aggregation efforts for large environments. It also can facilitate aggregation to take place at the Enterprise level. This can also simplify the level of control and amount of data required to be stored at the Enterprise GRC level.

Maintaining framework GRC program policies, KPI's and KRI's for RAS levels, business attestations, risk appetite levels, governance issue tracking, and committee charters and minutes in a single Enterprise GRC environment is conducive to supporting a central control environment for all key governance and Board reporting activity. This also supports and simplifies key Enterprise risk requirements for supporting the mission of an Enterprise GRC.

Aggregating and/or federating the key aligned risk indicators from environments, such as the ITGRC domain control environments associated with the key risk taxonomies, provides a centralized storage location for all key KPI and KRI metrics, Dashboard/ Scorecards, and other committee-level reporting results. This can take the form of storage of the results and minutes from the various operating committees including ITGRC and/or actual aggregation of federated or integrated data from the various ITGRC environments.

In summary, GRC system strategies require consideration of several decision factors: 1) Attempting to aggregate diverse and large volumes of IT operational data is required and can be difficult for critical time-sensitive data; 2) Multiple sources and data federations increases the level of system design complexity; 3) Many systems, networks, and security application, and database metrics often do not share a common standard integration or data format to provide meaningful information metrics.

Therefore, Federation or integration of EGRC data in varying levels of control as depicted in Figure 8.1, is a recommended concept for aggregating data for overall Enterprise GRC controls. In this model, the ITGRC Trusted Systems of record provides key RAS control metrics data that is aggregated within the ITGRC control environment and can be integrated to EGRC environments. This data drives ITGRC meetings and can be stored in a summary and/or aggregated format along with all other operational risk reporting environments within the Enterprise GRC Ecosystem environments.

Figure 8.1 EGRC Management Ecosystem

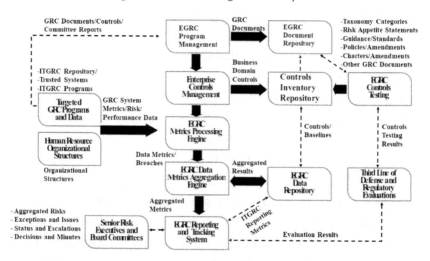

EGRC Ecosystem Solution Suppliers:

Several of the IT solution suppliers outlined in Chapter Seven ITGRC solutions are potential sources of generic GRC type functionality and can be considered as candidates for the overall EGRC Ecosystem solution. Their features are generally supporting as it relates to Enterprise GRC requirements for: compliance attestations, storage of policies/amendments, committee charters and minutes, and other GRC reporting and document artifacts.

In considering the various attributes of the software suppliers of GRC software, the Enterprise should evaluate the ease, complexity, and volume of data integrations required for the various system of records, data points, and the operational data aggregation capabilities within the target ITGRC system of record environments. These must be considered in defining the requirements and strategies for evaluating the integration, aggregation, and controlling of ITGRC data across the Enterprise. Additionally, operational IT domain software systems are complicated and focused upon domain specific functionality for operational control and management of the various IT domains. Because of this, Enterprises should carefully evaluate those suppliers that promote total solutions for all-purpose ITGRC domain functionality.

8.9 Enterprise ITGRC Reporting and Analytics

GRC business intelligence data through Enterprise GRC dashboards and scorecards are the primary aggregation point for risk data from the targeted ITGRC programs. These dashboards, alerts, and reports assist programs in the delivery of a dynamic view of ITGRC data for Enterprise risk oversight. The data in the dashboards and reports supports KPI and KRI metrics that align to the overall key operational risk taxonomies, ITGRC RAS, and senior Operating risk committees of the Enterprise.

A key component of the overall GRC and ITGRC technology strategy is ensuring that the correct level of integration occurs within the overall reporting hierarchies. This should be coupled with the correct business intelligence and analytical reporting tools selected for the GRC functions. Even more important is that the technology selected to support the GRC environments affords IT senior executives and Enterprise risk committees the ability to manage and conduct accurate oversight of the various GRC areas.

EGRC Hierarchical Reporting Category Levels:

As indicated, the level of dashboard/scorecard metrics presented for review by the particular oversight audience must be able to convey the level of ITGRC controls in an understandable manner and at an appropriate level of detail for the target audiences. As an example, the level of detail data and number of key indicators provided to the Board of Directors may be different then the level of metrics provided to the actual ITGRC operating committees or senior risk oversight groups. Figure 8.9 provides a hierarchical reporting concept for aggregating and providing levels of compliance and risk metric data that is recommended for oversight of ITGRC reporting by the IT Executive Committee.

Figure 8.9 EGRC Hierarchical Reporting Concept

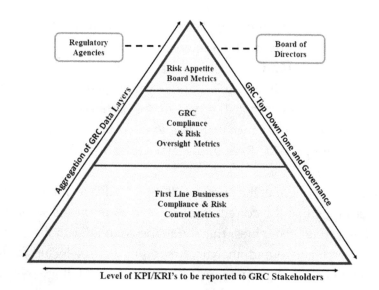

The frequency of dashboard, scorecard, and KPI/KRI's reporting should depend on the nature of the operational domain risk exposures, type indicators, technology environments, target executive audience, and as required by the senior operational domain committee, such as ITGRC. The frequencies and level of reporting required should be defined in the ITGRC framework and other GRC frameworks.

A minimum of three levels of reporting hierarchy are recommended in the various ITGRC and GRC frameworks. These levels include:

- Risk Appetite Metrics and Scorecards - Conveying the most critical summary metrics for the Enterprise for the Board Approved RAS. (e.g. Audience: Board members, Senior Operation Risk Committees, ITGRC, etc.).
- GRC Compliance and Risk Oversight Metrics - Provides subordinate-level detail to the ITGRC and other GRC committees

for overall performance of governance programs and level of risk exposures for the controls (*e.g.* Audience: Senior Operational Risk Committees, ITGRC and ITGRC sub-committees, etc.).

- FLOD Compliance and Risk Control Metrics - The most detailed level of metrics associated with IT and other operational controls (*e.g.* FLOD Controls - Audience: ITGRC sub-committees and IT organizational areas, Auditors, and Risk areas, etc.).

ITGRC Data and Analytical Organization:

All dashboard/scorecards metrics and reporting of data should be organized and structured to align with specific operational risk categories from the Enterprise standard operational risk taxonomies. The reporting and information can then be isolated based upon the specific IT business domain controls associated within these high-level operational risk taxonomies. Regardless of the reporting categories of risk defined for ITGRC or EGRC, the importance of utilizing standard reporting metrics, categorizations, and appropriate data levels is critical to IT and Enterprise executive understanding of ITGRC data. It provides them with an effective understanding of compliance and risk for the specific ITGRC business domains and the ability to quantify and predict risk directions.

ITGRC operational control and some ITGRC operational reporting categories can be structured into major control metrics areas similar to the following compliance and risk characteristics and concepts:

- Systems and Processing Risks - Risks associated with critical system availability, key IT process controls management, key IT operational and project delivery, access and securing of data, malicious technology and data attacks, obsolete technology, change management, system quality and data integrity.

The categories can include:

- Internal System Flaw: Risk due to failure or deficiency of internal systems or technologies. These can be triggered by hardware or software issues due to the inadequate planning in system design, technology architecture, business process design failures, delivery quality or operational system capacity.
- Process Management Errors: Risk because of flawed internal IT processes, controls, or systems. These can be triggered by operational control issues with the IT processes because of inadequate QA testing, maintenance, sub-par project management, or investment variances.
- IT Platform Processing Errors: Risk generated by inadequate or obsolete IT hardware and environmental platforms or facilities; or inadequate data storage, processing, and/or reporting.
- Data and Control Integrity: Risks because of data control, completeness, and accuracy of system transactions that are processed, aggregated, and/or reported by the various operating environments.

- IS/Cyber Risks - Risk associated with IT operations (including enterprise objectives, functions, Enterprise image, reputation), Enterprise assets, or individuals because of the potential for unauthorized data, data usage and/or disclosure, operational disruptions, IS environment modifications, or destruction of data and/or systems.

The categories can include:

- Data Loss: Data risk generated from an unauthorized access or use of systems, facilities, or networks environments to modify, destroy, steal, or restrict data information. This relates to inadequate applications, equipment or hardware security controls, inadequate monitoring, and/or ineffective identity and access management governance controls. It includes data breaches, external actor network intrusions, leaks of internal stakeholder/customer information, unauthorized disclosure of Enterprise data or information, data/system ransoms, encrypting and restricting access to Enterprise data.

- Disruptive Security Attacks: Risk due to intentional disruption, modification, or destruction of data, hardware, and/or information processing systems to cause operational business or economic impacts to the Enterprise. This relates to the lack of adequate environmental and system risk assessments, cyber-attack prevention planning and/or countermeasure testing, inadequate vulnerability management, inadequate Third-Party evaluations, inadequate cyber-threat intelligence, event management and response.

- Business Disruption Risk - Business risk associated with the continuity and resilience of mission-critical Enterprise business processes, operations, technologies, and environments, resulting from unexpected events, and/or significant natural hazard or technology disruption.

The categories can include:

- Systems/Technology Continuity Resilience: Risks from business impacts resulting from breakdowns of Enterprise systems or technology environments, as result of unexpected internal or external events. Includes loss of data centers, operational centers, inaccessible critical systems or due to environmental disruptions and recovery issues.
- Enterprise Business Continuity and Resilience: Risks from business or process disruption resulting from the inability

of Enterprise organizations to maintain or execute core operational processes. Includes the loss of physical assets and/or personnel who are responsible for executing operational and business processes, and recovery issues.

- Third-Party Supplier Risk - Risk associated with the of use suppliers, who provide the Enterprise with products and/or services on a continuing basis, and where vendor activity fails to meet Enterprise requirements, and/or business is not conducted in compliance with applicable laws and regulations. It includes operational failures or service disruptions, defective and faulty products, and contractual obligation issues.

Regardless of the reporting methodology that is used for management of ITGRC or EGRC programs, standard reporting metrics, risk categorizations, and appropriate hierarchical data reporting levels are critical to the Enterprise executives' ability to understand compliance and risk exposure for ITGRC business domains. The reporting data metrics should provide the basic ability to quantify and forecast ITGRC risk status for the Enterprise, from Trusted Data sources with appropriate levels of automation and integration/federation.

CHAPTER 9

Board ITGRC Governance

9.1 Board Oversight Drivers for ITGRC Activities

TODAY, MEMBERS OF the Board of Directors, and Executive management have a responsibility for oversight of the Technology and Security for systems and information. This is due to the well-publicized data breaches, such as Home Depot, Target, and Sony Corporation, Equifax, and even the 2016 US national election process; and as a result of major computer failures at national airlines, such as United, Delta, and British Airways. Each Board member and all CEO's of these Enterprises are focused like a laser beam on IT cyber and resilience technology, along with the associated IT investments required to defend against cyber-attacks and ensure computer availability. IT executives and IS officers hold equal responsibility for continued education for these Enterprise Boards on various new technology concepts and cyber-terms such as: Cyber-Actors, Identity Access, Malware, Ransomware, and other Cyber-terms. IT and IS executives are required to provide guidance and recommendations for the resilience level of Enterprise technology required to secure the IT network environments and the data of the Enterprise.

ITGRC Public Sector Oversight Drivers:

Members of the Boards for many public corporations have had the daunting task of overseeing IT capital investments and governance for many years prior to the recent security events. In fact, almost all capital expenditure projects requiring Board visibility and approval, have required ever-increasing board oversight and financial due diligence. This has been required legally since the Enron scandals in the early 2000s and the subsequent passage of the Federal Sarbanes-Oxley Act (SOX) 2002 regulations. These laws have required increased corporate accountability, governance, and financial disclosures/reporting in all public sector corporate firms by senior corporate executives.

Board Oversight Drivers in the Financial Industry:

In addition, specific industries including banking, brokerage, and insurance service firms have been under a multitude of additional regulatory changes and directions from their controlling agencies to increase Board oversight of not just cyber technology but also IT governance. These oversight areas include: application project and technology infrastructure investments; BCP and technology resilience planning/recovery; crisis and event management responses; release patching and change activities; and Third-Party service and product management. Privately held companies are also adopting and adhering to many of the public-sector governance and Board oversight practices.

Also, introduction at the turn of the twenty-first century of the Basel Banking Capital Accords and the subsequent Dodd-Frank reform regulations in 2010 have introduced further requirements on many of these financial sector firms. These increased requirements along with other regulatory focus has ratcheted up the level of corporate governance and oversight. This is true in the areas of operational risks, ITGRC domain environments, and Board of Directors IT governance. Against the backdrop of these changing directions and new regulations, the Board of Directors has become the increased target of independent accountability for ITGRC management by many regulatory agencies and industry Third-Party oversight groups.

The actual composition of publicly traded Boards and their independent affiliation nature are being interrogated along with the depth of the Board expertise and level of understanding of their Enterprise activities, and to ensure there is adequate monitoring of the various Enterprise IT operations. Boards are also being evaluated as to their understanding of their duties and responsibilities as they relate to overall Board oversight and ITGRC activities.

Additionally, many financial service firms are being examined to determine whether the Board members have adopted governance frameworks, policies, procedures, and monitoring IT operations on a continuous basis to ensure the firms are conducting safe and secure operations. During regulatory and audit cycles this has become prevalent in the area of technology operations and service delivery.

9.2 Board ITGRC Oversight Responsibilities

Public sector corporate Boards have a responsibility to their shareholders and customers, together with the Enterprise's senior executive management, to ensure that the Enterprise identifies, assesses, manages, and invests in the overall control of IT risks. The Boards must ensure that IT frameworks, policies, and controls are established for the Enterprise, and that these define the protocol and acceptable risk management levels of IT across the Enterprise.

Also, on an ongoing basis the Board needs to understand the impact and effects of all identified IT risks and ensure an ongoing planning and mitigation process for all of these IT risks, to include: IS, BCP, TRDR, ITSM, Change and Release Control, IT PPM and Project, IT Technology Obsolescence and Continuing Innovation, and Third-Party management and accountability risks.

Typically, the entire Board of Directors should be knowledgeable and exposed to all of the major IT risks associated with the delivery of service and products for the Enterprise. But specifically, most public boards will engage and appoint a series of committees that will focus on key elements of risk management, oversight, and governance, including Operational and ITGRC risks.

9.3 ITGRC Board Roles and Accountabilities

In most public sectors, Board governance protocols for most Enterprises have six to seven major oversight committees. There are three common standard committees that are focused on controls and risks. These are often defined as the Audit Committee, Risk Committee and Corporate Governance Committee. Each of these committees and their independent Board members execute the key accountabilities of their respective governance oversight as defined by their organizational charters.

Key Board Committee ITGRC Roles:

As it relates to ITGRC, the standard committees focus from a governance perspective are the: Audit, Corporate Governance, and Risk Committees. General responsibilities of these committees can include:

- Audit Control Committee - Assists the overall Board of Directors in meeting their responsibilities to the shareholders and investors, related to the soundness and integrity of financial statements, ITGRC activities related to IT controls and regulatory/legal requirements, and the performance of internal/external TLOD audit functions
- Risk Management Committee - Provides oversight of the Enterprise global risk frameworks and all of the various Enterprise risks. This is inclusive of all Operational risk and IT Risk Management. The Risk committee will review, approve,

and manage IT risk exposure, and as required, question and challenge IT strategy, direction, and management activities that can expose the Enterprise to adverse risk and/or breach the approved RAS for IT services and operational delivery.

- Enterprise Governance Committee - Develops and recommends to the overall board among other responsibilities, the various Enterprise governance principles applicable to Enterprise governance and operating principles of the Enterprise, and ensures key charters are established for the various boards committees.

Board Risk Committee ITGRC Accountabilities:

By far the most involved Board responsibility and focused activity for ITGRC governance in many Enterprises will be the engagement of the Board Risk Management Committee. Their activity will encompass the major IT organizational compliance and risk management oversight functions. This requires the primary approval of ITGRC key frameworks and policies, establishment of periodic basic approval and IT performance review cycles and evaluating program framework changes as business drivers and regulations dictate. Also, the board should ensure that various ITGRC frameworks are examined by internal and external independent auditors as the Enterprise TLOD, and any TLOD recommendation, and audit findings are resolved by the targeted IT organizational domains.

The Board Risk Committee should ensure that all required Operational risk, ITGRC frameworks, and IT control participants are knowledgeable in their positions and that they are provided the required training. These should be dictated as part of the ITGRC various frameworks. On a regular basis, the Board Risk Committee should participate in required framework activities as dictated by the IT domain policies, and receive required periodic updates on IT strategies, domain program activities, and overall IT operational activities. Both the Risk Committee and entire Board of Directors should be required to be included in the participation of various IT-based risk analysis, evaluation scenarios, and other types of risk simulations and exercises.

Additionally, depending upon the industry of the Enterprise, specific regulatory requirements may exist for Board and Risk committee activities. These may need to be incorporated into the various ITGRC primary and IT sub-domain frameworks and operational activities.

9.4 Board ITGRC Framework Controls

The ITGRC frameworks and policies should be developed by the respective IT domain SLOD control area but approved by both the targeted ITGRC senior and subordinate committees and the Board of Directors Risk Committees. Enterprise should have standard ITGRC framework programs that are associated with the domain risk assessments and standards associated with the defined ITGRC business domains.

Framework Approval and Control Requirements:

The Board Risk Committee should approve ITGRC frameworks and policies on a periodic basis. However, many of the standard IT domains need to be fully implemented, designed to meet the board requirements, and the RAS of the Enterprise. ITGRC frameworks and policies are foundational components for Board approval and governance of ITGRC areas. It is equally important to develop internal IT systematic controls for ongoing compliance, for Boards to require audits and random testing of these controls and ensure key executive officer accountability for each of these ITGRC domain activities.

Controls Design and Evaluation for the Board:

These internal controls can include: standards, procedures, processes, and monitoring designed to minimize and control the risks of the targeted ITGRC domains and achieve compliance within the Board-approved framework policies. These controls maybe, as it has been noted in Chapters Seven and Eight, inventoried in standard ITGRC and/or Enterprise risk control libraries. They can be associated to the key operational risk taxonomies and reported to the board for ensuring oversight of the various ITGRC compliance areas and controls. As defined, the Board should require the TLOD and reporting of testing of these ITGRC controls to the Audit and Risk Committees by the ITGRC committee chairman, and as required by the corporate governance framework, to the overall Board.

The Board expectations for TLOD exams and evaluations include: a sufficient level of detail review with an overall program evaluation of ITGRC activities. QA-level assessment of the various IT domain control; and compliance programs. In general, the TLOD independent testing of the ITGRC frameworks and controls should at a minimum include:

- Assessment of the overall adequacy and effectiveness of the various ITGRC compliance and controls. This should include: policies, procedures, processes, and control reporting, including SOX controls.
- Evaluations of IT executive management efforts to mitigate deficiencies in control effectiveness, previous evaluations and controls testing, and any outstanding findings.
- Reviews of the various ITGRC risk assessments, and a reasonableness test and alignment to the overall Board RAS defined for the various ITGRC domains, and any alignment of associated regulatory or specific IT-defined standards.
- Evaluations of ITGRC-compliance program participants training and organizational knowledge levels, and IT program organization structures.
- Performance by the TLOD participants of required risk-based testing of key ITGRC domain transactions and operational monitoring effectiveness.

- The results of such testing and evaluations by the TLOD, should be presented to both the key Board committees, and authorized by the Chief Internal Auditor and/or External Independent Audit Firm executives. While reporting of the ITGRC senior executive and CEO of the Enterprise are required operating requirements, a fiduciary obligation of the Board to its shareholders, investors, and customers is to ensure independent evaluations of the ITGRC framework and activities.

9.5 Board ITGRC Risk Appetite Statement Controls

The Board via the Risk Management Committee and other required Board committees (e.g. Audit Committee, etc.) oversees the Enterprise's performance for the approval of the various Operational Risk and IT Risk Appetite Statements. The Board in exercising their oversight role, should approve the RAS, review any required IT dashboards and scorecards, and regular reports from the senior ITGRC and Operational risk management committees. Each of the key Enterprise ITGRC domain committees will establish the various RAS for their respective areas for approval and reporting to the Board.

Risk Appetite Board Notifications:

As it relates to high risk events and incidents, the most senior Enterprise Risk officer should inform the Board Risk Committee and/ or Lead Director, when the ITGRC senior executive committee determines a pertinent or potential IT issue. This is especially true when risk elements can exceed the stated risk exposure of targeted ITGRC RAS threshold levels. The need to inform or escalate to the committee should be based upon quantitative metrics and facts that are supported by qualitative statements, risk direction and trend, and recommended mitigations and responses to such issues. The review should include new or potential threats or risk assessments associated with any of the ITGRC domain risks.

Some of the key issues that can be included in the consideration of Risk Appetite notification or escalation to the Risk Management committee include:

- Breaches approved RAS and related risk tolerances;
- Key audit results from 3LD examinations;
- Significant Trend direction changes for key RAS data;
- SOX related violations or material maters associated with ITGRC SOX controls;
- IT violations of applicable laws, regulations, or policies;
- IT-related events that can cause material adverse impacts to financial results, customers, or the reputation of the Enterprise.

ITGRC Program Performance Board Updates:

On a regular periodic basis, the Board Risk Committee, and at least annually, the full Board of Directors, often can be presented updates and reporting by the Senior ITGRC executive. This should represent the overall ITGRC domain compliance and risk activities and specific reporting on the metrics and thresholds associated with the Enterprise IT domain risk appetite statements.

Additionally, the Board Risk Committee can be provided a quantitative dashboard and scorecard that conveys in summary form the aggregate view of risk assessment based upon the key inherent and residual risk of ITGRC activities. These can include the standard Operational Risk definitions and risk categorizations established by the Enterprise risk framework.

9.6 ITGRC Program Board Activities

All Board members, no matter what their business background or experience, should be oriented to the specific general risk exposures and operating concepts for Enterprise IT. The key ITGRC accountability Board committees designated in the corporate governance framework and Board Risk Committee, maybe exposed in more detail to the overall IT Operational Risk frameworks of the Enterprise. As it relates to the framework, specific training can be provided as to their key responsibilities and accountabilities related to the ITGRC policies.

Additionally, the key ITGRC board committees can receive IT knowledge transfer and program exposure on a continuous basis at a required knowledge level. This will include reviews of evolving threat assessments, various technology exposures, and specific strategy concepts for each of the key IT domain program areas to include:

- Cyber threats, evolving cyber industry and associated national state intelligence, and operational exposures for the Enterprise.
- Technology obsolescence forecasts to include investment and service impact rationalization.
- Emerging IT innovations, future industry strategies, and perceived market disruptions; Competitive Enterprise IT advantages and service optimizations and performance.
- IT Resilience, cyber, and continuity capabilities, and participation in crisis response exercises.
- Key technology skill-sets inventories and personnel risks for turnover and retirement.
- Enterprise technology investment forecasts with three- and five-year timeframes.

9.7 Board ITGRC Program Monitoring and Reporting

At least annually, and per stated framework periodic updates, the Board Risk Committee should be presented with the required board ITGRC framework performance levels, risk exposures, and program compliance levels. At a minimum the following major categories of information can be included for each of the ITGRC program domain categories:

- Qualitative risk assessment program profiles to include: discussions of IT inherent and residual risk, risk trending direction, level of threats and impact considerations, and ITGRC program controls performance.
- Risk appetite performance metrics to include: quantitative metrics for the RAS-defined variables for conveying the status of the risk categories within the required performance tolerance levels, and assertion of any RAS breaches.
- Board level quantitative KPI and KRI metric domain dashboards/scorecards, as defined per the domain ITGRC program policy.
- Program key exceptions and issues with associated impacts, and root cause analysis with mitigation strategies.
- Results of key ITGRC program regulator examinations, findings, and mitigation strategies, and updates on resolution strategies.
- ITGRC program TLOD internal and external audit results, controls evaluations, and discussion of TLOD findings, and updates on issue progress and closure activities.

All reporting to the Board of Directors and Senior executives of the Enterprise requires reinforcement of the level of risks permitted within the RAS and ITGRC controls across the Enterprise. A certain level of risk is to be expected and permitted within the ITGRC Board-approved framework. This is due to the risk prevalent in all businesses' use of technology operations, services, and strategies. Enterprises can provide for this within their ITGRC and Enterprise framework, as dictated by the Board, for tolerance of IT Enterprise risk.

However, these risks require the appropriate top-down level of IT governance, control, and risk evaluation from the Board and senior executives. To accomplish this requires ITGRC control information and trusted data to be presented via a consistent, accurate, and timely report methodology. The ITGRC program, as presented in this book, needs to be optimized through efficient automation, due diligence reporting, and by integrating or federating ITGRC Ecosystems across the Enterprise.

Glossary of Terms

Access Rights - Computer system and technology users are granted permission to access a particular network, application, or operating environment via access logic and software. Access rights are a primary control for securing computer environments and are normally role-based for the varying access levels.

Active-Active - Computer technology architecture concept that provides for continuous processing between two identical network and processing environments often located within two separate physical data centers or logical processing environments to support failover with full redundancy of data and databases via identical applications, hardware, and network environments. Often referenced as "Continuous Operations".

Active Passive - Technology recovery design concept for data centers that uses two exact designed processing environments. One environment waits in a non-active or passive state for the active processing environment or equipment to be disrupted, and where data is replicated to the passive site in a manner that provides for minimum data loss.

Agile Development - A methodology and set of principles for development and delivery of requirements and software that promotes a collaborative model process. It uses iterative design and coding concepts, adaptive approaches, and products to deliver innovative solutions into the Enterprise. Program code is delivered in multiple phases by self-directed teams with cross-functional business input and DevOps SME's

All Hazard Planning - A Business Continuity planning strategy that is a risk-based approach used for creation of general baseline continuity plans and strategies to respond to business disruptions and/or major disaster events. It provides the ability for business units to plan for potential high- probability risk impacts.

API - Application Program Interface is a standard communication or program code set that provides standard logic coding structures for use in interfacing or integrating other computer programs, technology environments, or processes to software or other computer infrastructures.

Appendix J - FFIEC regulatory requirement that defines the guidelines for financial institutions to manage Third-Party suppliers of outsourced technology, issued in 2015.

ASP - (Application Service Provider) - Third-Party software suppliers that provide applications processing services and software functionality over the Internet to Enterprises in a fee-for-service operating model.

Authentication - A process for identification of the credentials of users or individuals that access computer and operating environments. The credentials can include: user names, id's, password, security tokens, or other secondary/tertiary access mechanisms.

Basel Accords - A set of banking standards and recommendations developed and issued by the Basel Committee on Banking Supervision over the last century (Basel 1, 2, and 3 Accords).

Best Practice Standards - Best Practices standards introduced as a set of techniques or methodologies across the IT industry, which have proven to be consistent in generating a repeatable result for management of IT technology and/or operations.

Big Data - IT terminology used to define a storage methodology and strategy for management and processing of large volumes and multiple layers of data stores and environments.

Biometric Authentication - A technology access methodology that identifies and validates users accessing computer or system environments that uses physical and individual human biometric attributes, such as fingerprint, vision, facial, or voice identification technology or mechanics.

BCP - A Business Continuity Strategy and/or Plan document or construct for documenting processes for continuation of business and/or resumption of services after and during a business interruption or disaster event that has resulted from natural hazards, man-made events, or operational impacts.

Black Art - a term applied to a mystical technique, as used in this book, to describe a project management capability of past project experience, political savvy, and skilled project managers.

Business Impact Analysis - A framework risk assessment and prioritization process within a BCP Program used to determine and evaluate the potential effects and exposure from impacts to critical business operations due to a disaster, man-made impact, or emergency.

Capacity Management - Component in the ITIL and COBIT methodologies for validating that IT applications and infrastructure environments are structured and sized for optimum processing and availability for both current and future business requirements.

Capital Expenditure - Financial term used to express the purchase of IT assets or other Enterprise equipment/facilities that require capital funding review by the Enterprise.

Change Control System - Automated system environment for managing any modifications to production or other IT environments throughout the Enterprise or within Data Centers.

Change Severity - As part of the ITSM methodology, it measures or assigns the level of priority and potential risk impact of a change to production environments for the Enterprise (e.g. High severity; etc.)

CCO - Chief Continuity Officer accountable for management of all technology resilience and business continuity in an Enterprise.

CIO - Chief Information Officer, often the highest authoritative officer, managing either the entire IT organization, and/or specific IT domains, such as application development and support, etc.

CISO - Chief Information Security Officer, an emerging role over the last ten to fifteen years, with accountability for cyber and IS activities within an IT organization.

Cloud Services - Cloud services are an internet-based technology operating model that provides computer processing environments and/or resources, or other technology services over the internet in a subscription. Service product.

CMDB - Configuration Management Database is a data repository that houses information regarding key components of data and components for all of the IT physical assets housed within IT and Enterprise environments and data centers.

CMS - Configuration Management System is an automated environment used to manage IT physical assists and component relationships, often in a federated environment.

COBIT - Control Objectives for Information and Related Technologies is a standard framework, and methodology for managing IT development and delivery environments, established by ISACA.

COBOL - Common Business Oriented Language is a legacy computer programming language used in most mainframe and some mid-range environments and systems. Developed in the 1950s, in 2018, COBOL remains one of the major programming languages used throughout the globe, with an estimated two-hundred-fifty to three-hundred+ billion lines of computer code in operation globally.

Concentration Risk - A risk term that represents an extremely high level of exposure for some business domains, such as credit risk, or in one particular risk category or component. For IT domains, it represents high numbers of vulnerabilities or services at risk in a particular location, or in one specific operating environment (e.g. high number of obsolete technologies in Data Center A, etc.)

Control Metrics - A set of variables and parameters that measures the effectiveness of ITGRC framework and program level controls and risk throughout the various IT operating domains.

Crisis Communication - A messaging and/or standard public announcement structure to maintain communication protocols and information dissemination during a specific Enterprise incident or IT-related outage that impacts customers or the public. Typically, standard messaging and crisis plans are developed by IT, BCP, IS, and risk management areas to support Crisis Communication.

CRO - Chief Risk Officer, often a senior Enterprise officer, accountable for managing financial, reputational, operational, legal and regulatory risk across the Enterprise. For the IT organization, the position is accountable to the senior IT organizational officer, and responsible for managing all ITGRC compliance and risk structures.

CSIRT - Cyber Security Intelligence and Incident Response Team, a group and/or groups of team members that are focused on continual evaluation, analysis, monitoring. and responding to cyber threats, vulnerabilities, and security risks across the Enterprise and IT environments.

CTO - Chief Technology Officer, who in most enterprises manages the overall IT operational and infrastructure environments, both delivery and support; in some organizations may manage development depending upon the IT culture or organizational strategy. In some Enterprise, the CTO maybe the highest IT executive or also the CIO.

Cyber Actors - Individuals or organizations that intentionally create and/or promote cyber threats against an Enterprise or governments. It includes organized crime, national state, internal employees, and/or political/social activists.

Data Breach - Represents an intentional data leak event or disclosure of customer or other Enterprise information as a result of cyber actor attacks or specific IT vulnerabilities

Data Center Tiers - A multi-tier category level of availability and redundancy, as developed by the Uptime Institute (Tier I to IV).

Data Corruption - Represents impacts to stored or processed data that renders the data unusable, unreadable, or inaccessible to IT operating environment, application, or business users. Sources are typically man-made (e.g. cyber-attack, programming errors, hardware failures, etc.).

Data Snaps - A storage technology data concept, used in back-up and recovery programs, or DR operating environments. It allows for multi-point-in-time capture of data or databases to assist in expediting recovery from some type of data corruption or other recovery event.

Data Vault - A storage environment that represent a historical point-in-time protective copy of data or databases that is often segregated from a network and/or available for recovery as a result of major data corruption events.

DDoS - Distributed Denial of Service is a type of cyber-attack where a cyber actor uses multiple Internet Protocol (IP) addresses to launch multiple (several thousands) simultaneous transaction accesses to a network or application service, over the internet, or to make a service unavailable to authorized users of the network or service.

Dependency Gap - In BCP and Technology Resilience, the difference between the availability of technology and dependent business process needs, as measured between the RTO of the technology and business process.

Dependent Processes - A business process that is dependent upon required IT application, infrastructures, or other upstream business processes.

DevOps - DevOps is a conceptual approach that introduces a close collaboration between various business lines, to include IT development and infrastructure operations, for promoting efficient and continuous IT delivery.

Disaster Recovery - A planning process, framework, and program to ensure the continuity and availability of technology environments or applications disrupted after a major natural or man-made event.

Dodd Frank - A federal law, Dodd-Frank Wall Street Reform and Consumer Protection Act (Public Law 111-203, H.R. 4173) passed by Congress in 2010 that introduced major changes of financial regulation in the United States to the banking industry.

DMZ - A technological architecture concept for isolation and design of the physical and logical layers of network boundaries (demilitarized zone).

DRaS - Disaster Recovery as a service is a type of Cloud service or product supplied to Enterprises to enable continuous services after a disaster or service interruption at a particular Enterprise location on a service-fee schedule with recovery through the Cloud and over the internet.

ENS - Emergency Notification System, an automated environment, that provides mass communication and messaging capabilities via phone, SMS text, smartphone, email, and alerting devices to alert stakeholders, employees, the public, or other entities as to an event or incident. It can provide instructions and next steps during an emergency or after an event.

Emergency Service Request - A request to expedite IT service repair or incident response for a specific IT event or disabled service response that requires priority-level attention to correct an IT problem or incident.

Encryption - A technology concept in security controls for encoding data and/or messages so that only an authorized person or system component can process or read the data or message.

Entitlements - A security control environment that grants permissions and usage privileges to a particular computer or system user to operate an IT application, network, or operating environment.

Evidentiary Results - Represents the efforts of applying key controls to compliance and due diligence activities in any compliance or risk program e.g. Third-Party due diligence, and often stored in a document control library (e.g. audits, questionnaires, validation reports, testing documents, etc.).

External Audits - An independent validation, testing, and/or inspection of a target methodology, program, or environment by outside Third-Party or industry body.

Fall Over Testing - A resilience testing technique that demonstrates and validates an operating environment or applications ability to continue processing or operations at an alternate location

Federal Heightened Standards - The Office of the Comptroller of the Currency (OCC) established final guidelines in September 2014 to strengthen the governance and risk management practices of large financial institutions > 50 Billion dollars. These established specific criteria for development of risk-based frameworks and roles across the banking industry.

Federated Cloud - An operational and delivery model that provides both internal and external services to end users or customers via logical network linked connections and technology.

Financial Control Systems - A group of Enterprise accounting, budgetary, and forecast systems or applications that provide the fiduciary financial control for an Enterprise.

Fin-Tech - An IT industry concept that represents a collection of external service suppliers providing new or innovative products and services to the financial industry and often seeded in the customer disintermediation of services.

GDPR - General Data Projection Regulation, a European Union Commission regulatory requirement to protect and strengthen data for European Union member citizens effective in 2Q2018. Firms failing to comply with requirements can incur large fines.

GRC - Governance, Risk, and Compliance represents the umbrella term for integration of Enterprise governance activities, management of the compliance to oversight programs, and the associated risk management activities of the Enterprise.

Hardware Configurations - Describes the physical and resource settings of particular IT asset or resources used in IT operating environments.

Help Desk - An IT organization resource area responsible for providing and assisting with information to support IT assets and environmental usage, and problem response.

Hot Site - A business continuity and resilience strategy where an alternate location is built and equipped to recover a data center or business operation in case of a major disaster or business outage, and where processing can be shifted, as a result, of such events.

HVAC - Heating, Ventilation, and Air-Conditioning, provides mechanical infrastructure for Data Centers and Operational buildings technology for management of indoor climate environments (e.g. cooling for raised floor areas, etc.)

Identity Access - An IS governance control that authorizes and enables assigned individuals to access specific application or technologies within IT and Enterprise environments.

Incident Management - A process and protocol for managing IT and other Enterprise events that can impact Enterprise customers, stakeholders, and employees

Inherent Risk - The risk of conducting IT operations or other Enterprise business activity, which can pose a threat, prior to any controls or mitigation strategies being in place to control the risk.

ISACA - ISACA is a nonprofit association that provides professional best practices and advocates these practices in the IT industry in key IT governance and risk management areas.

ISO - International Organization for Standards, develops and publishes key IT industry standards.

IT Domains - References organizational and/or operational environments within an IT organization.

ITGRC Ecosystems - Information Technology Governance Compliance and Risk, are a group of programs, automated systems, and processing environments used for managing the complex data relationships and controls for effective measurement and oversight of Information Technology services and operations.

IT Recovery Plan - In Disaster Recovery or Resilience programs, it defines a recovery strategy or document plan for recovery of specific infrastructure or application environments. It provides the protocol for recovery of the targeted plan focus. In ITIL, described as a, Service Continuity Plan (SCP).

ITIL - Information Technology Infrastructure Library is a best-practice methodology for management and alignment of IT services to business requirements and needs. ITIL is a registered trademark of the UK Government's Office of Government Commerce, who originated development of the standard.

ITSM - Information Technology Service Management represents a set of best processes and methodologies for managing the full-service IT delivery cycle.

Key Controls - ITGRC procedures to ensure repeatable and predictable results from a particular process or framework component. In SOX regulatory audit activity described as a Key Control.

Knowledge Database - ITSM automation environment that provides a centralized repository for information and knowledge of IT problems, activities, and services that supports IT organization ITSM activities.

KPI - Key Performance Indicators are used to measure the performance of a given set of controls for ITGRC domain areas.

KRI - Key Risk Indicators provide data about the level of exposure to a particular ITGRC domain operational risk area.

Lotus 1-2-3 - A major IBM PC-based spreadsheet application developed by Lotus Corporation, which replaced VisiCalc as the most popular PC based application in late 1980's.

Machine Assembler - One of the lowest levels of programming languages that has the set of commands that are similar to machine code.

Mainframe - Large business computers capable of processing large amounts of data and instructions and have the ability to manage access by multiple concurrent transactions sessions. Used for large bulk batch processing and critical applications, often operational in the insurance, financial, and airline industries.

Malware - Malicious software installed on a computer by cyber actor activity to disrupt computer operations, damage equipment, or collect data; includes computer viruses, spyware, and other computer attack software.

Metrics - Measurements used in ITGRC or GRC programs for management and evaluation of program controls, performance, and levels of risk.

Midrange - Computer server environments that execute middle-ware operating or distributed application environments.

Mirrored Processing Site - A mirrored processing site is a duplicate technology processing site or section of a data center, capable of providing the required technology, systems, and network access for users, and contains the same data as the processing site that the environment mirrors.

Mission Critical - A computer system or business process that is essential to the operations or execution in the Enterprise.

MSA - Master Service Agreement, a template used by legal or procurement organizations for managing Enterprise standard performance by a Third Party for specific IT domain and other Enterprise requirements in a contract relationship.

Network Appliance - Network addressable processing equipment designed for specific business purposes or execution on the network environment.

Network End-Points - A network end-point is an internet-capable network or hardware device accessible on an Enterprise network.

Network Perimeter - A boundary of network and external layers that provides an architecture of multiple levels of network defense and provides perimeter protection for internal Enterprise IT assets and networks (See DMZ).

Network Latency - a technology architecture term used to define delays in the data transmission from Point A to Point B, often described in terms of milliseconds or minutes delay.

NFPA - National Fire Protection Association, an independent association that sets specific codes and standards for building, processes, services design, and installation; NFPA1600 is one of the current DHS standards for Business Continuity processes.

NIST - National Institute of Standards, a Department of Commerce organization, founded in the early 1900s, that is responsible for setting and publishing specific standards for IT environmental domain activity, such as Information Security and other industrial or business activities and products; includes standards for measurement and/or product design.

NPV - Net Present Value is a financial term used to describe the calculation of the present value for an investment strategy or asset acquisition for IT purposes. The overall Cap-Ex evaluation depends upon NPV to support IT Project/Technology delivery and investments.

Operational Analytics - A methodology for analyzing, reporting, and managing information from IT operations data targeted to identify root cause problems, environmental variances, improve IT performance, and predict potential problems.

Patches - An IT software change to a specific operating environment, application, or IT infrastructure environment, often referenced in terms of IS security or operating environment updates.

PDU - Power Distribution Units are electrical devices used to control the distribution of power to individual computer equipment, servers, and workload racks within a Data Center Operational units.

Physical Security Controls - Protective security procedures and devices for controlling access to networks, facilities, computer applications, and operating environments.

Primary Data Center - An Enterprises Main Data Center facility used to centrally house production legacy computer applications, networks, and operating environments.

Production Migration - Product migration is the process for moving IT environmental or application updates into the production execution environments.

QA - Quality Assurance in the IT domain is a process for validating that the system and technologies delivered to production meet the requirements and specifications of the particular project or technology investment.

QC - Quality Control in governance and risk management for IT domains IT process delivery for validation of ITGRC controls.

RACI Model - A matrix table structure that describes participants of a process by their roles, tasks, and/or accountabilities in terms of: Responsible, Accountable, Consultative, and Informed activities.

Raised Floor - Used in Data Centers, a raised floor is a structural floor with removable tiles that is built above the base building concrete slab, to provide space for computer and network cables, specialized cooling pipes, and power cables.

Ransomware - Ransomware is a type of malware that a cyber-attacker installs on a computer that either limits the access to a system or locks the system or data files from access by a computer user.

RAS - Risk Appetite Statement defines a particular Enterprise risk area or IT domain acceptable risk level that an Enterprise can accept in the standard or exception processing or technology operating environments

RAS Breaches - Represents a threshold level violation detected and reported because of a specific limiting range deviation for the defined ITGRC or GRC control area.

RCSA - Risk Control Self-Assessment is a methodology used in risk management practices for qualitative assessment of the inherent risks of IT or business processes, and the effectiveness of specific controls.

Red Line - The process in contract management of identifying changes, additions and deletions of verbiage in a MSA or contract.

Release Management - A key component of the ITSM methodology that focuses on design, control, and management of specific periodic or scheduled release payloads of updates and/or new technology into production and other operating environments.

Replication - A database backup strategy and group of industry technologies for duplicating and distributing data and database objects from one environment to another environment (e.g. production to DR), and that uses industry software to synchronize the data between environments.

Residual Risk - The remaining risk and exposure after specific mitigating controls have been implemented to reduce or resolve inherent risk exposures.

Resilience Management - The practice of managing the availability of software, infrastructures, applications, and technologies at the highest level of access.

Resource Availability - Within the Project or Technology delivery cycle, represents the availability of assigned resources for time-on-task vs. non-project work activity (e.g. vacation, holidays, jury duty, etc.).

Reverse 911 - Mass communication technology used to notify residents and public communities via phone of an emergency event or provide specific instructions, e.g.: Shelter-in-Place, evacuation orders, etc.

Risk Sensitivity - A process used within Third-Party governance and risk management to further filter the risks of an Enterprise due to the use of Third Parties (e.g. levels of security risk, resilience, and other risks, etc.),

ROI - Return on Investment is a financial performance measurement used to evaluate the future profitability and financial benefits of technology investments.

RPG - Report Program Generator is a programming language developed by IBM in the mid-1950s and used on punch-card computers originally but still in use today in a more advanced language form and used on IBM computers (e.g. mid-range computers, etc.).

RPO - Recovery Point Objective represents the maximum allowable time and level of loss that a business can accept in data or information that could be lost from an IT or processing service interruption or due to an incident or impact event.

RTO - Recovery Time Objective represents the amount of time, and service level for business process, functions, applications, or technology systems that must be restored after a disaster or business/process disruption to avoid unacceptable outcomes to the business from the event

SaaS - Software as a Service is a software product licensing concept and delivery model where a software product is licensed on a subscription or rental basis, and is hosted by a Third-Party supplier. It is a product or service hosted within the Cloud (access over the internet).

Safe Harbor - A resilience and risk management data concept that uses off-line or off-network technology to preserve Enterprise data and protect the Enterprise from major data-corruption events, (e.g. data vault, etc.).

Scorecards - A category of performance and risk-reporting structures for consolidating a specific control area or IT domain group for tracking governance activities, (e.g. IT Domain Scorecards, etc.).

SCP - Service Continuity Plan is an ITIL construct template for defining the recovery concepts and strategies for a particular application, IT infrastructure, or operating environment.

SDC - Software Delivery Change is a grouped component, as defined in this book for SDLC or ITIL methodologies that focuses on the service and delivery and change management steps, within the defined Life Cycles.

SDLC - Software Development Life Cycle is a software development process concept that structures the software delivery steps, from requirements through design and specification, to testing and implementation.

Security Tokens - An IS control mechanism, either device or software, that is used to authenticate computer and network users to the environment, (e.g. hardware tokens, etc.)

Servers - As it relates to computer hardware, represents equipment that acts as a central network processing hub for access from other computers or network nodes often referred to as a Client-Server topology.

Service Catalog - A centralized repository of all of the Enterprise IT portfolio of services and products supplied to stakeholders in the Enterprise via shopping-cart metaphor.

SIG - Standard Information Gathering questionnaire used to provide specific information about a particular Third-Party organization, and the services or products they provide with focus on specific IT domains (e.g. security, resilience, financials, etc.).

SIG Lite - A simpler and abbreviated version of the full SIG and often used to pre-qualify Third Parties for further risk-sensitive analysis.

Six Sigma - A series of engineering concepts to help improve the quality and processes in technology and/or product delivery.

SLA - Service Level Agreement is a defined service commitment between either internal IT processing organizations, and/or Third Parties, to delivery specific services to the contracted customer, or internal Enterprise organizations. It defines the performance standards for the services and a specific response or service time for the service.

Smart Cards - A small credit-card-sized card that contains integrated circuit for storing security control and other credentials data for use in authentication functions. Often used where strong security control and authentication is required for technology access. EMV credit cards are an example of such cards.

SME - Subject Matter Experts represent personnel or areas with expertise or knowledge of a particular IT or Enterprise governance domain or operating environment.

SOC Reports - System and Organization Controls reporting is a series of standard reports (1,2,3) regarding specific internal controls areas (e.g. financial, security, resilience, data center, etc.) and methodologies used within the organization. Developed by the AICPA.

SOX - Sarbanes Oxley represents specific statutory financial reporting requirements that define control levels for various IT domains and controls. The Sarbanes-Oxley Act was passed by Congress, in 2002 for protection of shareholders, and provides specific public company compliance requirements.

Split Operations - Business continuity strategy where business processes or computer operations are divided or split between two or more sites, and where the workload is distributed between sites. One site is capable of assuming a full load when service is interrupted at the other site(s).

SQL Server - Microsoft software product that provides relationship database management services and structure. Released by Microsoft in the late 1980s, and a primary database technology used throughout the IT global industry.

Steering Committees - A specific group of stakeholders focused on decision processes, program, project performance, and key governance or management of a specific IT domain or Enterprise governance area.

Stoplight Reporting - A specific type of reporting structure used within ITGRC and Enterprise GRC reporting of performance and risk metric levels and/or score cards. Stoplight reports usually define levels of metrics or performance in terms of Red, Yellow, and Green, where Red indicates a problem.

Supplier Management System - A computerized system that provides management of Third-Party supplier data and a data repository of key supplier information and performance data.

Synchronous - Represents a type of communication transmission architecture for moving data between multiple sites at near real-time speeds. Asynchronous implies a delay in the transmission and at specified intervals for movement of data between sites.

SWAG Estimates - Scientific Wild Guess is a slang term used to define a rough estimate of time schedules or investment dollars, or a high-level estimate guess.

Technology Obsolescence - Represents a level of useful service to the Enterprise because of the introduction of newer market technologies, updated versions of the product or software, lack of functionality or optimization, or technology has reached useful end of life.

Technology Vulnerabilities - A technology design flaw or level of technical consistency or operating level that opens the technology to either performance, cyber, or Resilience threats.

Three Lines of Defense (3LD) - A corporate strategy for managing governance, compliance, and risk across the Enterprise that organizes three levels of defense: controls for various Enterprise risk management and domain areas; First Line (FLOD-Domain Function Execution); Second Line (SLOD-Monitoring and Control), Third Line (TLOD-Independent Audit validation).

Ticketing System - A software system that manages and controls the issuance, tracking, reporting, and update of service tickets issued by a Help Desk IT service organization or Analytics software for issues, special requests, or discovered anomalies.

Transfer to Hot Site - A disaster recovery strategy that provides for the movement of processing computer services to a duplicate or mirrored site that is enabled with a duplicate operating environment.

Transfer Work - A business continuity recovery strategy where work is transferred from a primary production or servicing site to a secondary site.

Trusted Data Sources - As used in this book, represents a defined technology source of data that is validated and managed by another technology, application, or federated system.

TVA - Threat Vulnerability Assessment is a risk methodology or process for identifying, quantifying, and/or ranking the level of a threat from a specific natural or man-made event, and/or the associated vulnerability of a specific asset for the enterprise supplier management system or database that represents the unique identification for a Third Party for reference in all other relationships and/or system that integrated or federate to the Third-Party supplier management system.

UpTime Institute - An independent research and consulting organization focused on development of data center performance, efficiency, and reliability for mission-critical corporate infrastructures. It assesses fees for both service evaluations and independent certifications.

Virtual Tape Library - A backup recovery technology that is used by IT organizations that operates with disk storage, simulates tape libraries or tape-volume drives, for use with existing storage tape technology application logic.

VisiCalc - VisiCalc was the first spreadsheet program designed by VisiCorp for the Apple computer, purchased by Lotus Corporation,

Lotus 1,2,3 replaced VisiCalc as the primary spreadsheet application for PC's.

Waterfall Delivery - Describes the IT SDLC methodology that represents a cascading process concept, where each of the component SDLC phases is normally a sequential step in the various phases from requirements to design, to testing, through implementation, and support.

Wireless Emergency Alerts - A free-form text alert used by government and emergency agencies to send specific notifications to include: weather threats, life threats, Amber alerts, important presidential events, etc. to cell phones and pagers.

Work from Home - A BCP recovery strategy where key personnel are authorized to initiate work from their home site or continue working from their home site to support business recovery and/or continuation of services.

Zero Day Attacks - Attacks that exploit existing vulnerabilities in an environment before a hardware patch or software update is released to the IT industry or public, or correction applied to an IT environment.

Exhibit List

Figure 1.2 Key IT Delivery Framework Controls 5

Figure 1.4 Project Portfolio Management Process 12

Figure 1.9 IT Project and Technology Delivery Ecosystem.............29

Figure 2.4 Key IT Service Management Delivery Controls.............41

Figure 2.5 IT Service Delivery Request - Change Cycle.................46

Figure 2.11 ITSM Life-Cycle Ecosystem 60

Figure 3.1 BIA Risk Assessment Process Concept..........................74

Figure 3.2 BCP BIA Risk Assessment Tiers 76

Figure 3.6 BCP Threat Assessment Automation Concept...............84

Figure 3.8 Sample BCP Dependency Capture Model 87

Figure 3.10 Emergency Notification - BCM Concept Model..........93

Figure 3.12 BC Management Ecosystem 101

Figure 4.3 Technology/Application Risk Assessment Process 113

Figure 4.4 Process Dependency - Technology Gap Model 119

Figure 4.7 IT Automated Management/Vulnerability Model 130

Figure 4.8 TRDR Dependency Capture Model 133

Figure 4.11 Technology Resilience/DR Management Ecosystem..140

Figure 5.1 IS Best Practice Principles Framework 153

Figure 5.3 IS Technology Risk Assessment Concept 158

Figure 5.11 IS Management Ecosystem 181

Figure 6.4 TSP Management Framework Process.........................196

Figure 6.5 Standard Assessment Practices 200

Figure 6.9 Third-Party Supplier Management Ecosystem.............211

Figure 7.5 ITGRC Controls Assessment and Automation Concepts 229

Figure 7.7 ITGRC Management Ecosystem 237

Figure 8.1 EGRC Management Ecosystem 256

Figure 8.9 EGRC Hierarchical Reporting Concept......................258

Index

3LD, 243–244, 246, 253, 271

Accenture, 166
Acceptance testing, 22
Access Permissions,
      163, 179
Active–Active, 116–
      117, 124–125
Active–Passive, 124
active–shooter, 70, 91
Adhoc, 91
ADLM, 58–59
aggregation
      delivery, 35
      GRC data, 254, 257
      integration, 78,179, 255
      ITGRC data, 232–235, 256
      organizational data, 238
      services, 201
      risk, 76, 106–107, 146
      Third–Party data, 212–213,
            221–222
Agile, 7, 18, 25
Agile Development
      Methodology, 7
Air Bus DS, 91
Alert Enterprise, 164
all–hazard, 85
Amazon, 123, 125, 189

analytics
      analytics engine, 231
      defect, 24
      executive, 219
      ITGRC, 238–240, 257
      operational, 56–57, 67,
            129–131, 140, 155, 174,
            182, 236
      predictive, 131
      Project, 12
      resilience, 140, 236
      security, 67. 155, 164, 174,
            179, 236
      Third–Party, 213
annual review requirements,
      206
anomalies
      BCP, 73
      delivery, 6, 8 – 9
      estimates, 16
      expenditures, 16
      ITGRC 73, 234, 237, 239–
            240
      ITSM, 57, 68
      security, 154, 166, 173 174
      testing, 21, 26, 136
      TRDR 112
      technology 129–130
      Third–Party, 198, 208–209
Anti–tamper, 173
APM Solutions, 131

Appendix J, 218–219

Application–Security Environmental Testing, 25

Application Service Providers, 192

applications, 1, 5, 34
ADLM, 58
asset controls, 42, 47, 165
code packaging, 27
change, 37, 61, 139, 171, 182
cloud, 121, 176
configurations, 50, 64, 68
DR, 112, 114, 118, 123–124, 136
federated, 137
framework, 50
ITGRC, 137–138, 211, 233
ITSM, 61
obsolescence, 108–109, 128, 141
recovery planning, 120
risks, 112–113, 114–115, 118–119, 156, 221, 260
process gap dependency, 87
secondary challenges, 117
security controls, 163–166, 170–171, 176–178
service disruptions, 120–121, 141
service KPI/KRI, 142–147, 183–187
service delivery gaps, 70–80, 82, 133

technology resilience, 108
testing, 134–135, 144–145, 166–167, 217

Assessments, 112

Architecture, Data, and Standards, 227

Archer, See Dell/EMC

ASP, 192, 199, 201

Aspect Security, 166

Asset Cost Tracking, 49

Asset Management, 42, 44, 47–49, 61–63, 69, 181

ATOS Identity/Access Management, 164

Audit Control Committee, 266

audits, 49–50, 152, 201, 205–206, 209, 212, 268

authentication, 150, 161–163, 166, 205

automated rules base, 231

Automated Source Code, 166

Automated Stress Testing, 25

Avatier Identity Management, 164

backups, 80, 121, 125–127, 129, 135, 168–170

Backup Generators, 121, 126

Basel Banking Capital Accords, 264

BCM, 71, 87–88, 92–94, 97–101, 138, 140, 236

BCP Management
    BCM) tools, 87
BCP recovery plans, 81
best practices, 6, 40, 68,
    126, 131, 134–135,
    172, 205
BIA, 73–79, 81, 83, 85, 87–89,
    96, 98, 103, 111, 115, 117
Big Data, 178–179
Biometrics, 162
Black Art, 17
BlueMedora, 131
BMC, 12, 43, 55
Board of Directors
    accountabilities, 73,
        151–153, 191, 226.
        245, 250–251, 263–265,
        267–268
    committees, 216, 226, 246,
        266
    governance, 160, 224
    performance results, 90,
        102,107, 142, 147, 248
    HR data, 93
    hierarchical reporting, 194,
        209,213, 241, 252–253,
        257, 271
    regulatory scrutiny, 265
    Risk Appetite Statements,
        247, 270
British Airways, 263
Business Continuity, 2, 37, 49,
    51, 70–75, 77, 79, 81, 83,
    85, 87, 89, 91, 93, 95, 97,
    99–107, 111, 168, 198–199,
    205,219, 236, 261
Business Continuity Risk, 71, 74,
    106
Business Disruption Risk, 261
Business Impact Analysis, 73–
    74, 97
Business Process Tiers,
    119
Business Recovery Tier, 75

CA, 12, 25
Call Center, 56, 95
Capacity Management, 69
Capex, 13, 28
Capital, 2–3, 13–16, 20–21, 28,
    30–32, 34, 227, 253, 264
Capital Expenditures 13, 227,
    264
centralized control, 233
Change Control, 11, 27, 36–37,
    40, 44, 61, 136, 236
Change Control Management, 11
Change Control officer, 37, 40
Change Severity, 53–54
Changepoint, 12
Checkmarx, 166
Checkpoint Software
    Technology, 174
Cherwell Software, 43, 55
Chief Continuity Officer, 278
Chief Information Officer, 3

Chief Risk Officer, 190, 224
Chief Technology Officer, 3
CI, 50–54, 57, 63–65, 68
CIO, 3, 7, 26, 37–38, 72, 191, 224
Cisco, 174, 180
CISO, 150
Clarizen, 12 Clear swift, 174
client–server distributed, 149
Cloud, 4, 7
    DRaaS, 121, 192
    emerging threats, 110, 149, 176–178, 189, 218–219
    federated, 43, 133, 137, 176, 234
    program solutions, 11–13, 20, 25, 49, 59, 98, 125, 164, 201, 234, 239
    service issues, 43, 52, 108–109, 110
    vulnerabilities, 70, 96, 121, 182,187, 191–192
CMDB, 51, 133
CMS, 51–52, 116, 132
Co–Location Sites, 123, 125
COBIT, 6, 39, 51, 120, 201, 225, 249
Cognizant, 25, 166
Cold Sites, 123, 125
Cold Start, 122
Command Centers, 83
Compliance, 2

BCP, 73, 101–102
Board of Directors, 253, 257–259, 262, 267–269, 271–272
business priority, 14, 30
CMDB, 27
controls, 224, 229, 232–233, 269
escalation, 241
framework, 193, 208–209, 225, 243
GRC, 238
information security, 142, 151, 170
industry standards, 49,64
ITGRC, 223
KPI/KRIs, 30, 104–105, 143–146, 212, 225, 232, 239–240, 247, 249–252, 259–261
License, 48
policy, 10, 48, 225–226, 228,
Regulatory, 77, 187, 214, 218, 220–221, 224, 243
Stakeholders, 215, 254, 269
SME, 9
taxonomy, 239
Third–Party, 192–193, 204, 208, 262
TRDR, 142, 143
Computer Associates, 43, 55, 164
Concentration Risk, 95–96, 104, 136–137 209, 218, 222

Configuration Items, 50, 64

Configuration Management, 27, 42, 48–52, 64, 99, 113, 139, 156, 181, 227, 235–236

Continuity Logic, 98

Continuity Software Availability Guard, 131

Contract Controls/Exceptions, 48, 203

contract templates, 194, 197, 202–203, 216

control breaches, 231, 234

control environments, 47, 59, 107, 162, 214, 228, 230, 255

CoreLogic, 99

Cost Expert Group, 18

Courion Access Assurance, 164

Crisis Management, 71, 90, 160, 201, 227

CRO, 191, 224, 229, 246

Cross Check Networks, 25

CSC, 25, 166

CSIRT, 155, 159–160, 173

CTO, 3, 7, 26, 37–38, 224

Customer Relationship Management System, 93, 100

Customer Service, 56, 77, 87

cyber actors, 159

cyber joint exercises, 217

Cyber Management, 149

Cyber Monitoring, 180

Cyber Security Intelligence and Incident Response Team, See CSIRT

dashboards, 24, 131, 155, 173, 238, 248–249, 251, 257, 270, 273

Data Breach, 209, 216

Data Center, 40, 69, 85, 97, 108–109, 112, 120–128, 134–137, 156, 177

Data Center Tier, 126, 134

data corruption, 168 –170

Data dog, 13

data governance,178

Data Snaps, 169

Data Vault, 170, 206

DDoS, 158

delivery controls, 2, 9–10, 14, 41, 68

delivery time–frame, 16

Dell/EMC, 98, 164, 174 210, 239

Deloitte, 25

Delta, 263

Demand Management Process, 10

demilitarized zone, See DMZ

Department Homeland Security, 99

Dependency Gaps, 95, 106, 109, 137, 146

Dependency Model, 119

dependency processes, 88–89

Dependent processes, 80, 83, 88, 105, 145, 193

Depreciation, 13, 28, 49, 64, 69

Desk Checks, 89, 105, 134, 145

DevOps, 7

Disaster Recovery, 49, 71, 108,
115, 120, 123, 125, 135, 222

Distributed Denial of Service,
See DDoS

DMD, 26

DMP, 10, 26

DMZ, 174

Dodd–Frank, 218, 264

Dow Jones, 201

DR Hot Sites, 123

DR Tier, 55, 114, 136

DR Tiers, 157

DRaaS, 123

DriveScale System, 131

due diligence, 3, 5–6, 31, 79,
94,157, 165, 175, 191–195,
197–200, 203–204, 207,
210, 212–214, 217, 221,
224, 264, 273

e–commerce, 149, 179

eBRP Solutions, 98

Ecosystem, 13, 26–29,
35,59–60, 97, 99–102,
107, 137–140, 179–
181, 188, 210–213,
233–238, 253, 255–
256

Emergency Changes, 65, 68

Emergency Mass
Communication, 91

Employee Safety, 78

encryption, 149–150, 178,
185, 205

End–to–End Testing, 22

ENS, 91–94, 97–100

Enterprise Governance
Committee, 267

Enterprise Human Resource
System, 93

Enterprise Risk Management
Committee, 40

Enterprise Risk Program, 72,
175, 223, 233, 239

Entitlements Rights, 163

Environmental Monitoring, 57,
151, 175

Equifax, 263

estimates, 16

EverBridge, 91

evidentiary, 209, 212

Executive Risk Committee,
152,226, 246

exit strategies, 216–217

F5, 174

fail–safe concept, 170

federated, 22, 51, 57, 60–61,
93, 102, 116, 133, 137, 167,
176, 181, 210–211, 213–214,
234–236, 251, 254–255

FFIEC, 218

Fin–Tech Industry, 218

Financial Control Systems,
27–28, 61

Fire protection, 127
firewalls, 150, 172, 182
First Line of Defense, 243
FLOD, 243–244, 259
Forensic, 154–155, 173
Full–Scale Disaster Recovery
    Testing, 135
Full–Scale Testing, 89
Functional Testing, 24, 89
Fusion Risk, 98

Galorath Seer Software, 18
gap analysis, 80–81,
    111, 118
GDPR, 155
General Ledger, 15, 28, 100
Geopolitical, 95, 193, 207, 209
Google, 123, 125, 189
Gramm–Leach–Bliley Act, 155
GRC, 199, 210–211, 222,
    238, 241, 243–245, 249,
    253–258
guidance, 71, 79, 110, 120,
    153, 155, 161, 195, 219,
    252, 263

Hardware and Software
    Inventory Controls Process,
    47
heatmaps, 240, 252
Help Desk, 46, 56
Help Desks Technology, 58
hierarchical reporting, 257–
    258

High Availability, 116
High Speed Data Transmission,
    124
Home Depot, 263
Hot Site, 83, 124
hoteling, 19
HPE, 12, 25, 43, 55, 125, 131,
    166, 174, 180
HTTP, 158
HVAC, 121, 125, 127

IBM, 12, 25, 38, 43, 55, 123,
    125, 162, 164, 166, 174,
    180, 189, 199, 210, 234, 239
Identity Access and
    Authentication Management,
    161, 180
In-place recovery, 134
Incident Management, 44, 58,
    99–100, 139, 182
Information Security, 9, 49, 51,
    72, 149–151, 153, 155–157,
    159, 161, 163, 165, 167,
    169, 171, 173, 175–177,
    179–183, 185, 187
Information Technology
Infrastructure Library, See ITIL
Infosys, 25
Infrastructure, 6–7, 9, 27, 30–31,
    36– 37, 39– 40, 42, 52, 78,
    109, 112, 117, 121–123,
    128–134, 139, 141, 171,
    173, 182, 201, 227, 264
inherent risks, 80–81, 85, 116,
    160, 191, 221

Innotas, 12, 43
Integration Testing, 22
International Organization for
Standards, See ISO
investment strategies, 116, 119–
120, 129, 144, 226
Iron Mountain, 125
IS Program and Policy, 227
IS Risk Assessment, 156–
158, 165, 180
IS Risk Tier Logic, 157
IS/Cyber Risks, 260
ISACA, 6
ISO, 152–153, 201, 249
ISO31000, 225
ISO 27000, 153
Issues Tracking, 57, 97, 230
IT audits, 50, 201
IT Domain, 1, 204, 223, 228,
230 232, 237, 239–241, 243,
247–248, 250, 254, 256,
267–269, 271–272
IT executive management, 62,
136, 225, 269
IT Inventories, 48
IT Operations Analytics, 57
IT Resilience, 67, 108–110, 132,
137, 140, 272
IT risk, 9, 30, 40, 52, 68, 78,
110–111, 117, 129–130,
148–149, 190–191, 193, 220,
223–225, 229–232, 239, 241,
246, 248, 266–267, 270
ITIL, 6, 38–39, 50–51, 58, 60,

120, 201, 225
ITRGC committee, 246
ITSM, 11, 36–43, 45, 47–55,
57–62, 67–69,130, 171, 182,
210, 214, 221, 225, 227,
244, 265
ITSM Life-Cycle, 37–39, 42–43,
45, 60, 69, 171

Juniper Networks, 174

key controls, 50, 208–209, 230–
231, 237, 247
Key Performance Indicators, See
KPI
Key Risk Indicators, See KRI,
key risk management control, 19
Knowledge Management, 44
Knowledge or Training Data, 100
KPI, 26. 62–66, 102, 104,
106–107, 131, 140, 142,
144–146, 148, 182, 186,
209, 213, 219–220, 228,
230, 232, 240–241,248–251,
254–255, 257–258, 273
KRI, 33-34. 67-68, 102, 106–
107, 140, 142, 146–148,
182, 184–186, 209, 213,
219–220, 222, 228, 230,
232, 240–241, 248–251,
254–255, 257–258, 273

Legal, 9, 15, 35, 77, 114, 155, 190, 194, 196–197, 202–204, 210, 215–216, 242–243, 246, 253, 266

License Compliance Management Control, 48

licensing, 52, 58, 61, 109, 124, 128 132, 139, 202

LogicMonitor, 131

LogRythm Security, 180

mainframe, 47, 112, 130, 164, 184

Malware, 154, 158–159, 168–170, 172–173, 179–180, 205, 249, 263

Management technology, 43, 59

manual, 48, 70, 80, 83, 214, 232–233

Master Service or Software License Agreement, See MSA

MC, 86–88, 95–96, 118, 207

Mcafee, 174

metric reporting, 240

Metric Stream, 98, 199, 210, 239

metrics, 44
    adjustments, 234
    BIA RTO, 76, 78
    breaches, 254
    consolidated, 238
    controls, 259
    forward looking, 248
    monitoring, 228
    operational, 172, 201, 247
    performance indicators, 30, 99, 144, 183, 239, 240–241, 251, 255, 257
    processing, 116, 233-234, 237, 250, 255, 259, 262
    RAS, 258, 273
    resources, 94, 144
    reporting, 234, 258, 262
    risk indicators, 34, 99, 107, 148, 209, 231, 234, 241, 255, 257
    rules, 116, 231
    scorecard, 251, 259
    testing, 90, 92
    thresholds, 248
    trending, 240, 250, 270–271
    trusted data, 213, 236, 255

MicroFocus, 25, 43, 180

Microsoft, 12, 25, 38, 43, 123, 125, 162, 164, 174, 18, 234

Microsoft Operations Framework, 38

mid-range, 7, 47, 164

MIR-3, 91

Mission Critical, 86, 90, 94, 107, 147, 201

Mission Mode, 91

mobile application testing, 25

Modulo, 98, 239

MSA, 202–203

National Institute of Standards and Policies, See NIST

natural hazard, 91, 261

Negotiating Business line, 204

Net Present Value, 14

Network Configurations, 139, 182

Network End-points, 183, 185–186

Network, Security, 40, 109, 182

NFPA, 201

NIST, 152–153, 201, 225, 249

Obsolescence, 14, 30, 49, 52, 64, 69, 109, 128, 159, 265, 272

OpenView, 131

Operational Analytics, 67, 129–130, 140, 155, 172–173, 182, 236

operational control, 128, 177, 210, 213–214, 256, 259–260

Operational Risk Management, 104, 144, 223, 242–246, 270

Operational Risk Taxonomies, 239, 248, 257, 259, 269

operational sustainability, 135

Oracle, 25, 162, 164, 183, 210, 234, 239

oversight

    BIA standard, 78

Board of Directors, 73, 101, 224, 245, 264, 270

Committees, 3, 224–225, 229, 231–232, 245–246, 257, 265–267, 269

Dashboards, 131, 270

escalation, 6, 73, 112

executive, 223–224, 232–233,

frameworks, 225,227, 241, 244, 246, 267

investments, 3,8, 16,

ITGRC 8, 225, 227, 246, 267, 269

IT changes, 39–40

outsourced technology, 37

policies, 71–72, 150–151, 227–228, 245

programs, 1–4, 6–10, 26, 33, 71–72, 77, 101, 110–112, 162. 189, 191, 208, 264

RAS, 270

risk management, 71, 257

Three lines of defense, 72, 110, 243–244

Trusted data, 239

Palo Alto Networks, 174

password controls, 159

patches, 37, 52, 68, 128, 150, 155, 170–173, 182, 185–186

PCB, 40, 54
PDU, 127
Pen-Test, See Penetration Testing
Penetration Testing, 23, 25, 29,
    35, 154, 166–167, 176, 185,
    187
Performance/Stress Testing, 23
Perimeter, 127, 152, 156, 177,
    180–182, 187, 205
Physical Security Control, 127
Plan Desk Checks, 89
PM training, 17
policy
    Accountability, 6, 37,
        73, 90, 150–152, 207,
        228,246
    changes/creation, 2, 6, 37,
        228, 243
    components, 73, 111, 152,
        197, 208, 226, 246, 273
    documents linkage, 111
    governance, 73, 111, 120,
        151, 226, 228, 241
    periodic review/approval,
        73–74, 112, 152, 228,
        243, 246
    programs, 37, 72–74, 86,
        88,90–91, 100, 111,
        150–152, 175, 184, 186,
        194–195, 197, 202, 207,
        228, 243, 246
Portfolio Prioritization, 14
Portfolio Project Databases, 12
PPM, 10–12, 15–18, 20, 24, 26,

28, 227, 244, 265
PPM Database, 12
Pre-Contract Evaluation, 196, 198
Predictive Analytics, 13
primary changes, 59
Problem Management, 42, 46,
    55, 57–59, 62, 66, 139, 182,
    236
Procurement, 15–16, 44, 47, 49,
    61, 63, 71, 110, 190, 196–
    197, 202, 204, 210, 216
production migrations, 47
Project Portfolio Management,
    10, 12
Project Portfolio Management
    Process, 12

QA, 21–26, 28–29, 33–34, 58,
    228,236, 251, 260, 269
Qualitative risk assessment, 273
Quality Assurance, 5, 21, 23–25,
    29, 32, 35, 228, 236, 251
quality control, 2, 79, 118,
    187, 209
Quick Ship, 125, 134

RACI, 73, 111
Raised Floor, 69, 127
Ransomware, 158, 263
RAS, 245, 246–248, 254–255,
    257– 258, 267–   271, 273
RAS breaches, 248, 273
RCSA, 230, 251

Recovery Planner, 98

Recovery Plans, 81, 120–121, 134– 135, 138, 141, 143– 147, 169, 211, 217

Recovery Point Objective, 7

Recovery procedures, 83, 154, 219

recovery strategies, 72, 81, 85, 90, 92, 96, 100, 110, 117, 120, 132

Recovery Time Objective, 75, 103

redline, 202

Regression Testing, 23

Regulatory
  business cases, 14, 30
  compliance, 2, 224, 241, 243
  Dodd Frank Law, 35
  requirements, 10, 13, 71, 82, 86, 179, 189, 192, 205, 214, 218, 220, 224, 230, 232, 266–268
  risk impacts, 35, 77, 114, 126, 187, 193, 269

Release Management, 27, 99, 139, 182, 187, 227, 236

replication, 64, 69, 113, 115, 117, 121–122, 124, 129–130, 168– 169

Reputation, 2, 35, 78, 85, 114, 155, 183, 187, 193, 209, 253, 260, 271

residual risk, 81, 220, 230, 252, 271, 273

resource assignment, 12, 14, 20, 28

Resource Availability, 18–20

resource hours, 16

Return on Investment, 11

Revenue, 14, 30, 77–78, 93, 253

Reverse, 91, 173

risk appetite, 85, 126, 209, 245– 247, 250, 254, 258, 270–271, 273

Risk Appetite Statements, See RAS

Risk Categories, 99, 193–195, 238, 243, 248, 252, 259, 273

Risk Committee, 152, 226, 241, 246, 266–268, 270–272

Risk Control and Assessment, 229

Risk Control Self-Assessment, 230

Risk Determination, 77, 117

Risk Management Committee, 40, 266–267, 270–271

Risk Profile Data, 99, 139, 181

risk sensitivity, 106, 207

risk weightings, 114

ROI, 11, 13–14, 30

RPO, 75, 114, 117

RTO, 75–76, 78–80, 86, 99, 103, 106–107, 109, 114, 117–118, 120, 122, 126, 133,137, 139, 142–143, 146–147, 181

SaaS, 11–12, 43, 47, 49, 59, 97, 101–102, 132, 164, 166

Safe-Harbor, 170

Salesforce.Com, 189

Sarbanes Oxley,
See also SOX

scanning tools, 166, 172

SCP, 120

SDLC, 4, 6–8, 10–11, 17, 21, 26, 28, 33, 45, 58–59

Second Line of Defense, 72, 110, 244

Secondary Challenge, 79

security appliances, 51, 130, 150, 172–173

Security gateways, 172

Security Tokens, 162

security violations, 23, 185–186, 209

Send Word Now, 91

Sensitive Data, 154, 157, 187, 192, 255

Service Aggregator, 99

Service Catalog, 44, 61

Service Desk, 44, 56, 66

Service Management, 6, 11, 27, 36–39, 41, 43–47, 49, 51, 53, 55, 57, 59, 61–63, 65, 67, 69, 77, 99, 120, 139, 236

Service Request Automated Management System (SRM), 46

Service Request Process, 41, 44

Servicenow, 43, 239

SIG, 199–200

SIG Lite, 200

SilverSky, 174

Single Sign-on, 162

Six Sigma Certification, 17

SLA, 45, 57, 63, 66–67, 77, 139, 82,198, 202, 208, 212–213, 216

SLOD, 72, 79, 110, 244, 268

Smart-Cards, 162

SME, 9, 78–79, 89, 111, 195–199, 202–204, 107–208, 210, 212–213, 215–216, 220–222,231

SMS text, 92–93

SOC, 200

Software as a Service, See SaaS

Software Management, 50

Sony Corporation, 263

Sophos, 174

SOX, 230, 238, 264, 269, 271

SP800, 153

split operations, 8, 123

Splunk, 174, 18

spreadsheet, 115

Steering Committee, 8, 152, 216

Stoplight, 240, 252

Strategic, 3–4, 8, 14, 30–31, 33, 98,107–108, 117, 122–123, 147, 155, 193, 207, 223, 244, 254

Strategic BCP, 98

sub-committees, 226–229, 232, 238, 240, 245–247, 259

Subject-Matter-Experts, 79, 195

Sungard AS, 98, 123, 125

Supplier Management System, 93

Supplier Questionnaire, 199

Supplier Stratification, 206

Swag Estimate, 18

Symantec, 174

Synchronous, 124

System Testing, 22

Systems and Processing Risks, 259

Table-Top Testing, 134, 136

Tabletop Exercise, 89

TARA, 111, 113–117, 120

TATA, 25, 166

Technology and Application Risk Assessment, See TARA

Technology Criticality Assessment, 115

Technology Dependency Gap Analysis, 81

technology obsolescence, 14, 49, 109,128, 159, 265, 272

Technology Resilience, 40, 51, 55, 108–115, 117, 119, 121, 123, 125, 127–129, 131–

147, 170, 205, 210, 236, 264

Technology Vulnerabilities, 128, 136

terrorism, 70

Third Line of Defense, 244

Third-Party

accountability, 204–206, 216, 265

assessments, 88, 198–199, 201–202

cloud services, 43, 70, 110, 123, 133, 182, 219

concentration risk, 96, 137

controls, 43, 88, 150, 152, 196–198, 208–209, 212–213

dependencies, 42, 58, 70, 75, 86, 105–106, 109, 118, 132, 137

environment, 99–100, 109, 133, 141

exceptions/exit strategies, 201–203, 216

federations, 99, 137

identifications, 86, 159, 174, 195, 207, 210

inventory, 93

ITGRC risks, 80, 82, 86, 96, 106, 113, 118, 121, 137, 150, 152, 159. 162, 175, 178, 182, 184, 187, 189, 190–194, 209, 219–221,

248, 261–262, 264, 265

notifications, 91–92, 94, 215

outsource, 189, 195

product suppliers, 11, 43,
49, 59, 80, 91, 97–98,
123, 125, 133, 164, 214

software, 1–2, 4, 28, 99, 116

source data, 139, 181, 211

stratifications, 206

test activity, 22, 145, 175–
176, 217–218

testing services, 25–26

Third-Party Supplier Risk, 190–
191, 193, 262

Threat Assessment Automation,
84

Threat Vulnerability Assessment,
83, 97, 100

Three Lines of Defense, See 3LD

Ticketing, 56–58, 62

Tier, 22, 53, 55–56, 75, 114–
117, 126–128, 134, 136, 43,
147, 157, 159–160, 165, 209

Tier Categories, 75, 116–117

Tivoli Unified Process, 38

TLOD, 244, 251, 266–267,
269–270, 273

transfers to hot site, 83

TRDR, 110–112, 114,
118–120, 130, 132–133,
135–147, 156–157, 160,
169, 194, 196, 201, 203,
207, 211–212, 214, 225,

227, 236, 244, 265

TRM software, 140

Trusted Data, 28–29, 60–61, 93–
94,98, 107, 139–140, 157,
181, 210, 213, 232–233,
235, 237, 239, 254, 262, 273

TrustWave, 174

TSP, 191, 193–200, 202–204,
207–216, 218–222

TSP inventory, 199, 207

TSP Life-Cycle Process, 210

TVA, 83–85

Unit Testing, 22

Uninterrupted Power Source,
See UPS

United Airlines, 263

Unix, 162

UPS, 69, 121, 127, 135, 169

UpTime Institute, 126

US Department of Commerce,
153

US national elections (2016),
263

Vericode, 25

Virtual Tape Library, 125

Virus, 172–174, 185, 205, 249

Voice Response Systems, 56

VoloRecovery, 91

WatchGuard Technologies, 174
Waterfall, 7
Websense, 174
WhatsupGold, 131
White Hat Security, 25, 166
WiPro, 166
Work Area Recovery, 83
work from home, 83
workflow, 12, 27–28, 55, 57–58,
    164, 167, 213
WorkFront, 12

XMatters, 91

Y2K, 149

Zero Day Threats, 173–174

About the Author

Geno Pandolfi was one of the first Chief Continuity Officers to be designated in the global banking IT industry as a "C" level executive officer. As a global Executive Director of Readiness Services for one of the largest banks in the United States, he was accountable for all enterprise resiliency and capacity management operations, including business continuity, disaster recovery, capacity and resiliency Management, risk assessment, and crisis management. He participated in standing executive GRC committee meetings and the preparation of multiple board risk updates on key compliance, resiliency, and technology activities.

He has more than forty years of industry experience in information technology and risk management domains, and has consulted on hundreds of IT strategy, governance, system/technology, infrastructure initiatives and programs across multiple industries to senior corporate and IT executives and is currently a senior management consultant to the IT industry. Also, he has authored several articles on IT operational risk and resiliency and has presented to multiple industry technology forums on these subjects.

Mr. Pandolfi holds an MBA from Fordham University in Management Science, BBA from Pace University in Computer Information Sciences, and attended the Amos Tuck Business School at Dartmouth MBA Update Program.

He is a Certified Business Continuity Lead Auditor by DRI*, and has architected, designed, and implemented multiple operational governance, compliance, and risk management software solutions over the last twenty years. (*Disaster Recovery Institute International).